CONTENTS

FOREWORD

Ireland is fortunate in the high quality of its national statistical services and in the degree of public availability of official statistics. This is especially true for the agricultural sector, for which there is a long tradition of data assembly and publication. More recently, information technology has greatly facilitated the dissemination of statistical information for small area units such as District Electoral Divisions, of which there are over 3,000 in the Republic.

Greater volumes of statistics are of limited benefit unless the data are presented in a readily understandable format, interpreted and used for the planning and management of public affairs. Computerised mapping techniques offer one means of reducing complex data sets to more simplified and visually attractive forms. In this atlas modern mapping packages are used mainly with census data from District Electoral Divisions to depict geographical variations in the Republic's land use, farming systems, livestock production, and cropping patterns. Where possible census statistics are supplemented by data made available from public administration sources.

While pasture for grazing livestock is the most extensive land use in the State's 4.4 million hectares of farmed land, the general picture emerging from the maps is one of complex local differences. These can be traced to a mix of factors including variations in natural resource qualities and climate, historical influences, economic and demographic circumstances, and public policies. The different farming regions of the country are now undergoing varying adjustment processes as the agricultural economy responds to economic forces, technological trends, and shifts in the direction of policy.

This atlas continues a scholarly tradition of agricultural mapping initiated by L. Dudley Stamp seventy years ago. It includes a number of new maps derived from data that had not been collected until the 1990s. In presenting the geography of Irish agriculture at the stage of entering an era of reform in the EU Common Agricultural Policy, the atlas provides a significant baseline from which future trends can be measured.

The compilation of the atlas originated from the Walsh Fellowships scheme, under which Teagasc supports young researchers in pursuing post-graduate degrees at Irish universities. Séamus Lafferty carried out much of the work while undertaking a Ph.D. Degree at the Department of Geography, National University of Ireland, Maynooth, and the progress achieved was due in great part to his skills, energy and perseverance. The successful completion and publication of the atlas is an exemplar of the research teamwork and inter-institutional cooperation intended under the Fellowships scheme. Accomplished researchers in Teagasc and NUI, Maynooth worked closely with a Walsh Fellow to combine experience with fresh ideas and the application of up to date geographical research techniques. Their collaboration and co-authorship adds a valuable contribution to the literature on Irish agriculture.

Teagasc gratefully acknowledges the financial support of the EU Structural Funds towards its Walsh Fellowships scheme. The atlas project was supported through the Research Stimulus Fund administered by the Department of Agriculture and Food to promote collaboration between research institutions. Thanks are due to each of the Regional Authorities and to FBD Trust Company for generous financial contributions towards the costs of publication.

Liam Downey
Director
Teagasc

ACKNOWLEDGEMENTS

This atlas is the outcome of an inter-institutional collaborative research partnership involving Teagasc, the European Union, the Department of Agriculture and Food, and the National University of Ireland, Maynooth. The authors acknowledge with gratitude the contributions of each partner. Teagasc generously supported the principal author under its Walsh Fellowships scheme and provided various forms of technical assistance to the project. Additional financial support was provided from the European Agricultural Guidance and Guarantee Fund through the Research Stimulus Fund established under the Operational Programme for Agriculture, Rural Development and Forestry, 1994-1999. The Department of Geography at NUI, Maynooth provided a conducive working environment and the technical facilities needed for preparing the maps contained in the atlas.

There are several individuals within the partner and other institutions to whom we are deeply indebted for their cooperation and assistance. In the first instance special thanks are extended to Dr Liam Downey, Director of Teagasc, both for his personal commitment to the project and for his initiative in fostering Teagasc - university collaboration through the Walsh Fellowships scheme. We are also grateful to Mr Eamonn Pitts, Head of the Rural Economy Research Centre, Teagasc, for his advice and interest in seeing the project through to publication. There are many others within Teagasc to whom we owe particular gratitude: Michael Cushion for his diligence and patience in assembling statistical data and helping in the painstaking tasks of reconciling various data sets; Tony McGarry for his care in proof-reading and checking statistical tables; Tony Leavy for assistance with the preparation and interpretation of data from public administration sources; and Perpetua McDonagh for helpful comments on drafts of the text. We are also grateful to Lena Gibbons for sustained and efficient secretarial services; to Charlie Godson, John Keating and Con O'Rourke for providing photographs; and to Seán Diamond and John Lee for help with assembling maps on soils and land suitability. Thanks are also due to numerous Teagasc personnel around the country who helped by way of their expertise and local knowledge.

Tony Smith and Michael Kelly from the Department of Agriculture and Food provided efficient and courteous administration of a generous grant from the Research Stimulus Fund while Dan Gahan and Michael Scullion from the same Department went to great lengths to make administrative data files available.

We owe a tremendous debt of gratitude to the staff of the Central Statistics Office in Cork who responded patiently and promptly to innumerable requests that often took them far beyond their normal duties. In particular special thanks go to Gerry Brady, Richie McMahon, Caroline Kelly, Harry McGovern and Jim Linehan – their efficiency, courtesy and good-humoured approach were much appreciated. We hope that we have added some value to their immensely rich database.

The greatest personal debts in the production of this atlas are due to the staff of the Department of Geography, NUI, Maynooth, in which much of the work took place. We want especially to acknowledge the invaluable technical, cartographic and editorial assistance and guidance provided by John Sweeney, Dennis Pringle, Rob Kitchin, and James Keenan. We would also like to thank the following for giving generously of their time, expertise and collegial support: Brendan Bartley, Proinnsias Breathnach, Ro Charlton, Patrick Duffy, Paul Gibson, Shelagh Waddington, Mary Weld, Céline McHugh, Daragh McDonough and Martin Whelan. We are also indebted to Gerry Boyle of the Department of Economics, NUI, Maynooth for advice and encouragement over the course of this project.

Numerous other organisations and individuals have been crucial to the completion of the atlas. For their concern about quality and the technical aspects of graphic design and layout we thank the staff of Eamon Sinnott and Partners – especially Eamon, Liam and Stephen who were tireless in their meticulous attention to detail. Their patience and understanding were stretched beyond the normal limits as they coped with successive amendments to the maps and text. We are also grateful for the technical support and advice provided by GAMMA and especially by Maura McGinn. For making available the digital boundary data on which the maps are organised we are indebted to the Ordnance Survey of Ireland. For meticulous proof-reading we acknowledge the assistance of Bill Tinley and Thomas Flavin. Thanks to Matthew Stout and James Keenan for preparing the soil and climate maps and to Ann Coughlan, Hazel Craigie, Ivan Devilly, Bryan Kehoe and Cormac Walsh for assistance with final editing, checking the tables and the preparation of graphs. Thanks also to Gillian Buckley whose photographic skills contributed enormously to the final product; to Dr Thomas Kabdebo and Paula Leavy-McCarthy for their efficiency and diligence in compiling the index and to Coillte and Steve Treacy of the Irish Farmers Journal for providing photographs.

Readers will be struck by the numerous references to the work of Professor Desmond A. Gillmor of the Department of Geography, Trinity College Dublin. Professor Gillmor's research, which spans over 30 years, covers all aspects of the agricultural geography of Ireland and we wish to acknowledge the inspirational and practical guidance which his studies provided in the compilation of this atlas. We also wish to thank him for his very constructive comments on an earlier version of the text.

Permission to reproduce copyright material has been received from Cork University Press (Figures 6 and 7), Routledge (Figures 8, 13 and 14), Teagasc (Figures 11 and 12) and Met Éireann (Figures 10 and 15); to all our grateful thanks.

As for the publication costs of the atlas, these could not have been borne without the generous financial assistance provided by Teagasc, the European Union and the Department of Agriculture and Food, the eight Regional Authorities, FBD Trust Company Ltd, the EU INTERREG programme, Shannon Development, Ballyhoura Development Ltd, KELT and Kildare County Council; to each sponsor our sincere thanks.

Finally, as usual, any errors or omissions remain the responsibility of the authors.

Séamus Lafferty
Patrick Commins
James A. Walsh
June 1999

LIST OF MAPS

LIST OF TABLES

LIST OF FIGURES

LIST OF ABBREVIATIONS

AAU	Agriculture area in use	FFO	Family Farm Operator
AWU	Annual Work Unit	LU	Livestock Unit
CAP	Common Agricultural Policy	RD	Rural District
CSO	Central Statistics Office	REPS	Rural Environment Protection Scheme
DED	District Electoral Division	SGM	Standard Gross Margin
ESU	European Size Unit		
FFI	Family Farm Income		
FIP	Farm Improvement Programme		

"*I watched this field for forty years
and my father before me watched it for forty more.
I know every rib of grass and every thistle
and every whitethorn bush that bounds it.*"

from 'The Field' by John B. Keane

Introduction

Irish Agriculture in Transition

Irish Agriculture in Transition – Introduction

Agriculture is the most important single industry in the economy of the Republic of Ireland. The agri-food sector generates about one-third of the Republic's net foreign earnings and employs one out of every eight people in the workforce. Of the total land area of approximately 7 million hectares, almost 5 million hectares are used for agricultural purposes, including forestry. Historically, the fortunes of the Irish people have been closely linked to life on the land. Culturally, themes drawn from farming and rural living have inspired Ireland's poets, dramatists and writers. Politically, and especially in the contemporary context of the Republic's participation in the European Union, the implications for its agricultural economy are a major consideration in the way Ireland negotiates its international trading relationships.

A knowledge of its agriculture is therefore essential to a full understanding of Ireland, and especially to knowing its rural geography. Despite the small size of the Republic and the fact that livestock rearing is by far the predominant farming activity there is still much geographical variation in farming systems. This spatial differentiation can be related to a range of physical, environmental, historical, economic and socio-cultural factors.

The pioneering work on mapping the geography of Irish agriculture was undertaken some 70 years ago by L. Dudley Stamp in his *Agricultural Atlas of Ireland*, published in 1931. In the late 1960s and 1970s D. A. Gillmor wrote many articles on aspects of the geography of agriculture in Ireland, and provided a detailed review of the 1970 census in his 1977 *Agriculture in the Republic of Ireland*. However, the first general atlas of Irish agriculture since Stamp's work, covering both the Republic and Northern Ireland, was *Agriculture in Ireland: A Census Atlas* compiled by A. A. Horner and colleagues and published in 1984. Taking advantage of developments in computer technology, these authors based their maps on a detailed analysis of the 1980 census of agriculture. They were therefore able to record the position for the early years of Ireland's membership of the European Community – an event which marked a new era for farming in both parts of the island.

Aim and Relevance

This present atlas updates and extends the information provided by the earlier publications. Its central aim is to present a detailed visual representation, with appropriate commentary, of the geographical variations in Irish agriculture as of 1991, the date of the latest census of agriculture. Where data permit, changes over time are traced for the 1980s and 1990s.

While there is already considerable information available on the country's farming industry, much of it treats the topic in aggregated statistical terms as a sector of the national economy. National and even county statistics can mask important local differentiation. Here, the focus is on presenting disaggregated statistical data so as to emphasise local territorial differences. It is particularly important to bring these spatial variations to light at a time when the agricultural economy is in the throes of a major transition – marked especially by the 1992 reforms of the Common Agricultural Policy (CAP) – from an expansionist phase to an era when policies are directed towards curtailing production in a number of commodities and re-shaping the use of agricultural land. This work, then, will also form a baseline against which to measure the future trends that will emerge in a changed economic and policy context.

Data Sources and New Data

This atlas was compiled from three main sources of information. Firstly, the principal database is the 1991 Census of Agriculture, undertaken by the Central Statistics Office, the information for which was available for small area units, namely, District Electoral Divisions (DEDs). There are some 3,400 DEDs in the State, of which all but 330 have some agricultural activity (Figure 1). Where appropriate, and despite difficulties arising from different enumeration procedures, change over the 1980s is mapped for Rural Districts (RDs) only. RDs are aggregates of DEDs (Figure 2) and the relevant number is 156 (i.e., treating Dublin as one). Secondly, some agricultural statistics are updated annually from Central Statistics Office surveys and, where possible, these are used in the accompanying regional statistical tables to track the 1991-97 trends. However, these figures are not valid for sub-county areas. Thirdly, where possible, use is made of administrative data supplied by the Department of Agriculture and Food to quantify the up-take and spatial distribution of selected policy measures, especially those arising from the 1992 reform of the CAP.

It would have been desirable to include Northern Ireland in the atlas but this was not possible. Apart from the practicalities of achieving data comparability, this project arose from work undertaken as part of a research programme co-financed by EU Structural Fund allocations for agricultural research in the Republic.

The atlas contains several new maps based on data that had not been collected prior to the 1991 Census of Agriculture. Thus, distinctive geographical patterns in the modes of land acquisition and land tenure are mapped in detail for the first time, along with data on farm fragmentation. Estimates of the value of farm output have been used to provide a basis for productivity maps. These, and the maps depicting characteristics of the farm labour force, provide new insights into the structural features of agricultural production throughout the State. The typology of specialist farm types compiled by the Central Statistics Office has been used to map the distributions of the main farming systems; these demonstrate the much greater diversity of farming types that are possible in the more favourable eastern and southern parts of the State. The overall perspective provided by the maps is one of complex local variations that, over time, have led to distinctive farming regions which are adjusting at different rates to processes of change resulting from decisions taken outside the regions and often beyond the State.

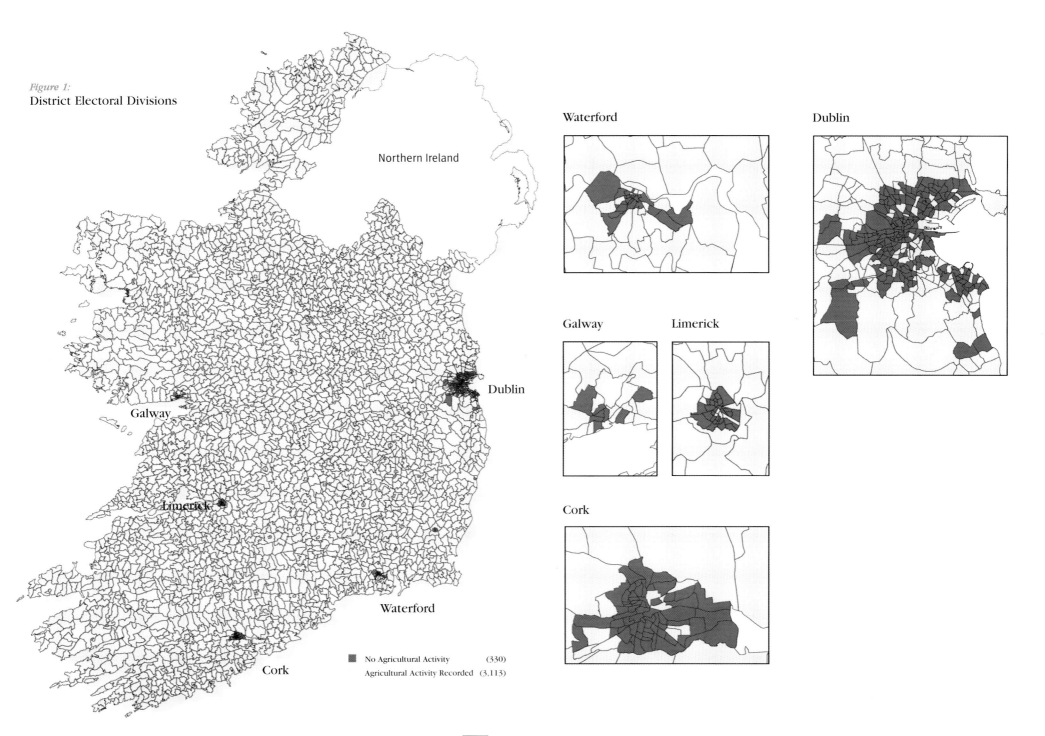

Figure 1:
District Electoral Divisions

Northern Ireland

Dublin

Galway

Limerick

Waterford

Cork

No Agricultural Activity (330)

Agricultural Activity Recorded (3,113)

Waterford

Dublin

Galway

Limerick

Cork

Methodology

Compared to earlier work on atlas production the present work was facilitated by two particular developments. One was the availability of greatly improved computer mapping techniques including facilities for colour reproduction. Almost all the maps were generated with the MapInfo mapping package. The second was the relative ease with which data sets can now be produced and transferred through modern information and communication technologies.

Nevertheless, the operational task of producing the atlas threw up numerous difficulties and issues requiring procedural decisions. Some of these problems typified those encountered in comparing data sets over periods of time – matters such as area boundary changes or changing definitions of census categorisations. Others were of a more technical nature – an example is the choice of an appropriate method for deciding the 'break points' in an array of data so as to adequately represent the differences between groupings of geographical areas. Decisions also had to be made on what to include in or omit from a range of possibilities. However, a description of these issues and the various technicalities involved in producing the maps is unlikely to be of interest except to the specialist reader. Details of the methodology adopted are therefore consigned to the Appendix.

In the majority of cases the class intervals for the maps are based on 'natural breaks' in the data. The number of districts represented by each class interval is shown in parentheses in the legend of each map.

Content and Structure

The atlas consists of over 100 maps which are accompanied by a descriptive commentary, together with statistical tables that summarise the numerical data at the level of the Regional Authority areas (Figure 4). The contents of the atlas are organised into a number of discrete parts. Before the presentation of the various maps and their associated commentary there is a general overview of the contemporary dynamics of change in the Irish agricultural economy (Section One). The Irish case illustrates many of the features of agricultural change recognised in more advanced countries. It is suggested that what is taking place is, in effect, a modern agricultural revolution driven by economic and technological forces and shaped by a range of public policies. Superimposed on an Irish resource structure and farming culture, which differs greatly across the State, this process of transformation produces a variegated geographical pattern in Ireland's agriculture.

Section Two presents the structural features of farming including, farm size, labour, mechanisation and productivity. Section Three deals with land use, covering pasture, hay, silage and arable cropping systems. The most important element of Irish farming, its livestock enterprises, is mapped in Section Four.

Section Five seeks to complement the census information presented in earlier sections by drawing on data from public administration files, where these data had been compiled for small-scale areas and made available to the authors. The maps in this section show geographical variations in the adoption of a number of 'new' policy measures, such as those for agri-environmental management and early farmer retirement. Finally, Section Six presents a short synthesis and some brief observations on future trends.

This atlas will provide a basis for a more thorough understanding of the complexities of agriculture and land use changes in the Republic of Ireland. It is hoped that it will be of particular assistance to those designing and implementing policies for agriculture and for rural and regional development. It should be of interest to geographers, economists and planners and indeed to the many others concerned for the Irish landscape and with understanding how the countryside is being shaped by the changes in farming practices.

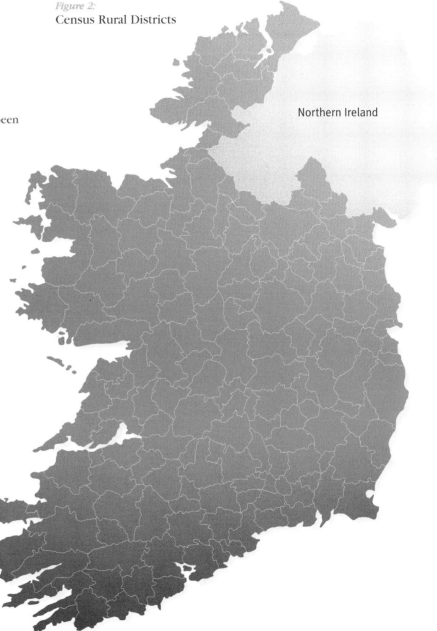

Figure 2:
Census Rural Districts

Northern Ireland

Figure 3:
Counties and Provinces

Figure 4:
Regional Authority Areas*

* In the statistical tables in this volume, the Border
region has been divided between Border (west)
and Border (east)

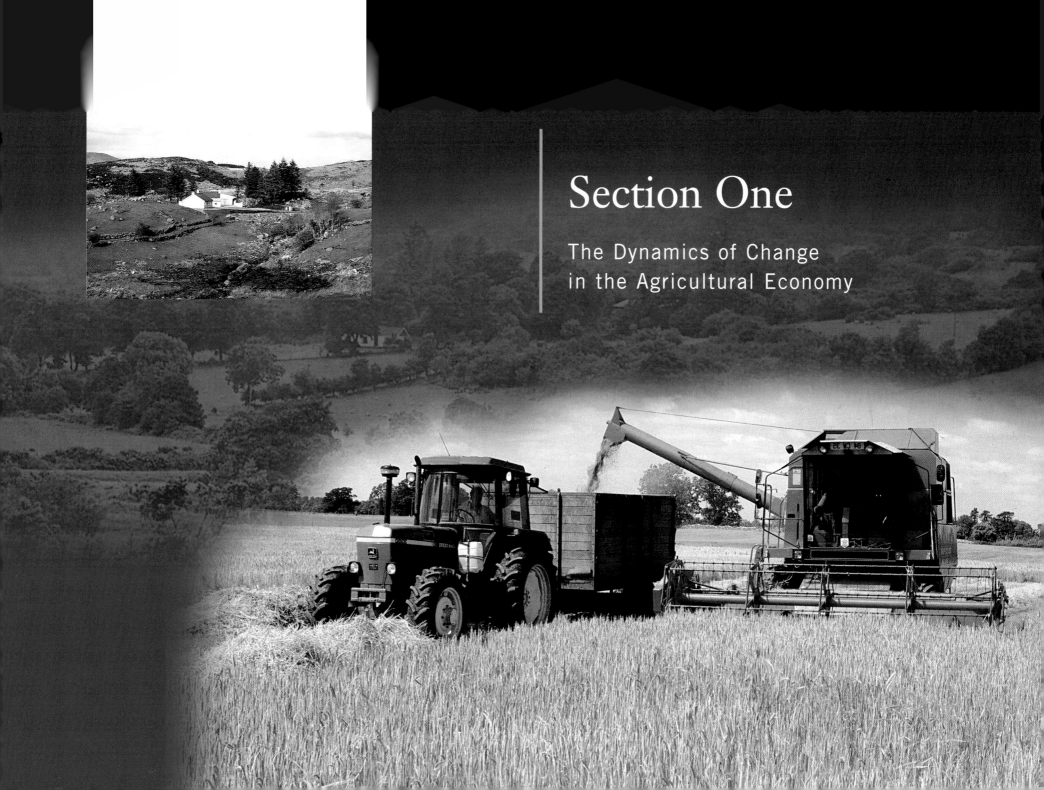

Section One

The Dynamics of Change
in the Agricultural Economy

The Modern Agricultural Revolution

*O*ver the past 40 years the more developed
countries of the world have experienced a modern
agricultural revolution. The impact of this
transformation has been such that society's priorities for
agriculture and land use have changed substantially.
Four decades ago the spectre of World War II food
shortages still haunted the countries of Europe,
a concern reflected in the 1957 Treaty of Rome.
Article 39 of the Treaty stressed the aim of improving
agricultural productivity, ensuring the security of food
supplies, and increasing the earnings of those working
on the land. Today, EU food supplies are in surplus
and the controlling of production is a main concern
of agricultural policy makers. Increasingly, farmers
are maintaining their living standards by earning
incomes outside of farming. Society is now more
concerned with the way its food is produced, the quality
and variety of that food, the sustainability of some
food production systems given their implications
for the environment, and the balanced development
of rural areas (CEC, 1998).

Two major phases in this longer-term pathway
of change have been identified (Ilberry *et al.*, 1997).
The first was a 'productivist' phase, from the 1950s
to the mid-1980s, characterised by technological
developments in agriculture, the modernisation
of farming structures and infrastructures
(e.g., in processing and marketing commodities),
and the expansion of output in a policy regime
dominated by high price supports for many
of the commodities produced.

Since the mid-1980s a second or 'post-productivist
transition' period has emerged in which the policy
focus has been on reducing supports for farm
productivity, stabilising or reducing farm output, giving
greater recognition to part-time farming, and
integrating agricultural practices with broader rural
economic, social and environmental objectives.

Ireland is an illustrative case of the modern
agricultural revolution. The central features of the
restructuring of the Irish agricultural economy have
been described elsewhere (Commins and Keane,
1994; Commins, 1996) and are represented in the maps
in this volume. The essence of the transformation
in Ireland has been higher productivity, but with
increasing differentiation of performance between
categories of farms and regions of the State.
The character and dynamics of change will be
discussed in detail presently but here we simply
record the main facts.

In the early 1950s there were some 500,000
people working on Irish farms compared to 120,000
today. This represents a decline from 38 per cent
to 10 per cent of the State's total labour force. At the
1961 Census of Population there were 210,000
persons who recorded their principal occupation
as that of 'farmer'. Currently, the corresponding figure
is little more than 100,000.

Despite this loss of labour the volume of Irish gross agricultural output has risen dramatically. Between 1971 and 1996 the total farm labour force declined by over half (54 per cent). Within the same period, however, the volume of gross agricultural output per person engaged in farming expanded more than threefold.

At the most general level of description Ireland has a two-tier farming economy which, territorially, roughly corresponds to a division of the State into the less prosperous west and north-west and the more favoured counties of the east and south.

A refinement of this division classifies the country into the 'Disadvantaged Areas' and other areas (see Figure 5). In 1997, in the east and south (the provinces of Leinster and Munster except for counties Longford, Clare, and Kerry, also West Cork) the value of average farm output was over twice that in the remainder of the State. The difference was more than three-fold if the comparison is confined to the regions of the South-East and West. While grazing intensity increased over many areas during the 1980s this was not the case in the more disadvantaged areas of the west (see *Map 95*).

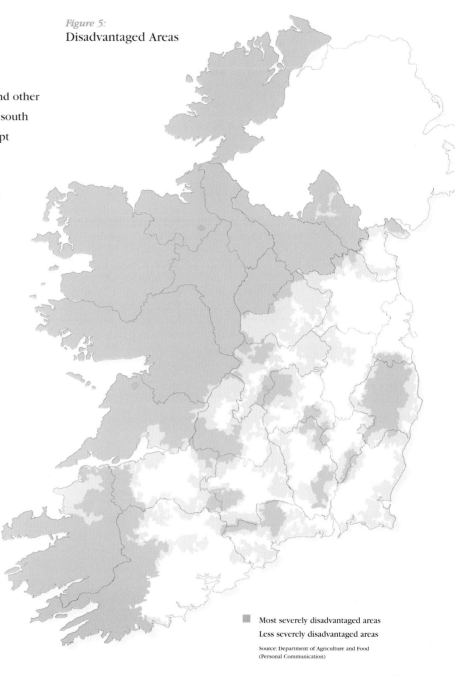

Figure 5:
Disadvantaged Areas

■ Most severely disadvantaged areas
Less severely disadvantaged areas

Source: Department of Agriculture and Food
(Personal Communication)

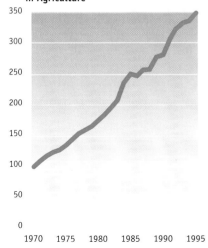

Index of Volume of Gross Output per Member of the Labour Force in Agriculture

350
300
250
200
150
100
50
0

1970 1975 1980 1985 1990 1995

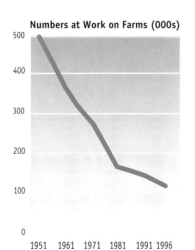

Numbers at Work on Farms (000s)

500
400
300
200
100
0

1951 1961 1971 1981 1991 1996

Explaining the Revolution in Agriculture

What accounts for this great exodus from farming and the growth in productivity? What are the driving forces and dynamics of modernisation and marginalisation in agriculture? How can we explain the geography of Irish agriculture in the sense that we can show why farming systems differ across the State?

There is not a single determining factor, but rather a combination of many reasons, some of which are not solely Irish in origin. Different disciplines and research specialisms tend to focus on some factors more than others but a comprehensive view would encompass the following:

(i) the natural resource base and its uneven potential throughout the State; this is clearly shown in Figures 6 to 9, and repeatedly reflected in the maps depicting the spatial distribution of farming activity and performance;

(ii) international economic forces, especially the relentless striving among producers and agri-business (and countries) for competitive advantage (e.g., by adopting labour saving technology or adapting to consumer preferences); inefficient farmers in particular cannot survive in this context;

(iii) public policies which are, broadly, of two kinds – those that propel change in the direction of greater economic rationalisation of farming structures (e.g., towards larger, economically viable holdings); and policies which have a palliative or modifying impact on rationalisation (e.g., by providing direct payments to farmers to offset price reductions, *Map 98*);

(iv) changes in the non-farm economy, especially those generating the expansion of employment which can 'pull' labour out of farming;

(v) cultural, institutional and historical factors, which vary in their influence among categories of farmer or geographical area, underlie certain farming traditions and practices (e.g., *Map 9* shows how farmers in the west of Ireland tend to transfer their holdings by making wills and allowing their properties to be inherited after their deaths, whereas in the east lifetime gift transfers and sales/purchases are more common). Congestion on the small holdings of the west can be traced to historical events;

(vi) the 'adaptive strategies' pursued by individual resource holders who, for example, may not always follow economic logic but whose behaviour is determined by their subjective motivations, goals, lifestyle preferences as well as their individual resources and capabilities.

Secondly, climatic conditions and topography have a major influence. Mountain and coastal areas in the west are subject to high rainfall. They also experience lower temperatures, a shorter growing season and are exposed to high winds and the risk of gales (see Figures 10 and 13-16).

The third significant aspect of the resource base is that the inferior tracts of land are mainly those on which small farms predominate. This is due to a complex of historical factors centred on colonisation, confiscation and population displacement which has created conditions of congestion on the poor quality land areas of the west and north. Moreover, the problem of small farm size is compounded by farm fragmentation (*Map 4*).

Many of the maps in this volume testify to the powerful influence of the resource base in the geographical distribution of agricultural activities. Layered over this relatively fixed set of basic resources is a complex of dynamic economic and technological forces, as well as an array of policy measures. The more significant of these are described in this section.

Against this explanatory framework, the following sections describe the general features of agricultural adjustment in the modern context, with particular reference to the more salient and specific changes observable in Ireland.

Geographical Differences in the Resource Base
Three factors are of central importance in determining the productive capacity of land and the range of farming enterprises it will support. One is that Irish soils vary considerably in potential and use range from one part of the State to another (Figure 6).

Land classified as 'difficult' for agriculture has been described as having stony and infertile soils, steep slopes, and rock outcrops (Lee and Gardiner, 1974; Gardiner and Radford, 1980; Gillmor, 1977). Generally, the west and north have the more difficult land, the percentages of such land in the provinces being: Connacht 57; Ulster 60; Munster 44; and Leinster 24 (Gillmor, 1977; p. 20). The more detailed distribution of Irish land according to its suitability for farming is shown in Figure 7.

Economic Forces – Demand and Supply in Farm Products

The capacity of a given population to consume food is limited. Thus, a basic characteristic of an agricultural economy is that the demand for its products is inelastic – that is, food consumption patterns generally will not change significantly even if prices are reduced. Similarly, increases in income, either for an individual or for a country, are unlikely to result in marked increases in demand. Therefore, demand is usually unresponsive with respect to both price and income, unless the total population expands. The replacement of agricultural materials by non-agricultural products (e.g. synthetics) exacerbates this demand problem.

Meanwhile, with the expansion of technical knowledge farmers can achieve high levels of production. The outcome of these demand and supply forces is a constant downward pressure on farmgate prices and farm incomes, which is accentuated when more and more of what the consumer pays goes to cover costs incurred in processing outside the farm.

In the face of these economic pressures farmers, individually and collectively, pursue a number of strategies – lowering costs, using new technology, enlarging the scale of the farm business, seeking other sources of income and advocating subsidisation policies of various kinds. The discussion which follows sets out how Irish farmers respond to their changing economic environment.

Technology and Rising Costs of Production

In a competitive market individual farmers realise that they cannot influence the price obtained for their products. They therefore seek to increase their incomes by raising output and utilising cost-reducing technology to do so. The term 'technology' is applied here in the broad sense, to incorporate not only mechanisation but also biochemical and information technology. Reliance on technology has three main consequences. The first is that while some innovations in technology may be 'scale-neutral', that is, applicable to farms of all sizes, most items are not neutral in their socio-economic impacts.

In other words, their successful adoption in practice calls for levels of resources, knowledge, skill and managerial ability which are not randomly distributed among the farm population. Machine technologies, especially, are scale-related (Walsh, 1992). In 1995 the asset value of machinery on Irish farms of over 100 hectares was 13 times their value on farms of between 10 and 20 hectares. A similar ratio existed in the case of machinery usage costs.

Since 1980, costs annually have generally been above 60 per cent of output value on the average farm, but were close to 70 per cent on farms over 100 hectares. The real impact of rising costs of production during the 1990s has been concealed to the extent that gross output figures are boosted by the inclusion of direct 'non-market' payments. This point is taken up in more detail later (see under 'The Role of Public Policy').

The third implication of dependence on technology is that farmers become integrated into wider networks of agri-business – those supplying credit and purchased inputs and those processing outputs. This wider context has its own set of technical and economic imperatives (e.g., for firms to be competitive) and these reinforce structural change at farm level. For instance, the efficiency demands and technological developments of agri-processing firms often require complementary investments by farmers themselves. Rather than incur these extra costs some farmers change to another farming system or cease production altogether.

Labour Outflow

One of the main functions of technology is to substitute for labour. We have already adverted to the longer-term decrease in the Irish farm labour force. This decline reflects both 'push' and 'pull' factors – the push of limited land and other resources and the pull of alternative sources of employment. It is significant that since 1951 the average annual rate of decline in the Irish farm labour force exceeded 3 per cent in two periods – in the 1970s and 1990s. These were years when there was a buoyant non-farm economy and employment rose by unprecedented rates.

The second implication of modern technology is that while it can lower costs per unit of output – especially for its early adopters – total costs per farm are not reduced. In fact total costs absorb a rising proportion of the increasing value of output per farm. From the 1950s to the 1970s total net expenses (direct costs plus overheads) on Irish farms ranged between 35 and 60 per cent of the value of gross farm output, though remaining below 50 per cent for nearly all farm size categories.

Enlargement of Farm Scale and Farm Consolidation

The pressure to maintain economic viability in farming obliges farm operators to enlarge the scale of their farm business by acquiring extra land and/or intensifying the scale of their farm operations. Equally, of course, the inadequacy of holding sizes limits the capacity of the farm household to 'reproduce' itself in the next generation. Farm enlargement in Ireland, albeit on a limited scale, is most pronounced in areas where small holdings are compounded by 'demographic failure' associated with the high incidence of farming households without direct successors (Hannan and Commins, 1993). In this volume *Map 6* and Tables 8 and 10 show that the demise of small holdings is greatest in those districts where there are high percentages of older farm holders and of farm holders who are not actively farming.

In general, however, because of rigidities in the Irish land tenure system (i.e., the virtual absence of long-term leasing and the limited scale of the land market) farm structural change is comparatively slow even in the face of the economic pressures noted above. Between 1984 and 1995 the average size of farm owned increased by only 2.5 hectares, to 29.2 hectares. Scale enlargement is more commonly achieved by renting in land, but such renting has become predominantly a feature of the larger farms (see *Map 13*) thus accentuating the differences in farming scale.

In the 1991 Census of Agriculture farms over 50 hectares represented 11.5 per cent of all farms in the State but these accounted for 23 per cent of farms renting in land and 51.1 per cent of the area rented.

The level of intensification on farms, as measured by livestock units per hectare, has also been increasing but, between 1984 and 1995, farms over 30 hectares showed the larger proportionate increases. This is reflected in a distinctive geographical pattern, as *Map 95* illustrates.

Concentration of Production

It will be understood from the above description of structural change that there has been a concentration of Irish agricultural production in a narrowing band of farm size groupings. In 1997, the larger-scale farms (over 16 European Size Units[1]), representing 34 per cent of all farms, operated 56 per cent of total utilised agricultural area, but produced 73 per cent of gross farm output. The tendency for production to become concentrated on the larger farms means, in effect, a pattern of regional concentration, as the following figures show:

Region	% of farms	% of Area	% Output
West[1]	57.3	47.2	36.4
East[2]	42.7	52.8	63.6

[1]Connacht and Ulster counties, together with Longford, Clare, Kerry, and West Cork
[2]Remainder of the State

Polarisation in Farm Incomes

The concentration of production on fewer farms creates a polarisation of farm incomes. The type of enterprise on the farm, rather than the size of the farm, has become the main discriminator between high and low income farms in Ireland. There has been a growing income divergence between farms with a dairy enterprise and those relying mainly on cattle and sheep (Commins, 1996). In 1997 the average farm income on dairy farms was £19,980, compared to £5,594 on 'cattle rearing' farms and £7,738 on mainly sheep farms, though, as will be shown later, most of the income on cattle and sheep farms comes from non-market, direct payments.

For similar farming systems, however, there were regional differences in the 1997 average farm income levels, as follows:

Region	Dairying	Dairying and other	Cattle rearing	Cattle other	Mainly sheep	Mainly tillage
West[1]	£14,640	£12,690	£5,228	£4,871	£7,505	£12,437
East[2]	£25,085	£21,739	£6,668	£6,640	£9,313	£15,095

[1]Connacht and Ulster counties, together with Longford, Clare, Kerry, and West Cork
[2]Remainder of the State

Reliance on Non-Farm Incomes

Over time, with the constant downward pressure on incomes derived from farming – and notwithstanding the supplementation of those incomes by both direct and indirect subsidies – farm households have come to rely increasingly on earnings from other sources. Between 1973 and 1994/95 the proportionate contribution of 'other employment' to Direct Household Income on farms (i.e., taking earnings of all persons into account but ignoring income transfers such as pensions) has generally doubled across all farm sizes.

Map 21, based on the 1991 census, shows the variation throughout the State in the proportion of farm households in which farming was not the sole occupation of the farm holder. In 1997 there was an estimated 42.5 per cent of farms on which the farm operator and/or spouse had non-farm earnings. If married farm operators only are taken into account this figure rises to 53 per cent.

The Role of Public Policy: The Impact of State and EU Income Supports

Because of the inherent instabilities in agricultural production and the longer-term tendencies for farms to be economically non-viable businesses, as well as the need, historically, to ensure food supplies, agriculture as an economic sector is distinctive in the universality and persistence of the public supports provided to it.

This support is evident in the provision of research and advisory services and in the funding of marketing structures but, especially, in the subsidisation of incomes. Three time phases of subsidisation can be discerned for Ireland.

The early phase was marked by guaranteed prices for farm commodities, a responsibility transferred from the Irish exchequer to the then EEC on accession to the Community in 1973. However, over time it was realised that price support policies skewed the distribution of income in favour of the larger volume producer and accentuated the differentiation between low-income and high-income farming. Gradually, farm price supports are being reduced.

A second phase of subsidisation – from the mid-1970s onwards – introduced 'compensatory allowances' to provide a reasonable level of income for farmers in 'less-favoured areas' where natural production conditions were difficult. While payments under this heading were modest they were biased towards low income farmers although this advantage was subsequently eroded by special premia payments made to all farmers.

With the 1992 reform of the CAP a third phase of subsidisation was established when (i) farmers were given special non-market premia to offset reductions in commodity prices; (ii) the non-productive (in the agricultural sense) functions of farming were explicitly acknowledged and farmers could obtain payments by opting for systems of farming which conserved the natural environment; and (iii) special incentives were provided to encourage diversification from conventional types of production.

The outcome of this evolution of income subsidisation has been that non-market payments have now become a major influence on farm income levels, especially on low income farms. In 1997 such payments amounted to £6,670 on the average Irish farm, or 61.8 per cent of average farm income. In fact, on cattle and sheep farms (typically the poorest earners of farming income) direct payments represented over 90 per cent of what was earned from farming. On western farms in 1997 direct payments accounted, on average, for £5,441 of the mean farm income of £7,931 (68.6 per cent); the corresponding figures in the east were £8,482 in direct payments on a farm income of £14,794 (57.3 per cent).

In this way policies have an ameliorative effect on the economic forces which tend to impel structural change and rationalisation of farm businesses, especially in the less favoured areas of the country.

Relief and soils

Physical factors have a major influence on systems of farming and their profitability. The significant advances in agricultural technology in recent decades have done little to alter the basic dependency between the quantity and quality of crop and livestock production and such physical factors as relief, soil and climatic conditions.

Ireland's relief could be described as predominantly low-lying with its saucer shaped physical morphology consisting of an outer rim of uplands around a reasonably undifferentiated central plain covering over one-third of the country (Figure 8). This form is due to a combination of variations in lithology (varying resistance to erosion) and the processes that occurred during the tertiary upheavals (c. 65 million years ago). The gently undulating central lowland plain lies atop the largest continuous stretch of carboniferous limestone in Europe.

The uplands of Ireland tend to be quite fragmented and, in fact, form what is a very discontinuous rim with lowland areas 'fingering' their way to the sea at several points along the western seaboard. The most significant break in the upland rim occurs over a 90 km stretch in the east, between Dundalk Bay and Dublin Bay (Johnson, 1994; Herries Davies and Stephens, 1978).

Within the 'central lowland' there is some diversity, ranging from the 'drumlin' region in its northern portion, which presents poor drainage and limitations for farming, to the 'ridge and valley' area in its southern portion. Here, upland areas of between 300 and 600 metres emerge amid broad fertile, relatively well drained, lowlands forming some of the best agricultural land in the State.

Figure 6:
Soils

Shallow brown earths
Grey-brown podzolics
Brown podzolics
Acid brown earths
Podzols
Gleys
Peats and peaty gleys

Source: Aalen *et al.* (1997)

Figure 7:
Land Use Capability

Wide
Somewhat limited
Limited
Very limited
Extremely limited

Source: Aalen *et al.* (1997)

Between these two regions lies what is perhaps the true 'lowland' region, characterised by glacial deposits varying in thickness from over 60 metres in the east to almost nothing in western locations (Johnson, 1994; Aalen *et al.*, 1997).

Soils are a vital link in understanding the geography of Irish agriculture. Irish soils vary greatly in type and hence in their range of uses (Gardiner and Radford, 1980). Figure 6 presents a very generalised summary of the distribution of the major soil types in Ireland. This spatial distribution is the result of the interaction of various factors, among which are the parent material from which the soil was derived, climate and relief.

In the case of Ireland most of the parent material consists of glacial drift which varies in its chemical and physical composition depending on the mixture of rocks from which it has been derived. The primary climatological influence on soils is the abundant rainfall resulting in leaching or the movement downward through the soil of minerals and nutrients. Relief is important in this context by virtue of its associations with climatic and vegetational changes so that areas of rugged relief tend to have poorer and shallower soils (Orme, 1970; Gillmor, 1977; Gardiner, 1979).

While any detailed discussion of soil types is outside the scope of this atlas, from Figure 6 it is evident that there is an intricate mosaic of soil types ranging from the good all purpose grey-brown podzolics of the midlands to the very limited peats and peaty gleys found extensively in the upland areas of the south-west, west and north-west. The predominantly gley soils in parts of the mid-west are also very limited due to impeded drainage except where some arterial drainage systems are put in place. The typically poor nutrient status of other soil types, such as the acid brown earths of the south-east and the brown podzolics in Cork, can be overcome with good management practices.

Figure 8:
Relief

Source: Sweeney (1997)

0 - 200m
200 - 600m
600m plus

Figure 9:
Number of Farm Types per DED 1991

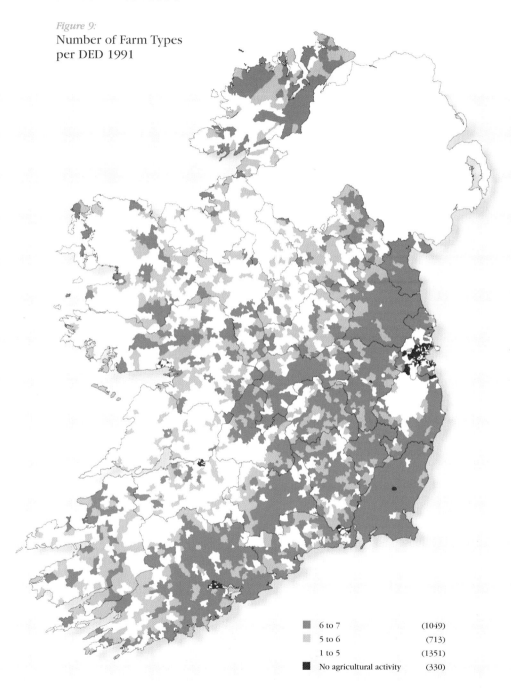

6 to 7	(1049)
5 to 6	(713)
1 to 5	(1351)
No agricultural activity	(330)

The land use capability of these various soil types is presented in Figure 7 in which the soils of the midlands, east and south have the widest use range. The mountainous areas are clearly the most limited although extensive parts of Connacht are in the limited, very limited and extremely limited categories.

The extent to which soils influence the geography of agricultural production can be seen clearly from Figure 9 in which those parts of the State with the greatest range of farming activities are shown to correlate strongly with those areas having soils with the widest use range.

Conclusion: Modernisation and Marginalisation

Four decades of change in the Irish farm economy have resulted in the modernisation and commercialisation of a core of Irish farms. Change has also contributed to the economic marginalisation – and even the demise – of many more. These processes are inextricably linked to the basic configuration of resources and farm size by which the less favoured west and north is distinguished from the remainder of the State. Superimposed on this resource structure is a range of other influences on change – the mix of policies, the impacts of technology and its implications for scale of farm business, variations in demographic characteristics, and in the availability of non-farm income-earning opportunities.

This pattern of modernisation and marginalisation seems set to continue over the next decade. Of the 128,000 farms in the State in 1997 (i.e., omitting the 20,000 very small holdings) only about 50,000 could be deemed economically and demographically viable in a strict sense. Of the remaining 80,000 farms (of which 60,000 are in the western counties) there are some 33,000 for which their non-viable status is cushioned by the farm operator and/or spouse having another source of earned income. Another 17,000 are operated mostly by older people with no off-farm employment and who are dependent mainly on social welfare payments. The problematic non-viable farms are the remaining 30,000 with low farm incomes (an average of £6,400 in 1996), no off-farm employment, and where the household is at a comparatively early stage of the family life cycle (Commins, 1999).

In many ways, then, the maps in this atlas, while mostly representing a snapshot at a point in time (the year 1991), also offer a preview of the geography of Irish agriculture for the early years of the new millennium.

Section Two

Structural Features
of Agricultural Production

Introduction

The geography of agricultural production in Ireland, as well as the direction of change in all of the principal farming types, is influenced by several factors as already noted. These interact in a manner that provides farms in some regions with distinctive sources of comparative advantage while in others, especially in the west and north-west, agricultural production and the capacity to adjust to commercial farming requirements are severely constrained. This section provides an overview of the geography of the main structural factors. Farm size, including the extent of fragmentation, is discussed at first, after which the various patterns of land acquisition are detailed. This is followed by an examination of key attributes of the farm labour force before proceeding to a consideration of farm mechanisation. Data on tractors are used as a proxy for identifying the geography of capital investment on farms. Finally, this section examines variations in productivity levels on farms which are related to, among other factors, contrasts in agricultural land potential.

Farm Size

The Central Statistics Office has defined a farm in the agricultural census as "a single unit, both technically and economically, which has a single management and which produces agricultural products" (CSO, 1994; p. 6). In 1991 there were just over 170,000 farms in the Republic of Ireland. The average size of farm varies considerably across regions and has a significant influence on the farm activities pursued by farmers and on their capacity to adjust to changing circumstances. Limited farm size has been one of the main structural problems faced by the 'modernising' agricultural sector in Ireland due to the dearth of land coming on the open market (Gillmor, 1979).

This inertia has resulted in little transfer of land outside the family and a resultant difficulty for farmers trying to increase the size of their holdings.

The average farm size in 1991 was 26.0 hectares which had increased to 29.4 hectares in 1997 (Table 1). At the regional level in 1991 the average varied from 36.5 hectares in the South-East to only 18.4 hectares in the West, with the smallest county average size of 16.2 hectares occurring in Mayo. Over 53 per cent of all farms in the State were less than 20 hectares in size with the largest concentration of small farms occurring in the Border and West regions. The largest farms were in the Dublin, Mid-East and South-East regions (the counties comprising each region are shown in Figure 4).

Large percentages (30 to 45 per cent) of farms in almost all regions are in the 20 to 50 hectare category. Over 18 per cent of farms in the South-East region are between 50 and 100 hectares while over 6 per cent in Dublin and the Mid-East regions are over 100 hectares. It is noteworthy that Dublin has a very high percentage of farms less than 10 hectares while also having a relatively high percentage of very large farms. These smaller farms are often associated with intensive vegetable and horticultural production for the Dublin market. Outside of Dublin, the regions with the smallest farms tend to correlate with the areas of poorest land quality, thus compounding the structural problem in these regions.

The origin of the 'small farm problem' in Ireland can be explained as an outcome of historical forces involving a number of phases of confiscation and settlement with large numbers of indigenous inhabitants displaced westwards to land of poorer quality. The resultant congestion in the west was exaggerated by the continuous sub-division of farms due to early marriages and the settlement of all sons on the land. Landlords promoting sub-division to increase their numbers of tenants as a means of increasing their power under the prevailing political system also contributed to the proliferation of small farms (Gillmor, 1991; Commins, 1993).

Map 1 presents the average farm size at District Electoral Division (DED) level and demonstrates its very distinctive geography. There is a clear dividing line from the Galway Bay area in the west to Dundalk in the east. The largest and second largest categories are mostly concentrated in the south and east. Some very large farms are also found in selected western districts especially in upland areas and in the Burren in north-west Clare. The physical size of a farm in these areas is less meaningful due to the poor quality of the land and the more extensive farming activities undertaken.

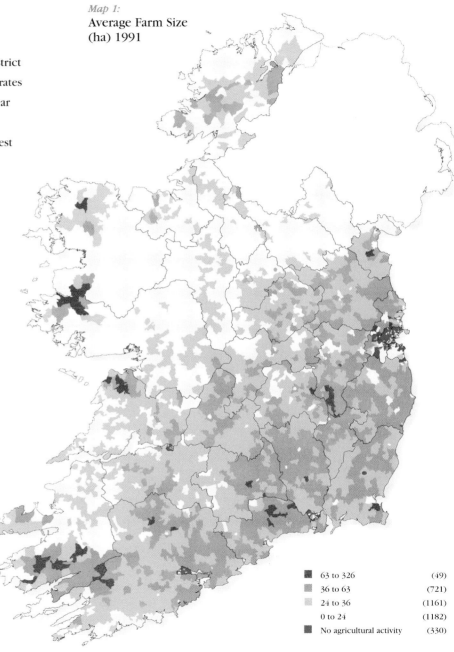

Map 1:
Average Farm Size (ha) 1991

63 to 326	(49)
36 to 63	(721)
24 to 36	(1161)
0 to 24	(1182)
No agricultural activity	(330)

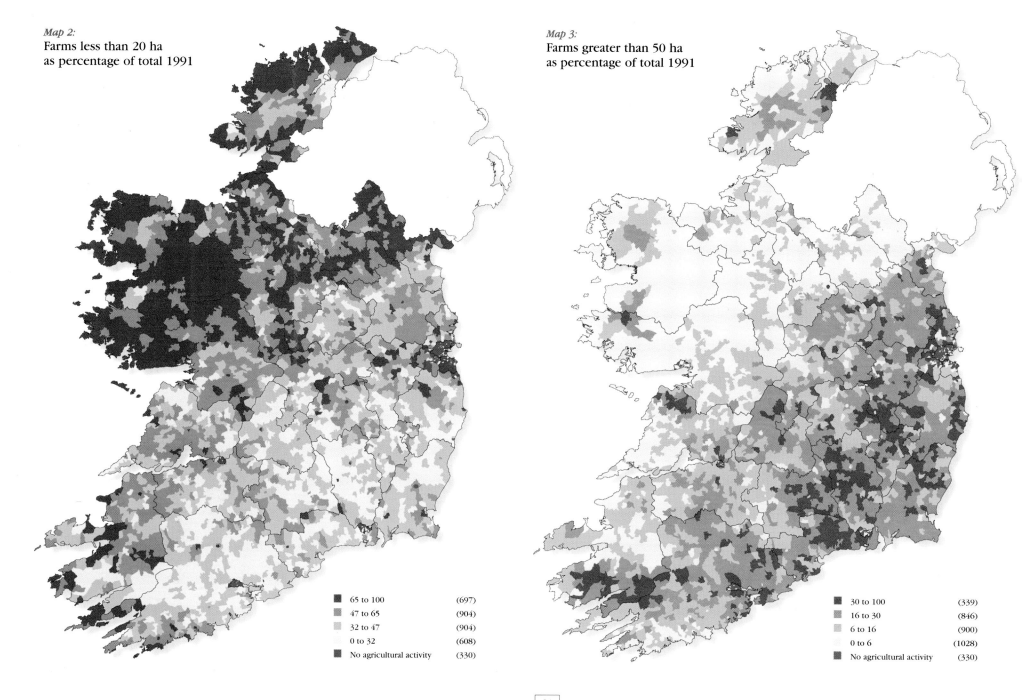

Map 2:
**Farms less than 20 ha
as percentage of total 1991**

Map 3:
**Farms greater than 50 ha
as percentage of total 1991**

	65 to 100	(697)
	47 to 65	(904)
	32 to 47	(904)
	0 to 32	(608)
	No agricultural activity	(330)

	30 to 100	(339)
	16 to 30	(846)
	6 to 16	(900)
	0 to 6	(1028)
	No agricultural activity	(330)

Maps 2 and *3* further illustrate the contrasts in farm size between the north-west and south-east. The top two intervals on *Map 2* represent areas in which more than 47 per cent of all farms are less than 20 hectares. This shows the severity of the small farm problem which is most acute in parts of Mayo, Galway, Roscommon and north Donegal. *Map 3* shows the obverse situation where in the top two categories over 16 per cent of all farms are greater than 50 hectares in size. This map is remarkable for the fact that the general north-western half of the State is almost totally undifferentiated while falling into the lowest interval (less than 6 per cent). Also of significance is the dairying region of Cavan/Monaghan which is classified in the lowest interval, as opposed to the dairying region of the south-west in which farms are significantly larger.

Table 1: Number of farms and percentage distribution by size (ha), 1991 and 1997

Region	No. of farms	Percentage of total					Average size (ha)
		<10 ha	10<20 ha	20<50 ha	50<100 ha	100+ ha	
Dublin	1,511	36.7	18.8	25.5	12.7	6.2	32.6
Mid-East	11,629	24.2	20.3	33.5	15.6	6.4	36.0
South-East	20,377	18.4	17.6	40.9	18.4	4.6	36.5
South-West	28,178	20.2	24.2	41.5	11.5	2.5	29.8
Mid-West	20,066	17.9	25.3	44.6	10.4	1.8	28.1
West	38,964	30.2	38.8	27.2	3.1	0.6	18.4
Border (west)	20,268	34.9	31.7	27.3	4.9	1.2	19.8
Border (east)	14,314	32.1	32.6	29.9	4.6	0.9	19.7
Midland	15,271	22.7	25.8	37.4	11.5	2.5	28.1
Ireland 1991	170,578	25.3	28.3	34.8	9.3	2.3	26.0
Ireland 1997	147,800	20.0	27.0	38.8	11.2	2.8	29.4

Source: Census of Agriculture 1991; Crops and Livestock Survey 1997.

Table 2: Percentage of farms classified by number of separate parcels, 1991

Region	Number of land parcels				
	1	2	3	4	5 plus
Dublin	56.8	20.8	10.5	5.1	6.9
Mid-East	60.1	25.3	9.4	3.2	2.1
South-East	45.3	29.6	13.9	5.7	5.6
South-West	52.6	29.8	10.2	4.1	3.3
Mid-West	46.2	31.2	13.6	5.1	3.9
West	38.6	32.2	15.5	6.8	7.0
Border (west)	53.0	29.2	10.1	4.3	3.4
Border (east)	52.0	29.5	11.5	4.2	2.8
Midland	49.3	29.8	12.4	4.6	3.9
Ireland	48.0	30.0	12.5	5.0	4.4

Source: Census of Agriculture 1991.

Farm Fragmentation

In addition to farms being small there is the added problem of farm fragmentation. Just over half of all farms in the State consist of two or more land parcels while almost 10 per cent comprise four or more parcels (Table 2). The Mid-East and Dublin regions appear to have the most consolidated farms with 60 per cent and 57 per cent respectively of farms being in one parcel. At the other extreme the West region has the most fragmented farm structure. Fragmentation has been a persistent problem in Ireland and has posed a substantial obstacle to improving farm efficiency (Scully, 1969; Gillmor, 1979).

Map 4 establishes that the geography of farm fragmentation is complex. Low levels of fragmentation are found in contrasting areas such as the flat terrain of much of the Mid-East and some of the upland areas in western districts. By contrast, high levels of fragmentation occur in east Galway and east Mayo (17 per cent of farms in Galway consist of four or more parcels) and also in the more arable farming areas in the south-east (in Wexford almost 14 per cent of farms consist of four or more parcels). In the latter areas, high levels of fragmentation may be associated with the practice of renting in or purchasing land.

Change in Size of Farms/Holdings

The change in enumeration procedures employed in the 1991 Census of Agriculture makes impossible any precise analysis of changes in farm size over the 1980s. However, given the historical stability of farm sizes in Ireland it is reasonable to assume that only minor changes have taken place and that the trends established in earlier decades have continued. As an illustration, *Map 5* presents the percentage change in the total number of holdings[2] over the 1960-80 period. In considering maps based on 'holdings' rather than 'farms' it is necessary to be aware of the distinction and some of the problems it presents. Holdings were enumerated on the basis of ownership of land rather than on who farmed it.

For this reason the number of holdings exceeded the number of true farms while also under-representing their size. This could have been due to separate holdings under the same management being recorded separately if they were not "in the same neighbourhood" and also due to farmers making 'strategic' decisions to report separate holdings.

Map 5 illustrates the general tendency for decreases in the total number of holdings over the period 1960 to 1980. The most obvious feature is that the greatest declines were in the areas of smallest holdings, namely the west and north. Clearly, small farms had become unviable economically and were amalgamated into larger units. Areas of increase were almost completely confined to the east and south.

Table 3: Total holdings[1] 1980 and change in holdings 1960-1980

Region	Total holdings 1980	Actual change 1960-80	Percentage change			
			<20 ha	20-60 ha	60-120 ha	>120 ha
Dublin	3,167	-1,067	-27.8	-18.1	-13.7	-6.0
Mid-East	18,910	-258	-4.9	8.9	-0.5	-16.9
South-East[2]	29,256	-2,027	-12.7	1.0	1.7	-14.9
South-West[2]	42,003	2,003	-8.6	1.6	-0.9	-8.6
Mid-West	29,281	-2,249	-12.7	2.5	-3.5	-15.7
West	59,381	-7,844	-16.1	15.5	-12.6	-22.4
Border (west)	36,022	-4,777	-15.5	6.2	6.6	-15.9
Border (east)	22,617	-4,113	-21.4	15.0	3.9	5.8
Midland	22,921	-2,412	-16.7	8.3	-3.2	-29.8
Ireland	263,558	-26,750	-14.6	5.6	-1.2	-16.4

[1] Excluding holdings less than 1 acre.
[2] For 1960 the number of holdings in Tipperary North and Tipperary South were estimated on the basis of 1980 distributions.
Source: Agricultural Statistics 1960; Agricultural Statistics 1980.

Declines in the total number of holdings were significantly greater in the Border and West regions than elsewhere (Table 3). The extent to which the overall pattern of change is influenced by variations in the size of holdings is evident from *Maps 6, 7,* and *8*.

Map 4:
Fragmented Farms* as percentage
of total 1991

■	64 to 100	(796)
▨	48 to 64	(1004)
▨	30 to 48	(899)
□	0 to 30	(414)
■	No agricultural activity	(330)

*Farms with two or more
parcels of land

Map 5:
Total Holdings
Percentage Change 1960-1980

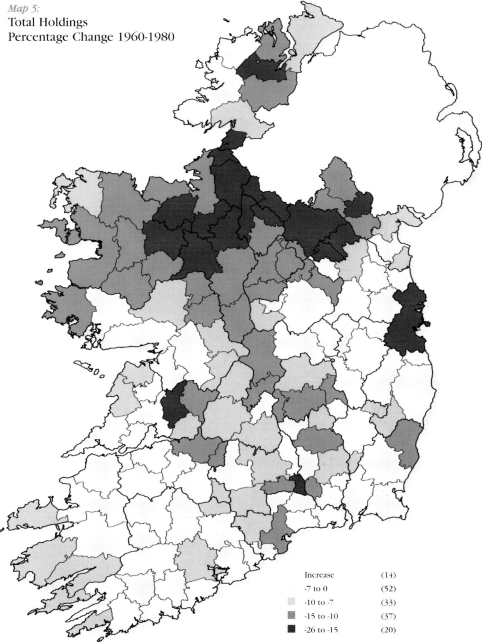

	Increase	(14)
	-7 to 0	(52)
	-10 to -7	(33)
	-15 to -10	(37)
	-26 to -15	(20)

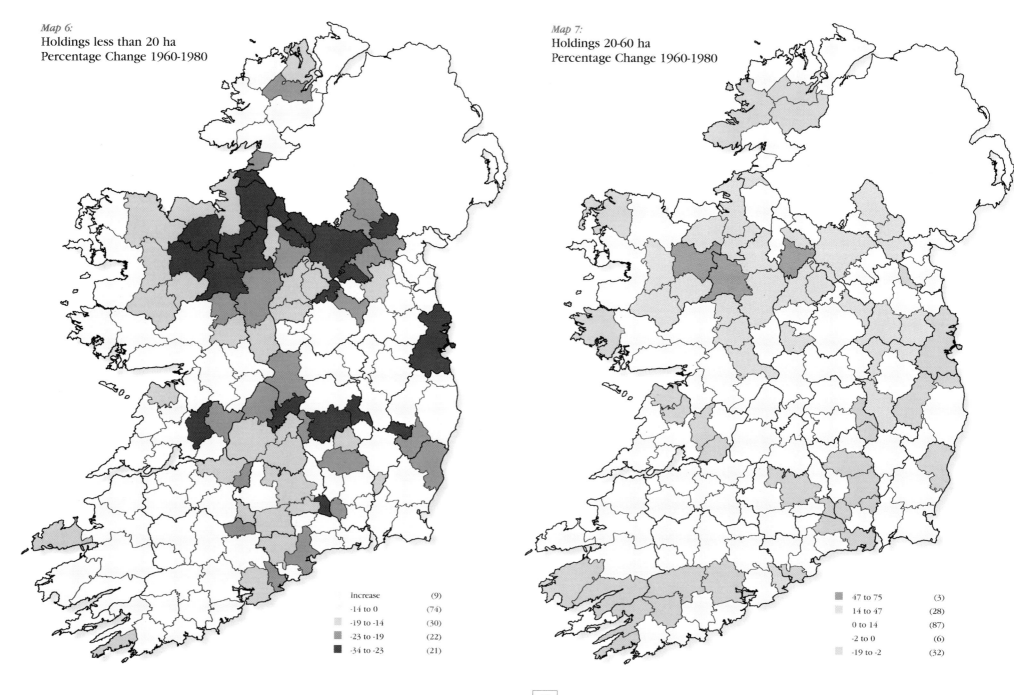

Map 6:
Holdings less than 20 ha
Percentage Change 1960-1980

Map 7:
Holdings 20-60 ha
Percentage Change 1960-1980

	Increase	(9)
	-14 to 0	(74)
	-19 to -14	(30)
	-23 to -19	(22)
	-34 to -23	(21)

	47 to 75	(3)
	14 to 47	(28)
	0 to 14	(87)
	-2 to 0	(6)
	-19 to -2	(32)

The greatest decline in holdings with less than 20 hectares occurred in parts of counties Mayo, Roscommon, Leitrim, Cavan and Monaghan *(Map 6)*. In a study of land use and mobility, Hannan and Commins (1993) found that three basic factors explained differences among Rural Districts in the rate of structural change in land holdings. These were: (i) the average size and quality of the resources owned by individual landholders; (ii) the varying degree of commercialisation in farming; and (iii) the opportunity for part-time farming. Regions with the greatest degree of change in land-holding structure were those with poorest resources, the least development in commercial agriculture and which were the most remote from employment in urban centres.

Map 7 shows increases in the 20 to 60 hectare category over large parts of the State, especially in those areas where there was a decline in the number of small holdings, confirming a gradual process of enlargement. The largest size category (>120 ha) showed declines everywhere with the exception of the Border (east) region and parts of the South-West plus some dispersed districts in other areas *(Map 8)*. Where increases are recorded the actual numbers involved are relatively small and to some extent they reflect a process of enlargement in districts with limited agricultural potential.

Land Tenure and Methods of Land Acquisition

In the early nineteenth century Irish farmers were predominantly tenant farmers who sub-divided their holdings among their sons. The Land Acts of the 1880s were aimed at replacing this system with one in which farmers could become owner-occupiers of their farms. So successful was land reform that Ireland now has the highest level of owner-occupancy of any country in the European Union. This history may account for the high social significance attached to land ownership in Ireland and indeed to the situation that has emerged in which Irish agriculture is characterised by low levels of land mobility resulting, in part, from the late transfer of family land (Gillmor, 1979; 1991). Late transfers can lead to a poor demographic structure among farm operators and to a lack of progress in terms of the adoption of new and efficient farm practices (Macra na Feirme, 1992). Land is often held by farmers who are not using it to its full potential while younger farmers, more capable and better qualified, are hampered in their efforts because they are unable to expand their farm size. Many factors have been advanced as influencing land transfer, including farm size, education levels, on-farm and off-farm income potential, as well as the policy environment in which farmers may be enticed to transfer land for pension, social welfare or tax relief purposes (Gillmor, 1991).

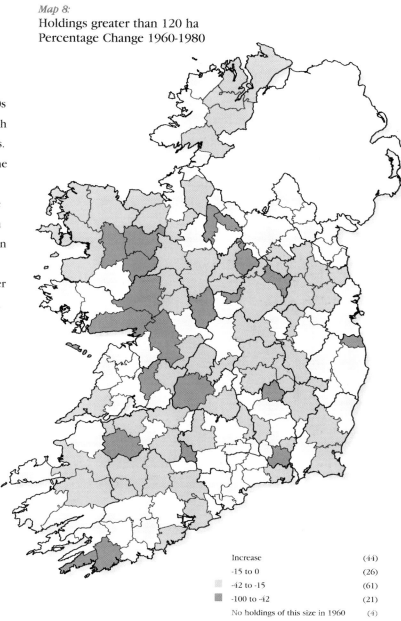

Map 8:
Holdings greater than 120 ha
Percentage Change 1960-1980

Increase (44)
-15 to 0 (26)
-42 to -15 (61)
-100 to -42 (21)
No holdings of this size in 1960 (4)

Acquisition by Inheritance

Table 4 summarises the regional variations in the 'means of acquisition' of farm land by the current owners, as of 1991. As expected, by far the most important means of acquisition in all regions is inheritance, that is, the passing on of land to a family member or relative after the death of the owner. Almost 45 per cent of the total area owned in the State was acquired by this method. Family transfers or 'gifts' account for the next largest share at 31.5 per cent, followed by purchase at 21.6 per cent. Behind these national figures lie substantial inter-regional and intra-regional variations. Acquisition by inheritance is very important in all parts of the State but its incidence is highest in the West, where it accounts for 53.5 per cent of the total area owned. The Border (west) is the next highest with 49 per cent. The West and Border (west) regions combined account for over 29 per cent of all land inherited while having just over 25 per cent of the total area owned in the State. This illustrates the degree of reluctance on the part of land holders to transfer land during their lifetime and, as *Map 9* shows, it is more a feature of the west and north-west. It is particularly important in Mayo where it accounts for 58 per cent of all farmed land. It is least important in the South-West where in many of the more intensively farmed districts the proportion is less than 20 per cent.

Table 4: Means of farm land acquisition by current owners as a percentage of total area owned (share of State total in parentheses), 1991.

Region	Inherited	Family Transfer	Purchased	Land Commission Grant	Other Means	Percentage of total owned
Dublin	43.9[1] (0.9)[2]	12.4 (0.4)	42.5 (1.8)	0.8 (0.5)	0.4 (0.5)	100 (0.9)
Mid-East	44.2 (9.0)	19.4 (5.6)	33.3 (14.0)	2.4 (13.5)	0.7 (8.4)	(100) 9.1
South-East	45.4 (17.0)	29.2 (15.6)	23.5 (18.3)	1.2 (12.2)	0.6 (15.0)	(100) 16.7
South-West	35.8 (15.4)	43.5 (26.5)	18.8 (16.7)	0.8 (8.9)	1.0 (27.8)	(100) 19.2
Mid-West	40.6 (11.8)	38.3 (15.8)	19.1 (11.5)	1.2 (9.8)	0.7 (12.7)	(100) 12.9
West	53.5 (19.8)	29.1 (15.3)	14.4 (11.1)	2.3 (23.2)	0.7 (15.3)	(100) 16.5
Border (west)	49.0 (9.5)	28.0 (7.7)	20.9 (8.4)	1.3 (7.0)	0.8 (9.1)	(100) 8.7
Border (east)	46.7 (6.5)	23.5 (4.6)	27.8 (8.0)	1.6 (6.1)	0.4 (3.6)	(100) 6.2
Midland	46.0 (10.1)	27.7 (8.6)	22.6 (10.3)	3.2 (18.9)	0.6 (7.8)	(100) 9.8
Ireland	44.6 (100)	31.5 (100)	21.6 (100)	1.6 (100)	0.7 (100)	100 (100)

[1] 43.9% of all land owned in Dublin is inherited.
[2] 0.9% of all inherited land in the State is in Dublin.
Source: Census of Agriculture 1991.

Farm land purchased as a percentage of total area owned, 1991

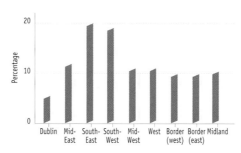

Acquisition by Family Transfer

Family transfer refers to land transferred prior to the death of the owner. It reflects situations where a planned approach to managing farm resources is more prevalent. As a means of transfer it is most important in the South-West and Mid-West regions where it accounts for 43.5 per cent and 38.3 per cent respectively of the total area owned. Indeed, while the South-West contains just over 19 per cent of the total area owned in the State it contains 26.5 per cent of all the land transferred by this means. The vast majority of land transfers in Ireland take place within the family network, which results in farms remaining "in the family name" for many generations. In a national survey Kelly (1982) estimated that in only 17 per cent of cases was the recipient of land not a relative of the previous owner. *Map 10* presents the 'family transfer' variable and highlights a general western bias although this type of transfer is particularly important in the South-West with proportions in excess of 50 per cent in a large number of districts. By contrast, family transfers are relatively uncommon throughout much of Mayo and parts of Sligo and Leitrim where there is a high incidence of inheritance. In the Mid-East family transfers are relatively infrequent, but here it is due to the greater prevalence of land acquisition through purchases (*Map 11*).

Map 9:
Land acquired by Inheritance
as percentage of area owned 1991

Map 10:
Land acquired by Family Transfer
as percentage of area owned 1991

■	63 to 100	(697)
■	44 to 63	(971)
■	23 to 44	(858)
	0 to 23	(587)
■	No agricultural activity	(330)

■	53 to 100	(539)
■	31 to 53	(705)
■	14 to 31	(946)
	0 to 14	(923)
■	No agricultural activity	(330)

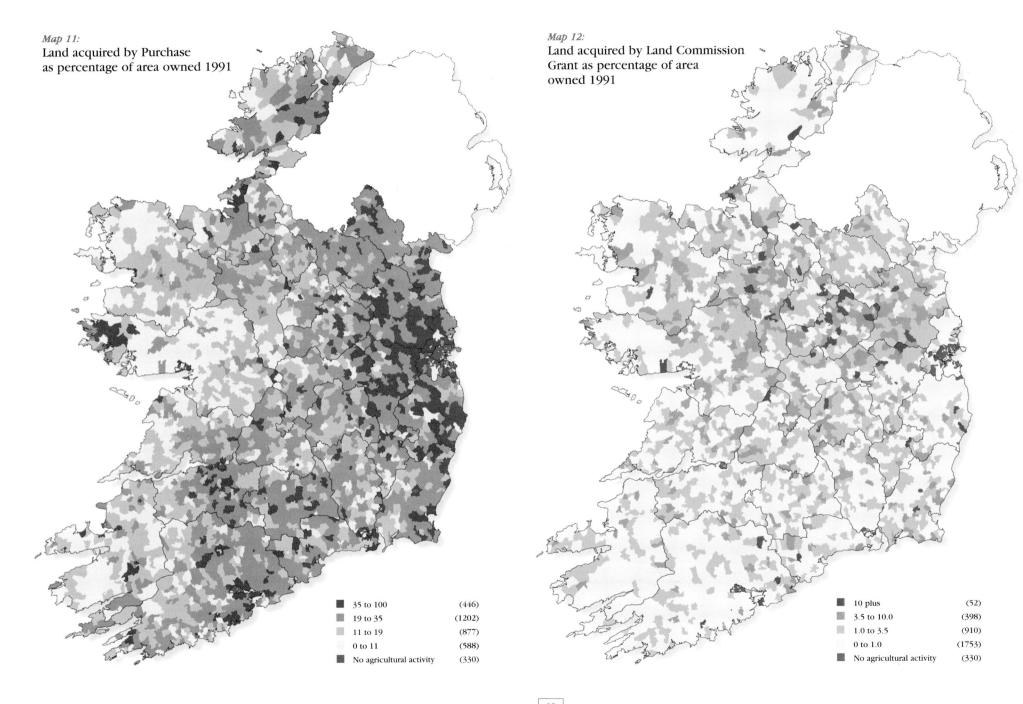

Map 11:
Land acquired by Purchase
as percentage of area owned 1991

Map 12:
Land acquired by Land Commission
Grant as percentage of area
owned 1991

■	35 to 100	(446)
■	19 to 35	(1202)
■	11 to 19	(877)
■	0 to 11	(588)
■	No agricultural activity	(330)

■	10 plus	(52)
■	3.5 to 10.0	(398)
■	1.0 to 3.5	(910)
■	0 to 1.0	(1753)
■	No agricultural activity	(330)

Acquisition by Purchase

Land acquired by purchase is of major importance in the Dublin and Mid-East regions where it accounts for 42.5 per cent and 33.3 per cent of the total area owned. *Map 11* clearly illustrates the significance of land purchases in the hinterland of the capital city. Another noteworthy feature is that land purchases are more important in the dairying region of counties Cavan and Monaghan than in parts of the southern dairy region, such as west Limerick, north Kerry and west Clare, where family transfers are more common. The orientation towards the land market in the east reflects a commercial logic where good quality land is regarded as a lucrative investment for large farmers as well as for other private and institutional investors. Urbanisation promotes additional demand for land and, by selling small parcels for residential or other development, farmers can gain the necessary capital to expand their farms by purchasing additional farm land.

Some exceptionally high levels of land acquisition by purchase are also evident in selected districts in parts of west Galway, north Sligo and west Cork. Such areas have experienced relatively high levels of immigration which may account for some of the land purchases.

Acquisition by Land Commission Grant

The fourth mode of acquisition, which is relatively unimportant in the overall context, accounting for only 1.6 per cent of total area owned, is through Land Commission grant allocation. The Irish Land Commission was established in 1881 to effect agrarian structural reform. Its role changed at several points in its history from rent-fixing and tenant purchase at its inception to bringing about enlargement of small uneconomic holdings and reduction of farm fragmentation in the latter years of its operation (Gillmor, 1979; 1991). Towards this end it had quite extensive powers of acquisition and distribution as well as the power to prevent the subdivision of a farm if this risked creating an economically non-viable farm.

The Land Commission was abolished in 1984 following the 1978 report of the Inter-departmental Committee on Land Structure Reform which accorded it only limited success in tackling the land structure problem, for reasons mainly outside the control of the Commission. The enlargement of 62,000 farm holdings since 1923 was not sufficient to eliminate the problem of congested areas and small farms. Of all land disbursed by the Commission, 23.2 per cent was in the West, followed by 18.9 per cent in the Midland and 13.5 per cent in the Mid-East regions (Table 4). However, less than 3 per cent of all land throughout most of these regions was acquired from the Land Commission.

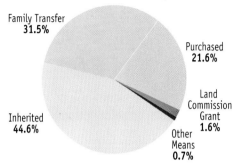

Means of Farm Land Acquisition

Family Transfer 31.5%

Purchased 21.6%

Land Commission Grant 1.6%

Other Means 0.7%

Inherited 44.6%

Map 12 illustrates the fact that by 1991 the influence of the Land Commission on modes of land acquisition had been reduced to minimal proportions. Over 56 per cent of all DEDs containing agricultural activity are classified as having farmers who obtained less than one per cent of all the area owned from the Land Commission. The main areas of activity for the Land Commission stretched from east Connacht, especially Roscommon, through the midland counties as far as Meath and north Kildare. Figures for Meath, Westmeath and Kildare reflect the impact of voluntary migration schemes that were in operation from 1934 until the 1970s whereby families (singly or in groups) were relocated from congested holdings in the west (Commins, 1993; Duffy, 1997). The exodus from the west of several thousand farm families in turn allowed for the enlargement of some holdings in that area.

Land Rented In

Due to the very small amount of land coming on the open market the extent of land rented in is an important feature of Irish farming. It can provide an insight into where intensive farming is practised, as for example on specialist tillage farms. A positive feature of land renting is that it introduces some flexibility by allowing more progressive farmers to expand their business while ensuring the land is utilised in a more productive fashion. A negative implication of short-term leasing is that it can be associated with a degree of insecurity which may be sufficient to inhibit good land management practices thereby leading to deterioration in land quality (Gillmor, 1979). Short-term leasing (usually 11 months) has emerged as the norm in Ireland due to the historical legacy of the landlord-tenant system. This was reinforced by the procedures of the Land Commission where permission was required for leases longer than 11 months, and since it also had the power to acquire land not being utilised to capacity, landholders were reluctant to get involved in long-term leases for fear of losing their land (Conway, 1986; Kelly, 1982).

Table 5: Land rented in[1], 1991

Region	% of farms with land rented in	% of AAU[2] rented in	Percentage distribution of farms by share of AAU rented in				
			100%	75-100%	50-75%	25-50%	<25%
Dublin	34.7	28.8	30.3	7.4	14.3	26.1	21.8
Mid-East	26.7	16.4	17.6	4.9	14.7	31.0	31.9
South East	29.7	13.6	16.5	4.2	10.2	26.8	42.4
South-West	20.6	12.3	20.8	4.5	11.5	28.9	34.3
Mid-West	20.4	10.2	17.0	3.6	10.0	30.3	39.0
West	15.4	9.5	12.0	3.5	14.7	38.5	31.3
Border (west)	21.7	14.5	25.5	4.8	16.6	30.1	23.0
Border (east)	23.6	12.8	12.0	2.9	13.3	36.1	35.8
Midland	20.5	10.8	14.5	4.3	13.2	32.9	35.1
Ireland	21.4	12.5	17.3	4.1	12.9	31.6	34.1

[1] Includes land rented in under long and short-term agreements.
[2] AAU refers to agricultural area utilised.
Source: Census of Agriculture 1991.

One-eighth of the total area used for agriculture is rented, although this varies considerably from 28.8 per cent in the Dublin region to 9.5 per cent in the West. It can be seen from Table 5 that 21.4 per cent of all farms have land rented in. This gives an average of 15.2 hectares per farm. On about two-thirds of farms the area rented in is less than 50 per cent of the total area farmed.

The incidence of renting in occurs on farms of all sizes although it is much more likely on large farms. For example, only about 13 per cent of farms with less than 20 hectares have land rented in.

For farms of between 50 and 100 hectares the proportion is 41 per cent and for those over 100 hectares the proportion rises to almost 50 per cent. On just over 1,900 farms with more than 100 hectares, the area rented in amounted to 23 per cent of the total rented area in the State.

Both Table 5 and *Map 13* illustrate the fact that most land renting activity takes place in the eastern half of the State and in east Donegal. Almost 35 per cent of all farms in the Dublin region have land rented in with 30 per cent of these renting their entire farming unit. The comparable figures are 15 per cent and 12 per cent for the West region.

The pattern summarised on *Map 13* can be largely explained by the association between the practice of renting in and type of farming. For example, 36.5 per cent of specialist tillage farms have large areas rented, on average 40 hectares per farm. Just over 30 per cent of mixed crops and livestock farms rent in on average 25 hectares. Almost 30 per cent of specialist dairy farms also have some land rented in, but the average area is much smaller at 12 hectares. The next highest incidence of renting in occurs on specialist sheep farms – 22.5 per cent of farms of this type have on average 19 hectares rented in. Renting in is least prevalent on specialist beef production farms being found on only 16 per cent of farms of this type.

Percentage of farms with land rented in

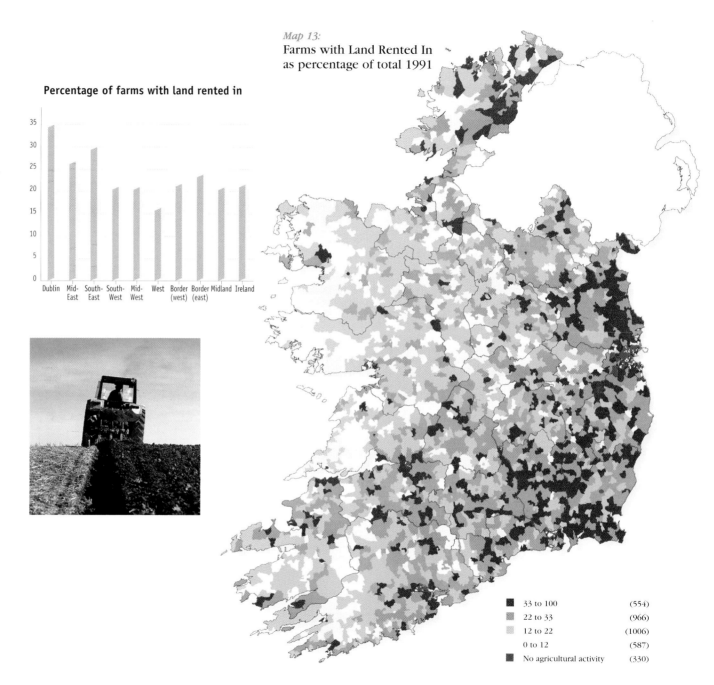

Map 13:
Farms with Land Rented In
as percentage of total 1991

33 to 100	(554)
22 to 33	(966)
12 to 22	(1006)
0 to 12	(587)
No agricultural activity	(330)

Map 14:

Commonage as percentage of total area farmed* 1991

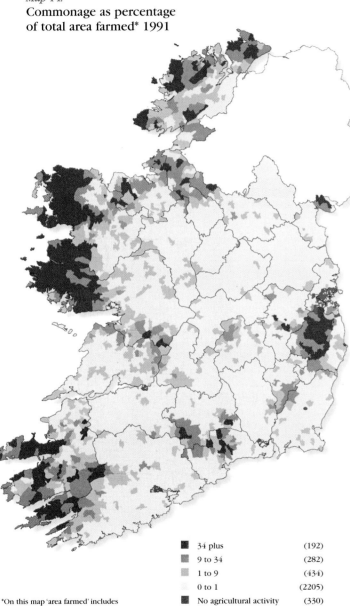

■ 34 plus	(192)
■ 9 to 34	(282)
■ 1 to 9	(434)
□ 0 to 1	(2205)
■ No agricultural activity	(330)

*On this map 'area farmed' includes area under commonage

Commonage

Commonage refers to land on which two or more farmers have grazing rights. It is used by just over 11,600 farms with an average area of almost 37 hectares per farm. While the majority of farms with commonage grazing rights are under 30 hectares there are a relatively small number – fewer than 200 – of large farms that have access to about one-third of the total commonage area. These are mostly on upland areas of poor land quality in counties Kerry, Cork, Clare, Galway, Mayo, Donegal and Wicklow. Commonage tends to be associated with less well-off farming areas and especially with mountain areas where it is used for grazing sheep *(Map 14)*. It is concentrated in the West, Border (west) and South-West regions where 12.2 per cent, 11.1 per cent and 8.8 per cent respectively of all farms have access to commonage; it accounts for 18.9 per cent, 13.9 per cent and 9.9 per cent respectively of the total area farmed (including commonage). Outside of the upland areas the map is almost completely undifferentiated showing that, over most of the State, commonage accounts for less than 2 per cent of the total area farmed.

Commonage can be a valuable addition to the owned land resources in marginal farming regions. Similar to land which is rented-in, commonage is subject to disimprovement due to having several 'sharers' which tends to lead to under-utilisation in general (Gillmor, 1979).

Table 6: Farms using Commonage, 1991

Region	Commonage as % of area farmed[1]	No. farms using Commonage	Number of farms using Commonage by size of farm (ha)				% of all farms using Commonage
			<5	5<30	30<100	>=100	
Dublin	8.7	63	12	41	6	4	4.2
Mid-East	8.8	427	29	201	180	17	3.7
South East	5.1	641	24	319	275	23	3.2
South-West	9.9	2,470	191	1,504	706	69	8.8
Mid-West	1.3	476	30	276	157	13	2.4
West	18.9	4,754	1,095	3,225	399	35	12.2
Border (west)	13.9	2,257	557	1,294	385	21	11.1
Border (east)	2.6	303	29	185	83	6	2.1
Midland	0.5	220	15	127	74	4	1.4
Ireland	8.8	11,611	1,982	7,172	2,265	192	6.8

[1] For this table 'area farmed' includes Commonage.
Source: Census of Agriculture 1991.

Under-utilisation occurs for a number of different reasons, including the non-commercial nature of the farms with which it is associated. Distance between the commonage and the main farm can also be a factor in how intensively it is utilised (Gillmor, 1977). However, given the huge increase in sheep numbers in the 1980s, some areas of commonage, especially in parts of Mayo, Kerry and Donegal, were seriously damaged from overgrazing due to excessive stocking levels.

Economic Size of Farms

In addition to assessing the physical size of farms, their fragmentation and the methods of land acquisition, it is helpful to consider their 'economic size'. Economic size is a measure of the scale of the farm business and is calculated in terms of European Size Units (ESUs).

Table 7: Percentage distribution of farms by European Size Units[1], 1991

Region	European Size Units (ESUs)					Average ESUs per farm
	0-4	4-8	8-16	16-40	40 plus	
Dublin	35.2	14.1	15.6	21.4	13.6	19.2
Mid-East	34.5	15.2	17.2	22.4	10.6	16.5
South-East	25.4	13.4	18.2	29.3	13.7	19.7
South-West	31.5	13.3	18.7	26.9	9.6	16.2
Mid-West	37.8	16.4	18.2	22.2	5.4	12.4
West	54.2	22.9	15.5	6.8	0.6	6.0
Border (west)	63.0	18.4	11.7	5.9	1.0	5.5
Border (east)	44.4	18.6	18.7	15.2	3.1	9.8
Midland	41.8	18.9	17.7	17.1	4.5	11.1
Ireland	42.7	17.6	16.8	17.3	5.6	11.6

[1] One European Size Unit = 1,200 ECU using 1986 standard gross margins.
Source: Census of Agriculture 1991.

ESUs are derived from standard gross margin (SGM) estimates for each farm based on the type of livestock and crops on the farm. For example, high SGMs are associated with tillage and dairying which tend to be concentrated in the Dublin and South-West regions, whereas in the West and Border (west) beef cattle and sheep generate low SGMs. Table 7 illustrates the significant differences in the average number of ESUs per farm across the regions. The highest values are found in the South-East followed closely by Dublin. The Mid-East and South-West are the next highest. These figures contrast very much with those for the Border (west) and West regions which have only approximately half the State average.

Almost two thirds of all farms in the Border (west) region have less than 4 ESUs, followed by the West region with 54.2 per cent.

The corresponding figures for the South-East and South-West are only 25.4 per cent and 31.5 per cent respectively. At the other extreme 43 per cent of all farms in the South-East generate more than 16 ESUs followed by the South-West with 36.5 per cent. Only about 7 per cent of farms belong to this category in the Border (west) and West regions.

The overall distribution of farms by economic size partitions the country along a line from Limerick to Dundalk (Map 15). The areas of largest economic size occur in the eastern and southern portion of the State, particularly counties Cork, Limerick, Tipperary South, Waterford, Kilkenny, Carlow, Wexford, Kildare and Dublin. The lowest category applies almost uniformly to counties Donegal (except the east), Leitrim, Sligo, Mayo, Galway, Roscommon, Longford and Clare.

Comparison of this map with that of average farm size (Map 1) produces broad agreement, with some notable exceptions. Donegal, for example, emerges with some differentiation in terms of the physical size of farms while it is totally (except for the eastern portion) in the lowest category in terms of economic size. Cavan and Monaghan have particularly small farms yet, due to the presence of dairying as well as pig, poultry and mushroom enterprises, they do not belong to the lowest economic size category. Also, dairying in north Kerry contributes to a favourable average economic size even though the average area of farms is relatively small.

Map 15:
Average Farm Size (ESUs*) 1991

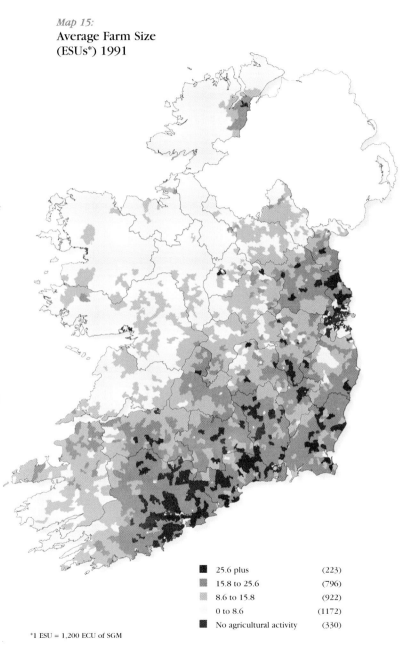

■	25.6 plus	(223)
■	15.8 to 25.6	(796)
■	8.6 to 15.8	(922)
	0 to 8.6	(1172)
■	No agricultural activity	(330)

*1 ESU = 1,200 ECU of SGM

Maps 16 and *17* provide further illustration of the strong geographical dimensions to the economic size of farms. *Map 16* shows that more than three quarters of all farms had less than 8 ESUs over extensive areas of counties Donegal, Leitrim, Sligo, Mayo, north Roscommon, west Galway, parts of Clare and the mountainous districts of Kerry. *Map 17* identifies the most prosperous farming regions of the State, namely, north Dublin, and eastwards from Cork to Wexford. The small-scale tillage and dairy region of east Donegal is illustrated to good effect in this map as the only notable area of reasonably prosperous farming in the north and west of the State.

ESUs cannot be used as a basis for making judgements on the nominal income of individual farms. Nevertheless, they can highlight relative disparities in terms of income-earning potential between different regions.

Maps 15-17 highlight the magnitude of the disparities in earning potential; the west and north emerge as areas of relatively lower economic potential from farming, with the situation improving as one moves south and eastwards. This regional variation is related to a range of factors including differences in farming systems and farm size, and variations in basic resource factors such as soil, climate and relief. In addition to these variables one must consider the demography of farmers and farm families, their education levels and disposition towards change and adaptation.

Only a minority of farming households now depend solely on income from the farm – that is when account is taken of all other sources including off-farm earnings and State transfer payments. However, the incidence of multiple income sources varies very much by region and size of farm (Frawley and Commins, 1996). A later map (*Map 21*) shows the distribution of farm holders for which farming is not the sole occupation.

Farm Labour Force[3] Characteristics

Farming in Ireland is almost totally a family enterprise. Of the 170,578 farms enumerated at the 1991 census 169,893 were classified as family farms. However, not all of those farms were operated by farmers; only some 122,500 operators of family farms recorded their current (or former) principal occupation as 'farmer'. About one-third of the remaining 47,400 were not even classified as part of the State's farm labour force (e.g., they had retired). There were some 122,000 farmers and their relatives 'at work' on Irish farms, compared to approximately 1,000 farm managers and 11,000 other workers (see Table 11). Data on the numbers in agricultural occupations, however, understate the volume of labour used on Irish farms. Given the nature of family farming it is understandable that family members who are not officially recorded as having agricultural occupations will in fact make contributions to farm work. Their inputs, as well as those of the 'official' farm labour force, are counted as shares of annual work units (AWUs) on the farm. One AWU is equal to 1,800 hours or more per person per annum.

In the following paragraphs, therefore, distinctions will be made between farm holders and other family members, and their labour inputs reckoned as annual work units.

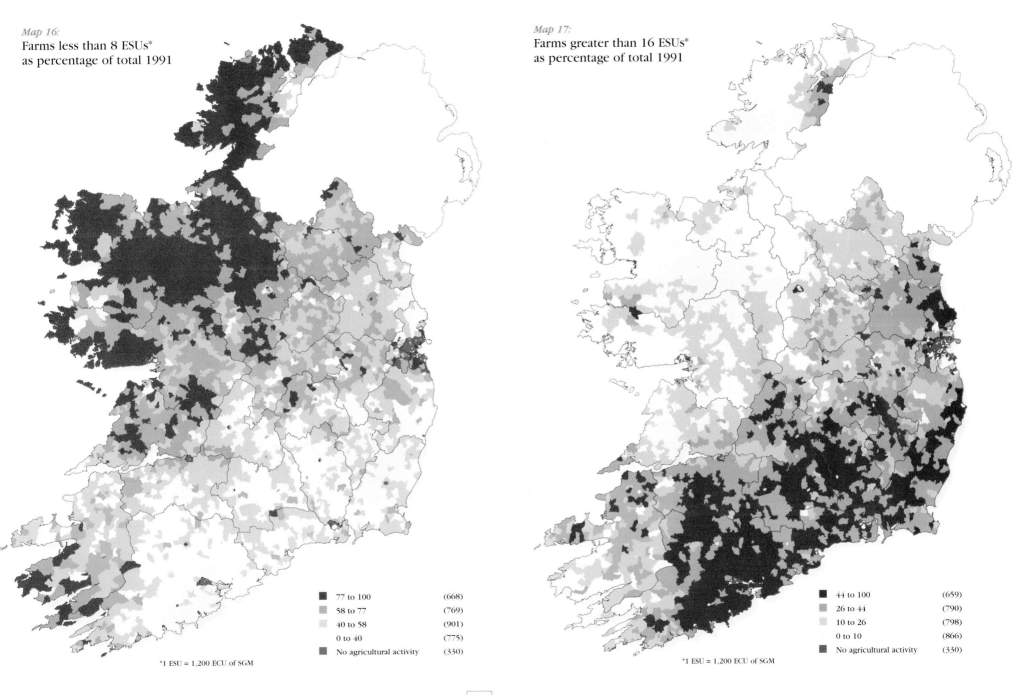

Map 16:

Farms less than 8 ESUs* as percentage of total 1991

	77 to 100	(668)
	58 to 77	(769)
	40 to 58	(901)
	0 to 40	(775)
	No agricultural activity	(330)

*1 ESU = 1,200 ECU of SGM

Map 17:

Farms greater than 16 ESUs* as percentage of total 1991

	44 to 100	(659)
	26 to 44	(790)
	10 to 26	(798)
	0 to 10	(866)
	No agricultural activity	(330)

*1 ESU = 1,200 ECU of SGM

Map 18:
Farm holders aged 65 years and over as percentage of total 1991

Map 19:
Farm holders aged under 45 years as percentage of total 1991

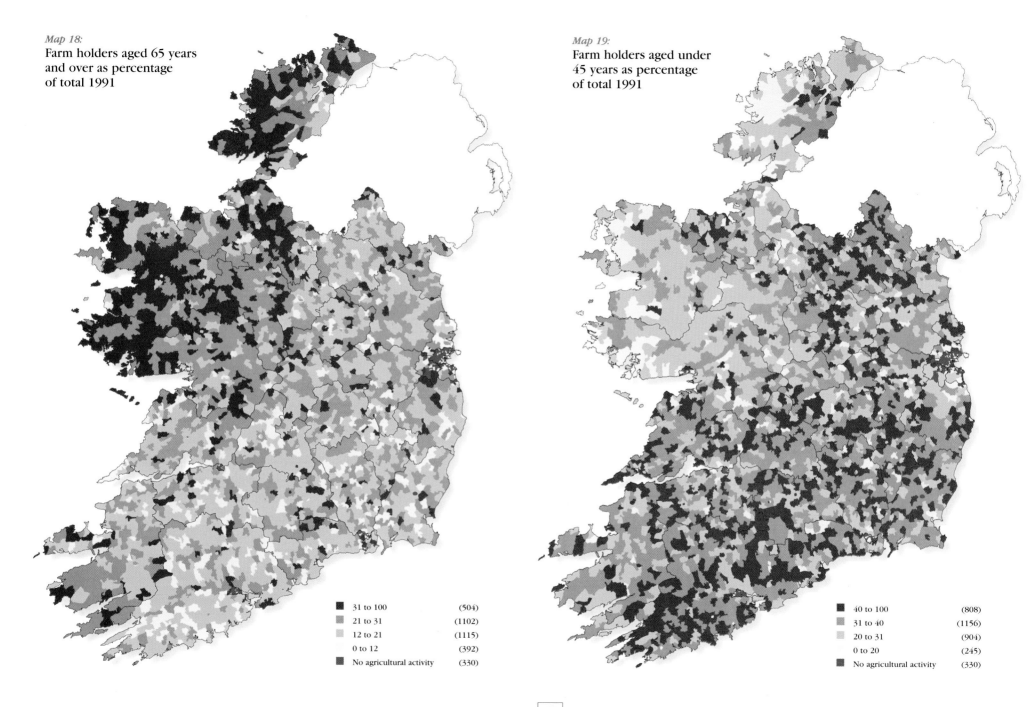

■ 31 to 100	(504)
■ 21 to 31	(1102)
■ 12 to 21	(1115)
□ 0 to 12	(392)
■ No agricultural activity	(330)

■ 40 to 100	(808)
■ 31 to 40	(1156)
■ 20 to 31	(904)
□ 0 to 20	(245)
■ No agricultural activity	(330)

Table 8: Percentage distribution of farm holders by age category, 1991 and 1997

Region	Percentage in each age category					Total farm holders
	<35	35-44	45-54	55-64	>65	
Dublin	10.2	21.0	24.4	24.3	20.2	1,468
Mid-East	13.5	20.8	22.7	22.5	20.6	11,477
South East	15.3	20.6	22.6	22.4	19.0	20,249
South-West	15.0	21.4	22.2	22.7	18.7	28,071
Mid-West	14.0	22.0	22.3	22.9	18.7	20,013
West	9.7	18.0	21.2	22.2	29.0	38,893
Border (west)	11.9	17.7	20.9	21.6	27.8	20,241
Border (east)	15.7	20.3	20.8	22.3	21.0	14,274
Midland	14.6	19.6	21.9	22.6	21.2	15,207
Ireland (1991)	13.2	19.9	21.8	22.4	22.8	169,893
Ireland (1997)	12.0	19.4	24.1	22.6	21.9	147,600

Source: Census of Agriculture 1991; Agricultural Labour Input 1997.

Farm Holders – Operators on Family Farms: Age Profile

The age profile of farm holders is of great significance in terms of its impact on the type of farming pursued and the longer-term viability and survival of the farm business. The older age structure of Irish farm holders has long been recognised as a problem. Scully (1969) noted that the high incidence of ageing farmers had a negative effect on farm productivity because of the difficulties associated with getting older farmers to accept new ideas and recommended farm practices.

In 1991, over 45 per cent of all farm holders were over 55 years; almost 23 per cent were more than 65 years (Table 8). Estimates from the CSO (1997) survey indicate that the age profile of farm holders

has become more 'middle-aged'. The proportion under 35 years has fallen during 1991-97, and this seems likely to be due to declining numbers of young entrants to farming careers.

Map 18 shows the location of the older farm holders as being predominantly in the north and west – the areas where farming is less commercially practiced and where farm succession is most problematic. Table 8 presents the regional breakdown of the age profile of farm holders. Younger farm holders (under 35 years) are found mostly in the eastern regions and in the South-West. Combining the percentages under 45 years shows that the figures are highest in the South-West, Mid-West, Border (east) and South-East regions. This geographical variation is borne out in greater detail on *Map 19*.

Importance of Farmwork as an Occupation for the Farm Holder

An increasingly relevant consideration in examining the structure of Irish agriculture is the importance of farmwork to the farm holder reckoned in terms of the proportion of his/her working time.

Table 9 presents the 1991 regional figures based on whether the holder classified farmwork as his/her sole, major or subsidiary occupation[4]. In the State over 73 per cent of farm holders regarded working on their own farms as their sole occupation.

Regionally, the lowest incidence of sole occupation is in the 'east' (Dublin and the Mid-East) and in the 'west', (Border (west) and the West). However, it would appear that the reasons underlying the comparatively low incidence of sole occupation farming differ between these two groups of regions.

This is suggested by the figures in Table 10 which shows the percentages of farm holders who were classified as 'not in the labour force' (e.g. because of retirement or being fully engaged in 'home duties'). It will be noted that whereas the percentages for the 'east' are lower than the national average those for the 'west' are generally higher – being over one-quarter in the Border (west).

Table 9: Percentage distribution of family farms classified by occupational importance of farmwork for the farm holder, 1991

Region	Total No. of family farms	Percentage distribution		
		Sole Occupation	Major Occupation	Subsidiary Occupation
Dublin	1,468	65.5	5.0	29.5
Mid-East	11,477	69.3	6.0	24.7
South-East	20,249	79.1	3.8	17.1
South-West	28,071	77.7	5.4	16.9
Mid-West	20,013	75.7	5.1	19.2
West	38,893	70.6	7.8	21.6
Border (west)	20,241	68.4	6.5	25.1
Border (east)	14,274	72.2	4.8	23.0
Midland	15,207	73.9	4.3	21.8
Ireland	169,893	73.4	5.7	20.8

Source: Census of Agriculture 1991.

Map 20:

Farm holders with Farm Work as Sole Occupation as percentage of total 1991

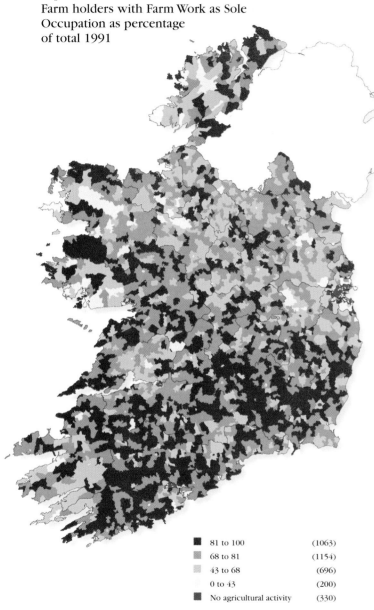

■ 81 to 100	(1063)
▨ 68 to 81	(1154)
░ 43 to 68	(696)
0 to 43	(200)
■ No agricultural activity	(330)

In fact, combining the figures for the Border (west) and West regions suggests that over 21 per cent of farm holders are not in the labour force – almost half of all such farm holders in the State. The inference to be drawn from this comparison (Tables 9 and 10) is that in the 'east' those landholders not involved in full-time farming tend to be in other gainful employment whereas in the 'west' this category of landholder includes a high proportion of persons who have disengaged from full-time economic activities or, perhaps, have never been in the labour force.

Map 20 presents the sole occupation variable which, while found everywhere, does have an orientation toward the southern part of the State as well as to western areas, although to a lesser extent. It appears strongest in the dairy region of the south-west and the tillage areas of the south and east.

Table 10: Percentage of Family Farm Operators (FFOs) not in the labour force, 1991

Region	Total FFOs	FFOs not in the labour force	% of total FFOs not in the labour force
Dublin	1,468	186	12.7
Mid-East	11,477	1,686	14.7
South-East	20,249	2,035	10.0
Midlands	15,207	2,209	14.5
South-West	28,071	3,513	12.5
Mid-West	20,013	2,332	11.7
West	38,893	7,529	19.4
Border (west)	20,241	5,332	26.3
Border (east)	14,274	2,167	15.2
Ireland	169,893	26,989	15.9

Source: Demographic, Social and Economic Situation of the Farming Community in 1991, CSO (1998a).

Over 80 per cent of farms are operated by sole occupation farmers in approximately one-third of all DEDs which are predominantly in the south-east and south-west.

A major source of differentiation between 'sole' and 'subsidiary' farm occupations relates to the area farmed. Where farming is the sole occupation the average farm size is 29.3 hectares while on subsidiary occupation farms it is only 14.3 hectares. Map 21 illustrates the percentage of all farms on which farming is a subsidiary occupation of the farm holder in the sense that the time spent on "gainful non-farming activity" exceeds that spent on farming. This map, in combination with Table 9, demonstrates that subsidiary occupation farming is least prevalent in the commercial farming areas, especially Cork, Limerick and eastwards towards south Wicklow and Wexford. In the South-West and South-East regions only 17 per cent of farm holders have farm work as a subsidiary occupation, compared to 29.5 per cent in Dublin and 25.1 per cent in the Border (west) region. In order for farm holders to have the option of making farming their subsidiary occupation there must exist the opportunity for off-farm employment. The chances of this are greater around Dublin and in the hinterlands of the major towns. The high incidence of subsidiary occupation farming in Donegal is due to the availability of jobs in fishing and tourism as well as to the fact that Donegal is quite industrialised in the Gaeltacht areas and around the expanding urban centre of Letterkenny.

Average Annual Work Units (AWUs)

As noted above, the numbers in agricultural occupations cannot be equated with the volume of labour used on Irish farms. Neither can the categorisations of landholders according to the importance of farm work. For the more accurate assessment of labour inputs we must have regard to the data on annual work units (AWUs).

Table 11: Total on-farm labour input (AWU)[1] (Share of regional total in parentheses), 1991

Region	Family labour	Regular non-family labour	Casual labour	Contract labour	Relief labour	Total labour input	Average input per farm
Dublin	1,944 (68.4)	575 (20.2)	285 (10.0)	35 (1.2)	3 (0.1)	2,842 (100)	1.88
Mid-East	14,529 (80.8)	2,619 (14.6)	493 (2.7)	306 (1.7)	42 (0.2)	17,989 (100)	1.55
South-East	31,132 (87.2)	2,639 (7.4)	971 (2.7)	814 (2.3)	139 (0.4)	35,695 (100)	1.75
South-West	42,638 (92.9)	1,537 (3.3)	694 (1.5)	892 (1.9)	124 (0.3)	45,885 (100)	1.63
Mid-West	28,428 (94.5)	709 (2.4)	346 (1.1)	526 (1.7)	85 (0.3)	30,094 (100)	1.50
West	51,980 (97.1)	627 (1.2)	266 (0.5)	643 (1.2)	7 (0.0)	53,523 (100)	1.37
Border (west)	24,074 (96.3)	467 (1.9)	230 (0.9)	205 (0.8)	12 (0.0)	24,988 (100)	1.23
Border (east)	18,303 (91.6)	995 (5.0)	369 (1.8)	286 (1.4)	23 (0.1)	19,976 (100)	1.40
Midland	21,149 (93.0)	853 (3.8)	334 (1.5)	371 (1.6)	33 (0.1)	22,740 (100)	1.49
Ireland	23,4177 (92.3)	11,021 (4.3)	3,988 (1.6)	4,078 (1.6)	468 (0.2)	253,732 (100)	1.49

[1]One AWU is equal to 1800 hours or more per person per annum.
Source: Census of Agriculture 1991.

Table 11 shows that over 92 per cent of the labour input on all farms in the State is family labour. Regular non-family labour accounts for only 4.3 per cent while casual and contract labour account for 1.6 per cent each. Relief farm labour is hardly significant at 0.2 per cent of the total. There exists considerable regional variation in these figures, however, with family labour accounting for over 96 per cent in both the Border (west) and West regions, while its share in the Dublin region is only 68.4 per cent. Regular non-family labour is most important in the Dublin and Mid-East regions at 20.2 per cent and 14.6 per cent respectively while accounting for only 1.2 per cent in the West region. There is a tradition of hired labour on large farms in tillage areas. Again, casual labour is most important in Dublin while hardly featuring in the more western regions. Contract and relief labour tends to be associated primarily with the dairy and tillage areas of the South-East, South-West and Mid-West regions.

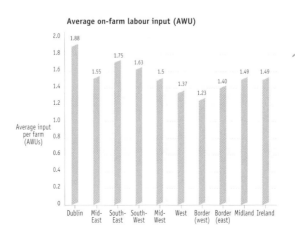

Average on-farm labour input (AWU)

Dublin	1.88
Mid-East	1.55
South-East	1.75
South-West	1.63
Mid-West	1.5
West	1.37
Border (west)	1.23
Border (east)	1.40
Midland	1.49
Ireland	1.49

Average input per farm (AWUs)

Map 21:

Farm holders with Farm Work as Subsidiary Occupation as percentage of total 1991

- ■ 35 to 100 (377)
- ▨ 19 to 35 (1121)
- ▧ 11 to 19 (913)
- ☐ 0 to 11 (702)
- ■ No agricultural activity (330)

Dublin has the highest labour input with 1.88 AWU per farm, followed by the South-East, South-West and Mid-West regions. The high labour input in Dublin reflects the intensive nature of the market gardening enterprises in the county. The Border (west) has the least labour intensive input of any region in the State. This fact is well illustrated on *Map 22* as most of Donegal and north Connacht emerge in the lowest interval with the areas of most intensive labour input occurring around Cork, eastwards to Wexford, north Dublin and east Donegal.

Table 12: Sources of regular farm labour input in the State, 1991 and 1997

Category of Worker	1991			1997			% Change 1991-1997	
	Persons (000s)	AWU (000s)	% of AWU[1]	Persons (000s)	AWU (000s)	% of AWU[1]	Persons	AWU[1]
Farmholder	169.9	142.9	56	147.6	122.1	59	-13.1	-14.6
Spouse	72.0	53.0	21	54.4	33.9	16	-17.6	-36.0
Other family	57.3	38.2	15	66.0	32.3	16	+15.0	-15.4
All family	299.3	234.2	92	268.0	188.3	91	-10.5	-19.6
Non-family[2]	13.4	11.0	4	13.9	8.9	4	+ 3.7	-19.1
Total[3]	312.7	245.2	97	281.9	197.2	96	- 9.8	-19.6

[1]AWU = Annual Work Units; One AWU = 1,800 hours or more per person per annum.
[2]Regular workers only.
[3]Non-regular labour inputs omitted.
Source: Census of Agriculture 1991; Agricultural Labour Input 1997.

It is of interest to note which category of family members contribute labour inputs and how their relative contributions have been changing in recent years. Information on this question for the State as a whole is provided in Table 12 . Firstly, it will be seen that the numbers of family members involved in farm work declined by 10.5 per cent between 1991 and 1997. Significantly, however, their labour inputs decreased at almost double this rate – by 19.6 percent. Obviously, as well as the falling number of workers the amount of work per person is also being reduced. Secondly, the labour inputs by farm holders' spouses have fallen remarkably since 1991. Other data (McDonagh *et al.*, 1999) indicate that proportionately more spouses have been working off the farm in recent years. Thirdly, although the absolute amount of farm work undertaken by farm holders is being reduced their relative contribution is increasing; more than likely, while the numbers of farms are declining proportionately more are being operated by the holder alone. Fourthly, more 'other family members' are becoming involved in farm work so that their relative contribution remained stable during 1991-97, although their absolute inputs declined.

Map 22:
**Labour Units (AWUs*)
per farm 1991**

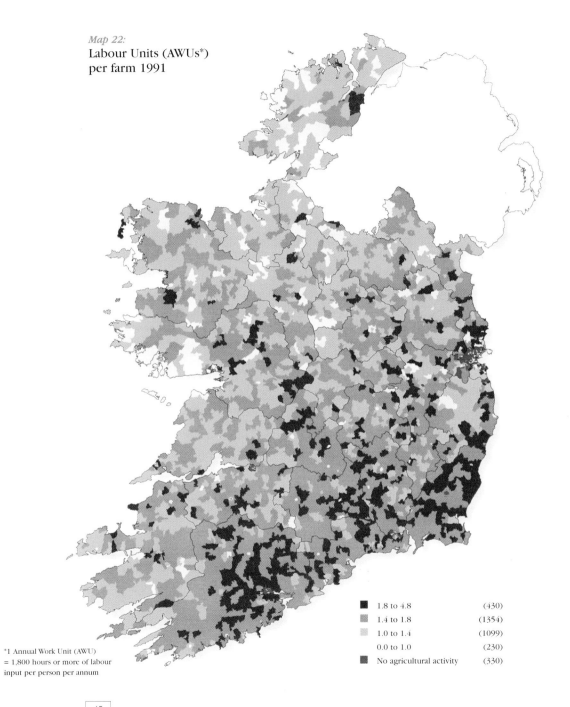

■ 1.8 to 4.8	(430)
▨ 1.4 to 1.8	(1354)
▨ 1.0 to 1.4	(1099)
▢ 0.0 to 1.0	(230)
■ No agricultural activity	(330)

*1 Annual Work Unit (AWU)
= 1,800 hours or more of labour
input per person per annum

Mechanisation

Increased mechanisation has been a vital component in the modernisation of farming. It has enabled increased crop and livestock yields, reduced the labour input and consequently increased productivity per labour unit and per hectare of land. Mechanisation has been manifest in a wide variety of ways and has impacted on almost every aspect of farming. It ranges from the introduction of milking machines to potato pickers, from grain silos to automated cow-feeding systems and from combine harvesters to crop sprayers.

The single biggest technological advance was the development of the tractor which replaced the horse and, to a large extent, facilitated much of the subsequent mechanisation. The number and density of tractors have proved to be a useful summary index of total farm mechanisation and, more broadly, of capital investment on farms.

The first gasoline tractor was produced in the United States in 1882 and by the 1920s tractors were used in Britain and Ireland, albeit in relatively small numbers. Walsh (1992) has traced the adoption process associated with tractors in Ireland and demonstrated that there has been a spatial diffusion pattern westwards. In 1928 their main concentration was in the east and south with localised concentrations around Dublin, in Ardee and Dundalk in county Louth, Athy in Kildare, around Cork city and in east and north Donegal. These areas were, for the most part, characterised by flat terrain and large farms and thus were more suited to mechanisation. They were also the main areas of arable crop production for which mechanisation was an attractive labour-saving option.

The general eastern and southern bias in the location of tractors remains evident today, as *Maps 23-28* illustrate. *Map 23* shows that the highest densities of tractors occur in Cork, Kilkenny, Carlow and Wexford while the lowest densities are in the most marginal farming areas in the west and north-west (Table 13).

The spatial contrasts in the intensity of mechanisation are more evident from *Maps 24-27* which show variations in the different size categories of tractors. The highest density of the smallest tractors is in the north and west. Districts where more than 46 per cent of tractors have the less than 35 horse power (HP) rating are particularly prevalent in west and north Donegal, large parts of Leitrim, west Mayo and west Galway. The greatest density of smaller tractors in the east occurs in the Wicklow uplands. While this category of tractor is not the most important in any region, it is most prevalent in the Border (west) and West regions where it accounts for 32.1 per cent and 27.1 per cent of all tractors respectively (Table 13).

Table 13: Total number of tractors and regional percentages, 1991

Region	Percentage distribution					Tractors per 10 farms
	<35 HP	35-51 HP	51-80 HP	>80 HP	Total	
Dublin	10.8	27.8	37.4	24.1	1,887	12.5
Mid-East	12.7	25.3	39.0	23.1	12,101	10.4
South East	8.5	27.3	44.0	20.2	23,470	11.5
South-West	13.4	32.5	38.4	15.7	29,763	10.6
Mid-West	14.3	41.4	35.4	9.0	19,548	9.7
West	27.1	47.2	22.1	3.7	26,054	6.7
Border (west)	32.1	42.8	19.9	5.2	15,612	7.7
Border (east)	19.4	34.9	32.0	13.8	14,161	9.9
Midland	17.2	35.4	34.4	13.1	15,153	9.9
Ireland	17.7	36.1	33.4	12.8	157,749	9.2

Source: Census of Agriculture 1991.

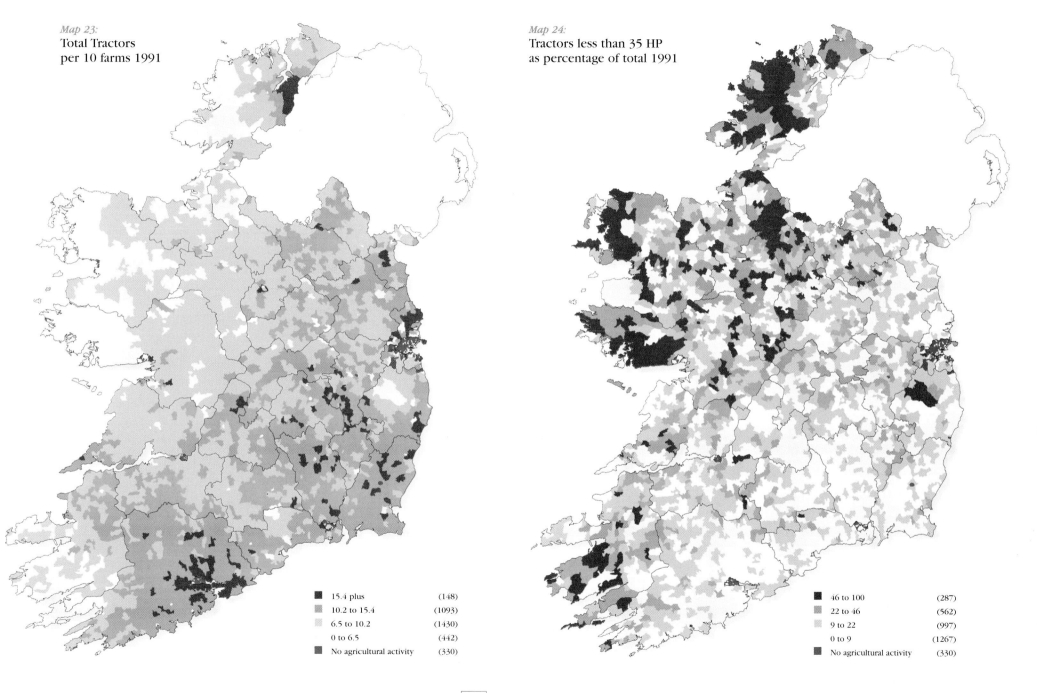

Map 23:
Total Tractors
per 10 farms 1991

Map 24:
Tractors less than 35 HP
as percentage of total 1991

■	15.4 plus	(148)
■	10.2 to 15.4	(1093)
■	6.5 to 10.2	(1430)
	0 to 6.5	(442)
■	No agricultural activity	(330)

■	46 to 100	(287)
■	22 to 46	(562)
■	9 to 22	(997)
	0 to 9	(1267)
■	No agricultural activity	(330)

Map 25:

Tractors 35-51 HP as
percentage of total 1991

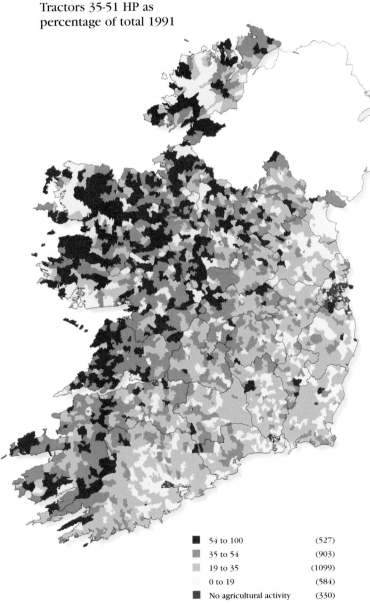

■ 54 to 100	(527)
▨ 35 to 54	(903)
▨ 19 to 35	(1099)
▢ 0 to 19	(584)
■ No agricultural activity	(330)

The modal size category of tractors in 1991 was the 35-51 HP group followed closely by the 51-80 HP range. Table 13 indicates that the 35-51 HP category is most important in the West, Border (west) and Mid-West regions where it accounts for over 40 per cent of all tractors. This is in contrast to the 51-80 HP category which is most important in the South-East, Mid-East, South-West and Dublin regions. From *Map 25,* 35-51 HP tractors are most prevalent north and west of a line from Mizen Head in county Cork to Dundalk in county Louth while the 51-80 HP tractors, on *Map 26*, are mostly to the south and east of this line. The dividing line is moved further south and eastwards for the largest category (> 80 HP) which is most important in north Dublin, Louth, Meath, southwards towards Wexford and in south and central Cork (*Map 27*). In the West and Border (west) regions this category accounts for 5 per cent or less of all tractors.

Table 14: Percentage change in number of tractors, 1980-1991

Region	<35 HP	35-51 HP	51-80 HP	80+ HP	Total
Dublin	-32.3	-12.5	-11.9	354.0	4.8
Mid-East	-19.3	-30.5	7.2	132.8	1.7
South-East	-35.5	-29.7	21.6	238.3	6.2
South-West	-11.3	-20.7	37.7	325.0	14.0
Mid-West	-31.9	-16.6	72.9	338.5	7.4
West	-12.9	13.8	98.1	382.0	18.4
Border (west)	-12.1	-7.2	72.4	307.0	4.8
Border (east)	-33.0	-17.7	56.0	387.5	5.7
Midland	-23.5	-21.1	44.6	230.0	5.2
Ireland	-19.9	-13.9	44.7	265.8	10.3

Source: Derived from: Agricultural Statistics 1980; Census of Agriculture 1991.
Note: 1980 figures used to produce these percentages were rounded to the nearest 100.

The total number of tractors in the State increased exponentially in the 1960s and 1970s after which the rate of expansion moderated as the majority of farms were mechanised at that stage. *Map 28* presents the percentage change in total numbers of tractors between 1980 and 1991 while Table 14 presents the regional figures. The total number of tractors increased in all regions over the period with the largest increases in the West and the smallest in the Mid-East. The numbers of small tractors decreased everywhere with the largest decrease in the South-East in contrast to much smaller declines in the South-West, West and Border (west) regions. The 35-51 HP category also decreased everywhere with the exception of the West where the increase was quite significant at almost 14 per cent. In contrast, the 51-80 HP category increased in all regions with the exception of Dublin where there was a decline of almost 12 per cent. The largest increases were in the West and Border (west) regions. The number of the most powerful tractors (>80 HP) increased dramatically in all regions with the highest percentage increases in the Border (east), the West and the Mid-West. These figures reflect the relatively small numbers in these regions in 1980.

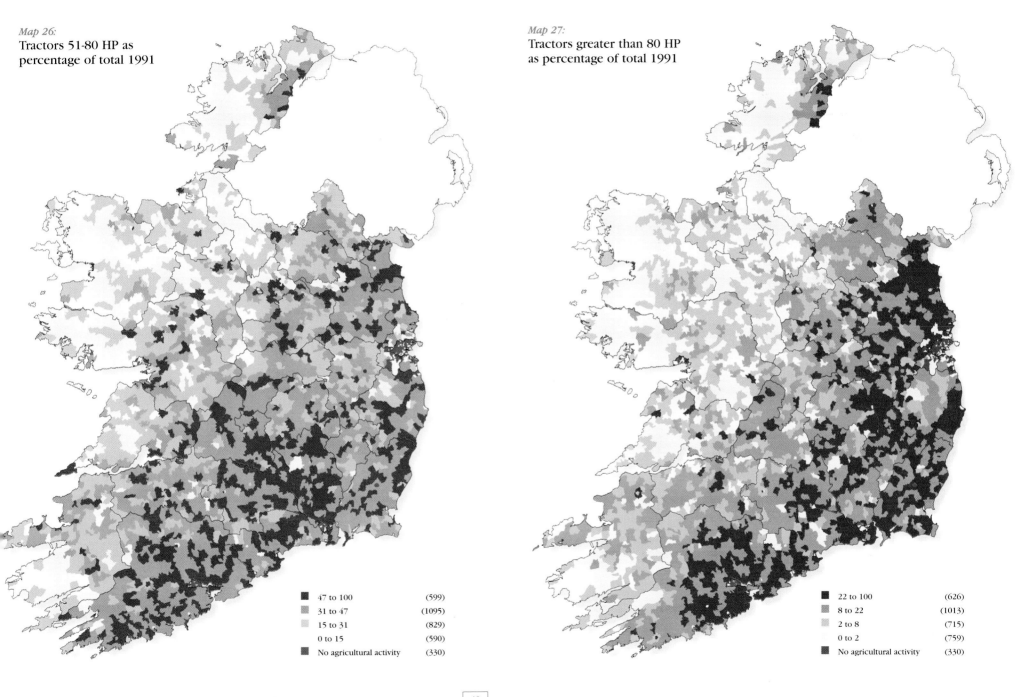

Map 26:
**Tractors 51-80 HP as
percentage of total 1991**

Map 27:
**Tractors greater than 80 HP
as percentage of total 1991**

■	47 to 100	(599)
■	31 to 47	(1095)
■	15 to 31	(829)
	0 to 15	(590)
■	No agricultural activity	(330)

■	22 to 100	(626)
■	8 to 22	(1013)
■	2 to 8	(715)
	0 to 2	(759)
■	No agricultural activity	(330)

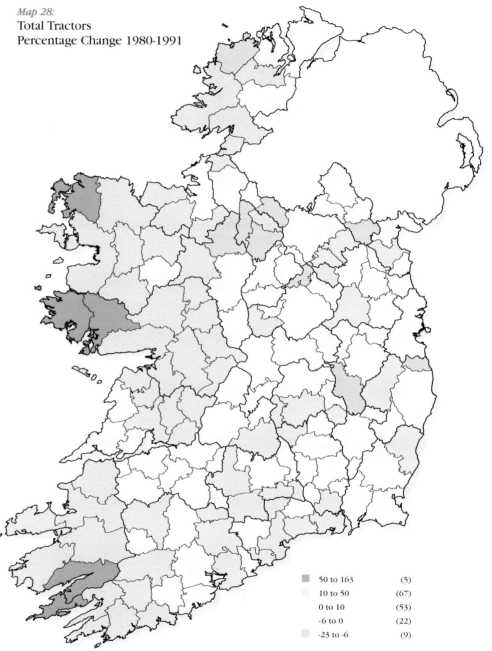

Map 28:
Total Tractors
Percentage Change 1980-1991

The trends emerging from Tables 13 and 14 represent the declines in the numbers of smaller tractors in general and the increasing incidence of larger tractors in western counties. These patterns accord in a general way with those established as a result of diffusion processes in earlier periods (Walsh, 1992). These trends in general are evident from *Map 28* where the largest increases in total tractors occurred in western areas while most of the decrease occurred in the east. The decrease may be indicative of farmers replacing smaller tractors with fewer larger ones. The substantial decline in total tractor numbers in west Donegal and in Leitrim is likely to be associated with the overall decline in farming in these areas as well as to a greater reliance on agricultural contractors by small-scale, part-time farmers.

50 to 163	(5)
10 to 50	(67)
0 to 10	(53)
-6 to 0	(22)
-23 to -6	(9)

Farm Based Productivity Measures

It has long been established that Irish agriculture is characterised by pronounced spatial variation in the productivity of farms. However, due to data constraints, it has always been difficult to estimate this variation. As noted, the 1991 Census of Agriculture has, for the first time, collected information on the labour input on farms. Subsequently, the CSO calculated estimates of standard gross margins for each district. These figures, which in turn are aggregated into European Size Units (ESUs), provide the first detailed insight to the spatial variations in farm productivity. Productivity can be related to a large number of variables including land quality, size of farm, enterprise type, farmer demographics, available labour and accessibility to markets. Some of these factors have already been discussed and their spatial patterns illustrated while others will be alluded to in subsequent sections.

Table 15: Productivity measures, 1991

Region	Total ESUs per ha AAU[1]	Index of ESUs[2] per ha AAU (Irl = 100)	Total ESUs per AWU[3]	Index of ESUs per AWU (Irl = 100)
Dublin	0.59	131	10.21	131
Mid-East	0.46	102	10.63	136
South-East	0.54	120	11.27	144
South-West	0.55	122	9.96	128
Mid-West	0.44	98	8.27	106
West	0.32	71	4.35	56
Border (west)	0.28	62	4.44	57
Border (east)	0.50	111	7.01	90
Midland	0.40	89	7.49	96
Ireland	0.45	100	7.81	100

[1] AAU = Agricultural Area Utilised.
[2] ESU = European Size Unit (1 ESU = 1,200 ECU).
[3] AWU = Annual Work Unit (1 AWU = 1,800 hours or more per person per annum).

Source: Derived from Census of Agriculture 1991.

In 1991 the average number of ESUs per hectare of area farmed in the State was 0.45, and it ranged from 0.28 in the Border (west) to 0.59 in Dublin (Table 15). *Map 29* presents the distribution of gross margins per hectare. The intensive dairying regions of Cork, north Kerry, Limerick and parts of Tipperary and Waterford have the highest levels of productivity. The tillage areas of the south-east and north Dublin are also highly productive as is the dairying region of the north-east, although to a lesser extent than the south-west due to poorer land quality and smaller average farm size. Again west Donegal, Leitrim, Sligo, Mayo, Roscommon, Galway, the midlands, Clare and south-west Kerry have the lowest levels.

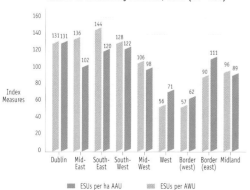

Indices of Productivity Measures, 1991 (Irl = 100)

ESUs per ha AAU   ESUs per AWU

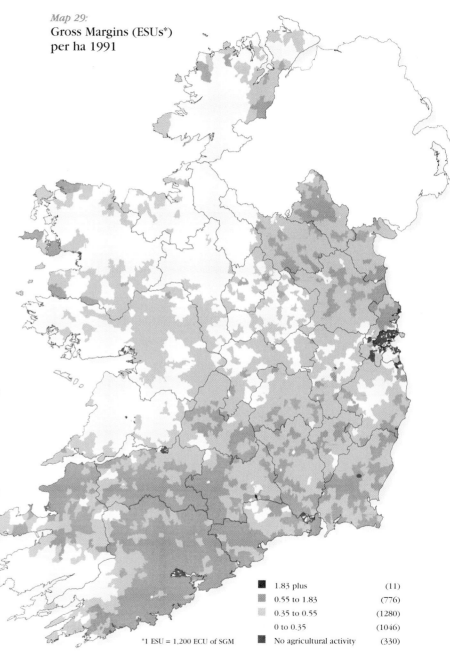

Map 29:
Gross Margins (ESUs*) per ha 1991

■ 1.83 plus	(11)
▨ 0.55 to 1.83	(776)
░ 0.35 to 0.55	(1280)
0 to 0.35	(1046)
■ No agricultural activity	(330)

*1 ESU = 1,200 ECU of SGM

An alternative measure of productivity is the value of output per labour unit. The average number of ESUs per AWU for the State is 7.8 but it ranges from 4.35 in the West to 10 or more in the Dublin, Mid-East and South-East regions (Table 15). *Map 30* identifies the areas of highest productivity by this measure as occurring in Meath, north Dublin and Louth, and in east Munster generally. North Connacht and particularly Leitrim, Sligo and north Roscommon show very low economic returns per unit of labour input due to the predominance of more extensive sheep and cattle rearing systems.

Maps 31 and *32* use indices calculated by reference to the State average to demonstrate the variations in productivity. The very low relative productivity levels in the north-west and most of the marginal areas along the west coast are brought out more clearly. The main differences between the two distributions relate to the values for parts of the Border (east) and areas in counties Kildare and Wicklow.

In the former areas where there is a tradition of intensive dairy farming, large pig and poultry rearing enterprises and labour-intensive mushroom-growing units, productivity levels per hectare are above average while the levels per labour unit are below average. By contrast, in parts of Kildare and Wicklow output levels per hectare are below average, possibly due to the heavy reliance on cattle production, while output per labour unit is above average due to a combination of large farms and high levels of mechanisation.

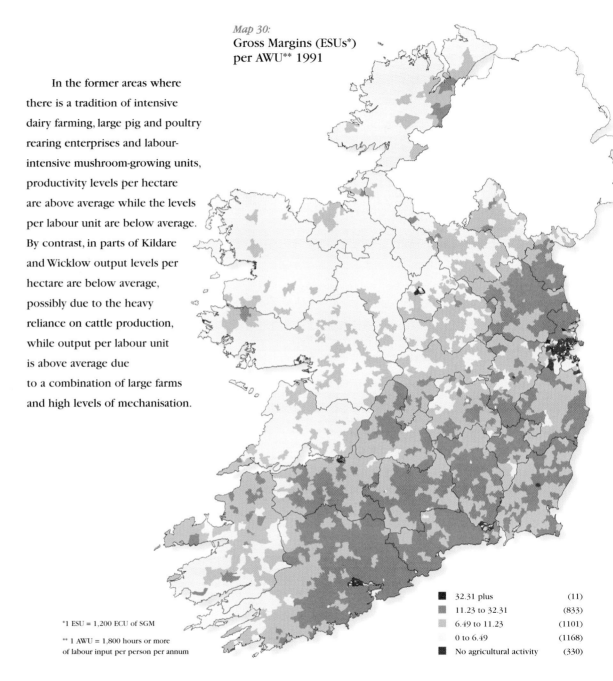

Map 30:
Gross Margins (ESUs*) per AWU** 1991

*1 ESU = 1,200 ECU of SGM

** 1 AWU = 1,800 hours or more of labour input per person per annum

■	32.31 plus	(11)
■	11.23 to 32.31	(833)
▨	6.49 to 11.23	(1101)
□	0 to 6.49	(1168)
■	No agricultural activity	(330)

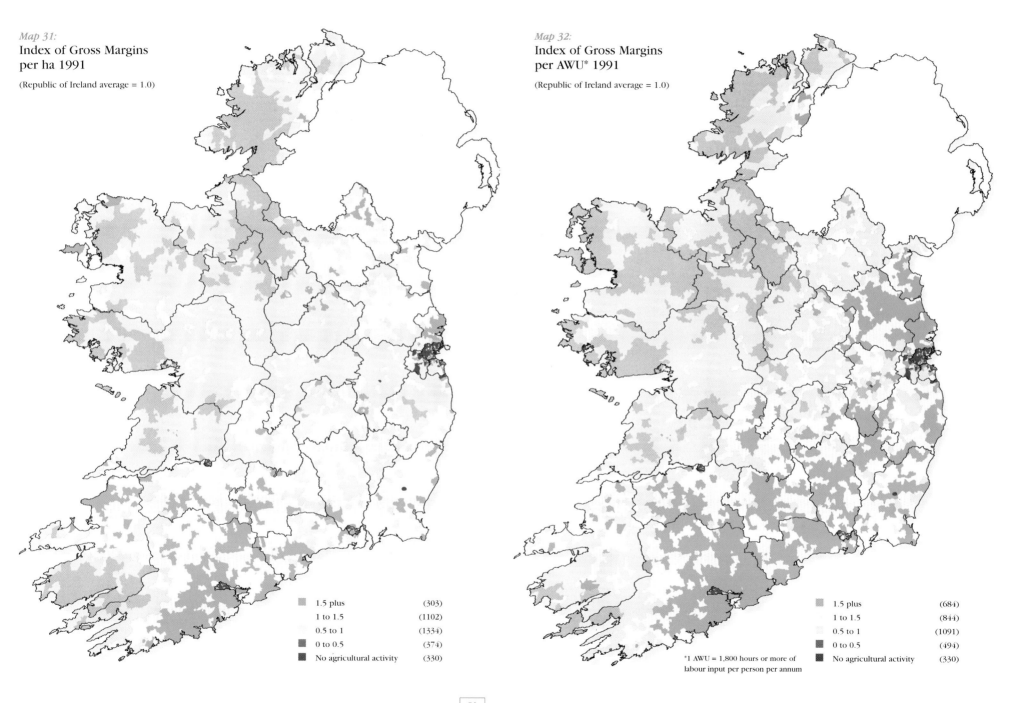

Map 31:

Index of Gross Margins per ha 1991

(Republic of Ireland average = 1.0)

	1.5 plus	(303)
	1 to 1.5	(1102)
	0.5 to 1	(1334)
	0 to 0.5	(374)
	No agricultural activity	(330)

Map 32:

Index of Gross Margins per AWU* 1991

(Republic of Ireland average = 1.0)

	1.5 plus	(684)
	1 to 1.5	(844)
	0.5 to 1	(1091)
	0 to 0.5	(494)
	No agricultural activity	(330)

*1 AWU = 1,800 hours or more of labour input per person per annum

Four decades of change in the Irish farm economy have resulted in the modernisation and commercialisation of a core of Irish farms. Change has also contributed to the economic marginalisation - and even the demise - of many more.

Section Three

Principal Agricultural
Land Uses

Introduction

Traditionally, Irish agriculture has been quite diverse geographically with many types of farming found, to some extent, in most parts of the State. This section examines the various land use categories of importance and, where possible within the constraints imposed by the data, provides a summary of the principal changes that have occurred during the 1980s. In addition, regional level data are presented to update the 1991 analysis; these in many cases highlight differences in general trends between the 1980s and 1990s. The trends of the 1990s are partly in response to 'the MacSharry reforms' of the CAP in 1992.

In this and the following sections reference is made to farms classified by type of specialism (e.g., specialist[5] sheep). Details of this system of classification are given in CSO (1994), and summarised in the Appendix.

The principal land use categories used in the Agricultural Census of Ireland 1991 were tillage (including all cereals, root and green crops, fruit and horticulture), silage, hay, pasture and rough grazing in use. The total area under all these categories combined is referred to as the agricultural area utilised (AAU) and amounts to over 4.4 million hectares for the State.

Of this, pasture comprises the largest share at 50.6 per cent, followed by silage at 17.2 per cent and rough grazing at 14.5 per cent, with hay and tillage accounting for almost 9 per cent each. If commonage (426,124 hectares) is added to this figure the total area farmed accounts for almost 71 per cent of the total land area of the State.

Pasture

Pasture used for grazing livestock is the most extensive form of land use, accounting for just over half of the total area used for agriculture in the State in 1991. The importance of pasture land stems from favourable climatic conditions, allowing for a prolonged growing season, and from soil limitations and the traditional importance of livestock production to the agricultural economy (Horner et al., 1984). Thus, pasture was recorded on 89 per cent of all farms in 1991.

The significance of pasture as a land use is greatest in the Midland, Border (east), Mid-West and West regions (Table 16). Map 33 illustrates the percentage of the total agricultural area in each DED accounted for by pasture[6]. It is clearly of greatest importance in the east Connacht, Midland and mid-to north-east Munster regions. This is to be expected given that these are the main beef cattle grazing areas of the State. The districts where pasture is least significant are mostly upland areas where rough grazing is the dominant land use.

Map 34 and Table 17 show the change in the area under pasture between 1980 and 1991. While the overall recorded area declined by more than one-fifth (part of which may be accounted for by changed methods of enumeration), the loss in the north-west was almost three times the rate of loss in the south-east. A modest increase in the total area has occurred in the 1990s (Table 18) reversing the regional trends of the 1980s.

Table 16: Percentage distribution of principal agricultural land uses, 1991 and 1997

Region	Pasture	Silage	Hay and permanent meadow	Rough grazing	Total crops, fruit and horticulture	Area farmed (ha)
Dublin	37.2	7.1	7.2	4.5	44.0	49,212
Mid-East	52.0	14.6	8.6	6.3	18.4	418,546
South-East	49.7	19.3	8.2	5.7	17.1	743,676
South-West	43.4	20.9	5.1	22.2	8.5	837,356
Mid-West	54.5	20.1	11.3	11.6	2.5	563,371
West	54.4	13.5	10.6	19.9	1.4	718,779
Border (west)	45.4	9.2	9.7	32.8	2.9	400,826
Border (east)	55.8	21.0	9.7	5.8	7.8	281,430
Midland	56.6	17.5	10.4	7.0	8.6	428,558
Ireland 1991	50.6	17.2	8.9	14.5	8.8	4,441,755
Ireland 1997	51.3	21.0	7.6	10.7	9.4	4,431,600

Source: Census of Agriculture 1991; Crops and Livestock survey 1997.

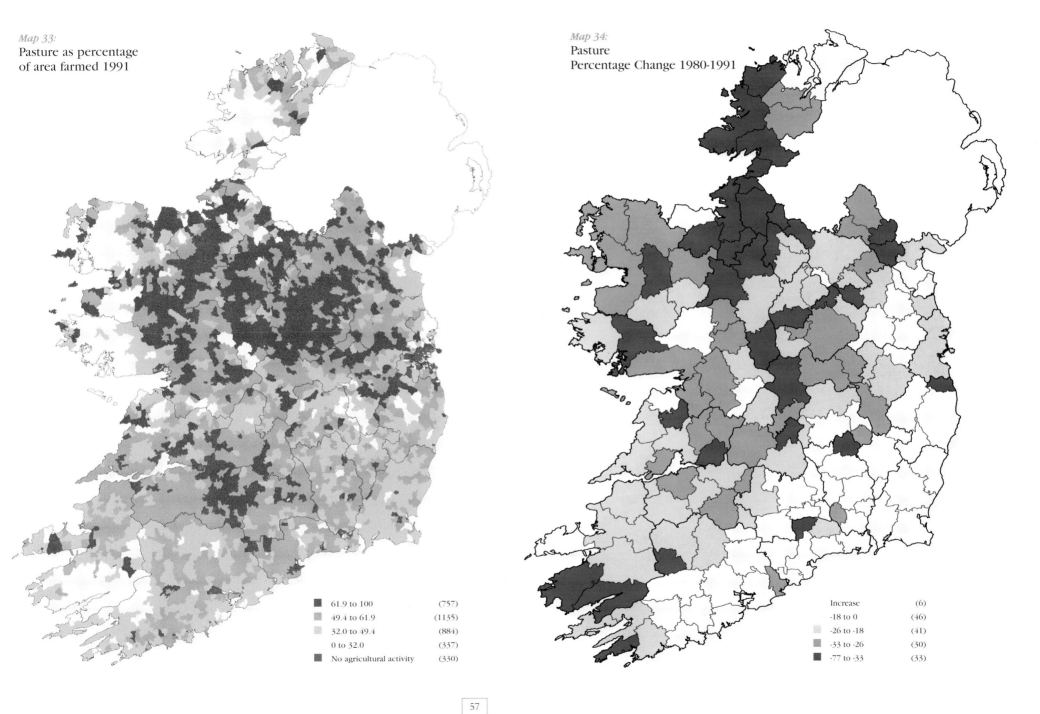

Map 33:
Pasture as percentage
of area farmed 1991

■	61.9 to 100	(757)
■	49.4 to 61.9	(1135)
■	32.0 to 49.4	(884)
	0 to 32.0	(337)
■	No agricultural activity	(330)

Map 34:
Pasture
Percentage Change 1980-1991

	Increase	(6)
	-18 to 0	(46)
■	-26 to -18	(41)
■	-33 to -26	(30)
■	-77 to -33	(33)

Silage

After pasture the next most important land use is silage production which, in 1991, took place on 17.2 per cent of the total area farmed in the State. Silage was grown on approximately 48 per cent of all farms. It is especially associated with dairying, being grown on 83 per cent of farms of this type. By contrast, it was found on only 36 per cent of specialist beef farms and on an even smaller proportion (26 per cent) of specialist sheep farms. Furthermore, the average area grown on the latter category of farms was much smaller so that only 3 per cent of the total silage area was grown on specialist sheep farms. These contrasts by farm type help to explain the pattern depicted on *Map 35*.

The highest percentages were in the Border (east), South-West and Mid-West regions. Within the South-East region, Waterford, Tipperary South and Kilkenny were also important. These are the main dairying regions where farming is generally more intensive and where silage-making represents the most efficient method of harvesting fodder for winter feeding. This map masks the significant difference in the intensities and yields of silage production between the dairy farms of the north-east and those of the south-west. While both these areas fall into the top interval on the map the south-west enjoys a substantial natural advantage for grass production in terms of a considerably extended growing season (see Figure 10).

Hay

Historically, hay was the predominant winter fodder for livestock throughout the State. While in 1991 the total area under hay was only about half that under silage, hay continued to be harvested on a large number of farms. It was grown on approximately 60 per cent of all farms with an average area per farm of 3.8 hectares; the average area under silage was 9.4 hectares. Hay was grown on approximately two-thirds of specialist beef farms, on which the total area grown was almost identical to the area of silage. It was also produced on 58 per cent of specialist dairy farms though the total area grown on these farms was equivalent to only one-fifth of the area of silage. Hay was also of some importance on specialist sheep farms, forming a component of the land use on 48 per cent of these farms, where it was slightly more favoured than silage as a form of winter fodder.

Hay is now relatively less important than silage in every region with the exception of the Border (west). *Map 36* shows that while hay accounts for approximately 9 per cent of the total AAU in the State the proportions are more than double this amount in parts of Leitrim, Roscommon, south-west Galway and west Clare. These are typically smaller farming districts where farming is strongly oriented towards low intensity cattle production and where the demographic profile of farms would suggest that they are likely to be late adopters of changes in farming practices.

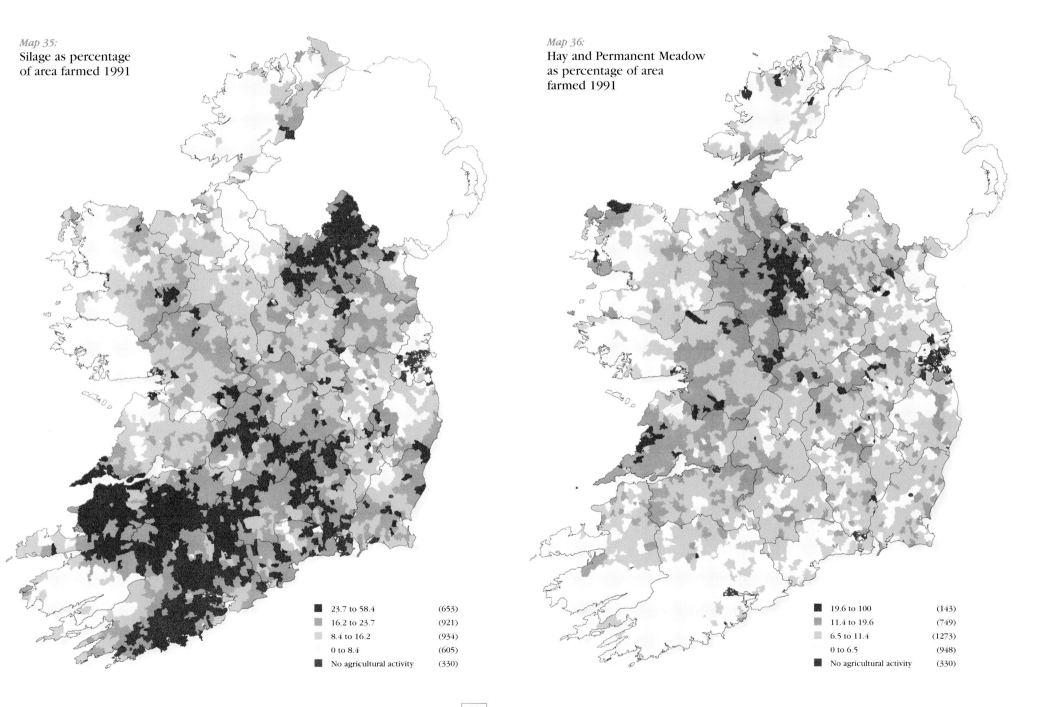

Map 35:
**Silage as percentage
of area farmed 1991**

Map 36:
**Hay and Permanent Meadow
as percentage of area
farmed 1991**

■	23.7 to 58.4	(653)
▨	16.2 to 23.7	(921)
▨	8.4 to 16.2	(934)
	0 to 8.4	(605)
■	No agricultural activity	(330)

■	19.6 to 100	(143)
▨	11.4 to 19.6	(749)
▨	6.5 to 11.4	(1273)
	0 to 6.5	(948)
■	No agricultural activity	(330)

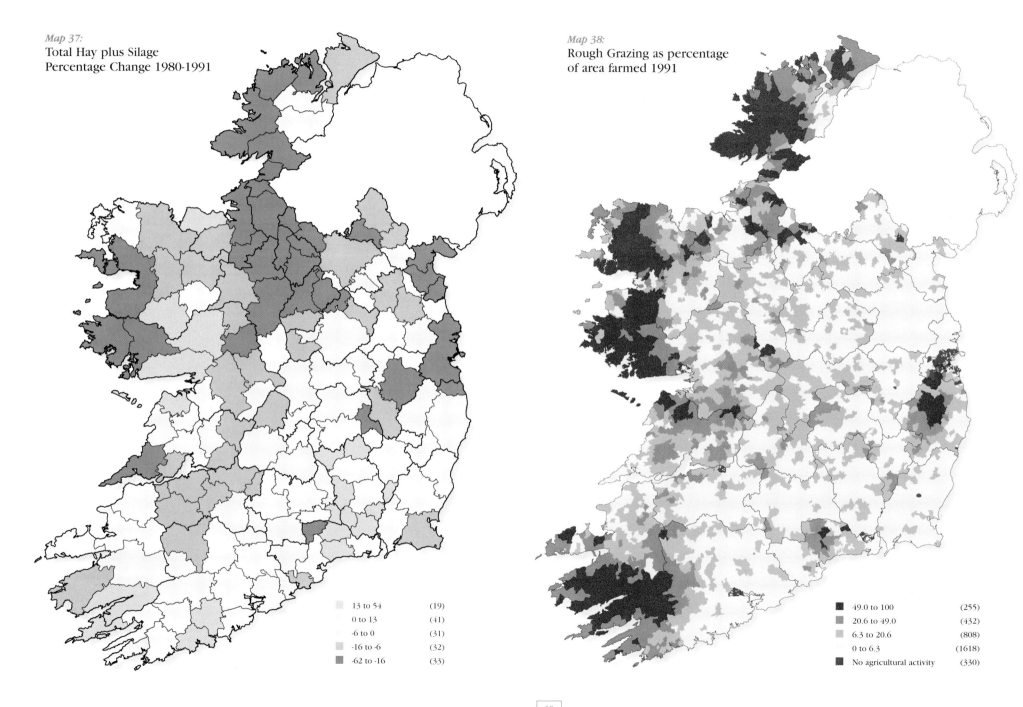

Map 37:
Total Hay plus Silage
Percentage Change 1980-1991

13 to 54	(19)
0 to 13	(41)
-6 to 0	(31)
-16 to -6	(32)
-62 to -16	(33)

Map 38:
Rough Grazing as percentage
of area farmed 1991

49.0 to 100	(255)
20.6 to 49.0	(432)
6.3 to 20.6	(808)
0 to 6.3	(1618)
No agricultural activity	(330)

As silage and hay were enumerated together in the 1980 census it is not possible to measure the increase in the production of silage. Undoubtedly there was an increase in the area under silage and a corresponding decline in the area under hay. The continuing increase in the quantity of silage produced is primarily related to the unfavourable climate for hay but it has also been aided by relatively recent advances in technology. The introduction of 'baled silage' has reduced the level of investment required in physical structures associated with the older techniques of silage production and feeding, and has brought silage making more within the reach of smaller farmers. Between 1980 and 1991 the combined areas under hay and silage declined by 4.5 per cent (Table 17). However, there were extreme contrasts between the increase of 5.3 per cent in the South-East and the decline of almost 19 per cent in the Border (west) region (*Map 37*).

Table 18 shows that between 1991 and 1997 the combined area under hay and silage increased by 111,300 hectares through a combination of an increase of 166,800 hectares of silage and a decline of 55,500 hectares in the area under hay. Regionally, silage production has increased everywhere with the largest increases in the Border (west) and West regions, where silage making was least prevalent in 1991. Meanwhile, areas under hay have declined everywhere apart from the South-West, with the greatest declines in the Mid-West followed by the Border (west) and West regions.

Table 17: Change in area under hay plus silage, pasture and AAU[1], 1980-1991

Region	Total area under hay plus silage (ha) 1991	% change under hay plus silage	Total area under pasture (ha) 1991	% change pasture	Total AAU[1] (ha) 1991	% change AAU[1] 1980-91
Dublin	7,000	-25.3	18,300	-19.7	53,900	-6.9
Mid-East	97,300	-3.4	217,900	-16.5	458,900	-11.6
South-East	204,300	5.3	369,900	-12.2	783,700	-7.7
South-West	217,800	1.6	363,600	-18.3	929,100	-10.3
Mid-West	177,100	-6.9	307,300	-26.3	570,800	-19.4
West	173,800	-5.6	391,300	-27.7	886,200	-15.7
Border (west)	75,600	-18.7	182,000	-34.3	465,600	-20.2
Border (east)	86,200	-14.2	157,000	-27.2	289,000	-19.1
Midland	119,500	-5.6	242,100	-26.2	431,100	-20.3
Ireland	1,158,700	-4.5	2,249,400	-23.2	4,868,300	-14.7

Source: Agricultural Statistics 1980; Census of Agriculture 1991.
[1] Total area farmed (including commonage).

Rough Grazing

Rough grazing is a somewhat difficult land use to enumerate in that it lacks a clear definition and is open to different interpretations on the part of farmers. It is generally taken to equate to "grazed mountain land" and as such is particularly associated with upland areas. It accounts for 14.5 per cent of the total agricultural land in the State and occurs on approximately 32 per cent of all farms. Regionally, it occupies as much as 32.8 per cent in the Border (west), 22.2 per cent in the South-West and 19.9 per cent in the West (Table 16). It is especially important in Donegal where it accounts for almost half of the total area farmed. Rough grazing land is mostly on farms which specialise in sheep or beef production. Approximately 30 per cent of the total area of rough grazing is found on just over 7,000 specialist sheep farms which represent 47 per cent of farms in this category.

Another 33 per cent of the total area of this land use was recorded on 23,800 specialist beef farms, one-third of the total in this category. The association of this land use with specific farm types is clearly evident from *Map 38* which highlights, in particular, the significance of this land use in upland areas and its almost total absence from most of the east and south of the State.

Table 18: Actual and percentage change in area under pasture, silage, hay and rough grazing, 1991-1997

Region	Pasture	Silage	Hay	Rough Grazing
Dublin	1,400 (-7.8)*	1,100 (32.5)	-100 (-4.1)	100 (5.1)
Mid-East	9,133 (-4.2)	10,608 (17.3)	-4,045 (-11.2)	1,383 (-5.3)
South-East	15,797 (-4.3)	20,072 (14.0)	-7,082 (-11.6)	898 (-21.3)
South-West	2,024 (0.6)	24,052 (13.7)	3,577 (8.4)	47,555 (-25.7)
Mid-West	4,511 (1.5)	23,162 (20.5)	-14,437 (-22.6)	18,993 (-29.2)
West	25,988 (6.6)	38,254 (39.3)	-14,797 (-19.3)	38,876 (-27.1)
Border (west)	16,103 (8.8)	15,869 (43.2)	-7,799 (-20.0)	40,174 (-30.6)
Border (east)	1,642 (-1.0)	16,524 (28.0)	-2,869 (-10.6)	1,728 (-10.6)
Midland	3,145 (1.3)	17,082 (22.8)	-7,863 (-17.7)	10,641 (-35.3)
Ireland	23,765 (1.1)	166,752 (21.8)	-55,461 (-14.1)	168,218 (-26.2)

Source: Census of Agriculture 1991; Crops and Livestock Survey 1997.
* Percentage change 1991-1997 given in parentheses.

Figure 10:
The Grass Growing Season in Ireland

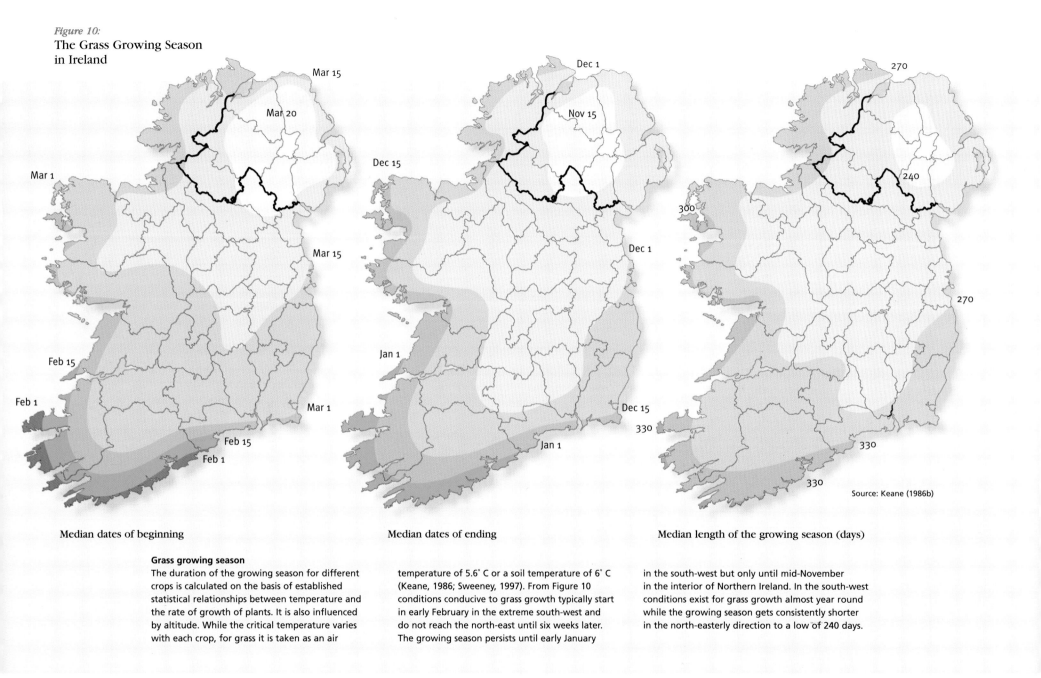

Median dates of beginning

Median dates of ending

Median length of the growing season (days)

Source: Keane (1986b)

Grass growing season

The duration of the growing season for different crops is calculated on the basis of established statistical relationships between temperature and the rate of growth of plants. It is also influenced by altitude. While the critical temperature varies with each crop, for grass it is taken as an air temperature of 5.6° C or a soil temperature of 6° C (Keane, 1986; Sweeney, 1997). From Figure 10 conditions conducive to grass growth typically start in early February in the extreme south-west and do not reach the north-east until six weeks later. The growing season persists until early January in the south-west but only until mid-November in the interior of Northern Ireland. In the south-west conditions exist for grass growth almost year round while the growing season gets consistently shorter in the north-easterly direction to a low of 240 days.

Figure 11:
Soil Suitability for Grazing

Figure 12:
Soil Suitability for Tillage

Soil suitability for grazing

In assessing the suitability of soil for agriculture the physical characteristics of the soil itself, as well as the environmental conditions (especially climate) in which it is situated, must be taken into account. The degree of suitability or limitation is based on factors such as wetness, liability to flooding, slope, rockiness, elevation and susceptibility to poaching.Based on these factors, together with climatic variables, a ranking of soils in terms of their suitability for grassland has been established (Keane, 1986; Lee, 1991).

Figure 11 shows that a large portion of the State falls into the high suitability category – indicative of the relatively undemanding nature of grass. The low suitability category is confined almost entirely to mountainous areas of the west and north-west due to the soil limitations and high rainfall amounts.

Soil suitability for tillage

The most suitable land for tillage is largely confined to the south and east. In addition to having the highest incidence of the most suitable soils for tillage, these areas also have the most suitable climate in terms of having lower rainfall amounts, higher temperatures and more hours of sunshine than western and northern areas. Least suitable for tillage crops are the mountainous regions which are associated with peat soils as well as those lowland areas with gley soils. Comparison of this map with Figure 11 indicates the substantially more restricted area of the State suitable for arable cropping as opposed to grazing.

High
Moderately high
Moderate
Moderately low
Low
Unclassified

Highly suitable
Suitable
Moderately suitable
Marginally suitable
Unsuitable

Source: Lee and Diamond (1972)

Source: Gardiner (1981)

Tillage

Tillage refers to the production of arable crops and includes cereals, root and green crops, and horticultural produce. Arable farming has traditionally played a minor role in Irish agriculture accounting for only 8.8 per cent of the total area farmed in the State in 1991, with cereals representing 77 per cent of this amount. Tillage accounted for 6.7 per cent of gross agricultural output in 1997 compared with 8.8 per cent in 1991 and approximately 12.0 per cent in 1980. In 1991 tillage crops were grown on over 41,000 farms, 24 per cent of the total in 1991. However, half of the total arable area is concentrated on just over 5,000 specialist tillage farms (farms on which tillage crops contribute over two-thirds of the farms' standard gross margin). Within this subset there were 2,200 large specialist tillage farms, with an average of 66.5 hectares of crops that accounted for 37 per cent of the total arable area. Tillage farming is therefore mostly concentrated on large farms where a higher than average proportion of the farm operators are aged under 45 years (45 per cent of specialist tillage farmers compared with 33 per cent of all farmers). The average economic size of these farms is approximately twice the average for all farms.

Table 19: Percentage share of principal tillage crops in each region, 1991

Region	Cereals	Oilseed Rape	Potatoes	Sugar Beet	Total Tillage[2]
Dublin	5.0[1]	6.2	15.4	0.2	5.5
Mid-East	21.0	45.1	21.1	7.8	19.7
South-East	33.1	7.7	14.8	46.4	32.5
South-West	16.8	6.4	14.3	31.4	18.1
Mid-West	3.7	0.4	2.7	3.1	3.6
West	2.3	0.5	4.2	0.9	2.6
Border (west)	2.6	2.3	16.6	0.0	3.0
Border (east)	5.8	29.0	7.7	0.3	5.6
Midland	9.7	2.4	3.2	9.9	9.4
Ireland	100	100	100	100	100

Source: Census of Agriculture 1991.
[1] 5.0% of all cereals are grown in Dublin.
[2] Includes all crops, fruit and horticulture.

The main regions of arable land use are the South-East, Mid-East and South-West (Table 19). The distribution of specialist tillage is highly concentrated within these regions (*Map 39*). The pattern is primarily a product of the limiting physical factors which hinder arable farming throughout many parts of the State, namely soil, climate, relief and drainage conditions (Figure 12).

Probably the most important factor in this list is climate because the development of cereal crops is greatly affected by temperature and excess precipitation (Keane, 1986b). The drier and sunnier climate of the southern parts of the State (Figures 13 and 14) aid the ripening of crops and help to prevent disease which tends to be more prevalent in wetter areas. The most suitable tillage soils have a light to medium texture and are free draining, making them easily 'tilled'.

These soil types are found mainly in the south and east and hence, together with the climatic advantages, provide those regions with the widest range of options in terms of crop selection (Gardiner and Radford, 1980).

The economic importance of specialist tillage farms is displayed in *Map 40* and summarised at regional level in Table 20. By far the highest incidence of this type of farming is in parts of north Dublin, Louth, Meath and Kildare and some dispersed districts of east Cork and Wexford. By contrast, specialist tillage farming accounts for under 2 per cent of the total value of regional output in the Mid-West, West and Border (west) regions.

Table 20: Indicators of significance of tillage farming, 1991

Region	Number of Specialist Tillage farms	Specialist Tillage farms as % of all farms	% of Specialist Tillage farms within State	% of total ESUs accounted for by tillage
Dublin	408	27.0*	8.1**	} 19***
Mid-East	908	7.8	18.0	
South-East	1,306	6.4	26.0	8
South-West	1,016	3.6	20.2	5
Mid-West	187	1.0	3.7	1
West	126	0.3	2.5	0
Border (west)	226	1.1	4.5	3
Border (east)	354	2.5	7.0	5
Midland	500	3.3	10.0	5
Ireland	5,031	2.9	100	6

*27% of all farms in Dublin are specialist tillage.
** 8.1% of all specialist tillage farms in the State are in Dublin.
***Dublin and Mid-East Combined.
Source: Census of Agriculture 1991.

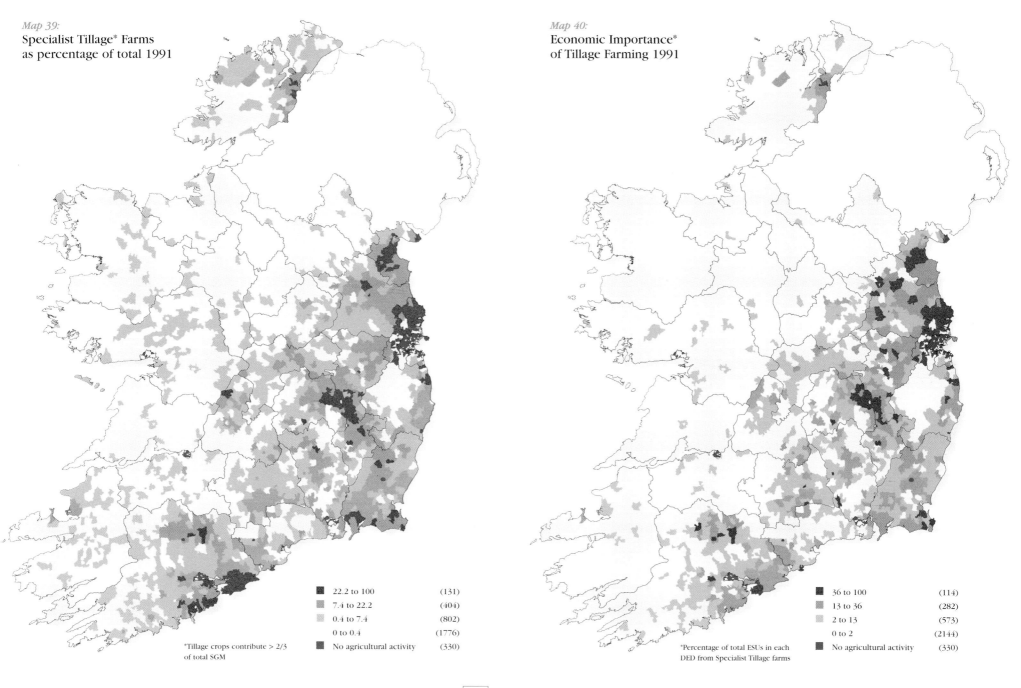

Map 39:
**Specialist Tillage* Farms
as percentage of total 1991**

Map 40:
**Economic Importance*
of Tillage Farming 1991**

■	22.2 to 100	(131)
	7.4 to 22.2	(404)
	0.4 to 7.4	(802)
	0 to 0.4	(1776)
■	No agricultural activity	(330)

*Tillage crops contribute > 2/3
of total SGM

■	36 to 100	(114)
	13 to 36	(282)
	2 to 13	(573)
	0 to 2	(2144)
■	No agricultural activity	(330)

*Percentage of total ESUs in each
DED from Specialist Tillage farms

Cereal Crops

In 1991 cereal crops, principally barley and wheat, accounted for 7 per cent of the total area farmed or 77 per cent of the total tilled area. Some cereals were grown on 23,183 farms, 13.6 per cent of the total. While in the past the area under cereals was much more extensive, there has been a tendency towards concentration of production on fewer farms. The concentration has occured in areas which have distinct comparative advantages in soil and climatic conditions, as well as in farm structure. In 1991 farms with cereals grew on average 13 hectares, with cereal crops grown predominantly on larger farms (*Map 41*). Half of the total cereals area was on 4,370 specialist tillage farms with an average area grown of 34 hectares. In a significant number of cases extensive areas of cereals are grown by a small number of farms on land rented in.

Cereal growing is geographically concentrated. The proportion of all farms with some cereals is in excess of 38 per cent (almost treble the State average) in about 15 per cent of the DEDs. These are very much concentrated in parts of the east and south with some outlying districts in east Galway and north-east Donegal (*Map 42*). In parts of Louth, Dublin, Kildare, Wexford and Cork the share of agricultural land under cereals is more than four times the State average.

Table 19 shows that almost 71 per cent of all cereals are produced between the South-East (33.1 per cent), Mid-East (21.0 per cent) and South-West (16.8 per cent) regions. The exceptions to the south and east orientation are east Donegal, which has a tradition of arable farming, and north and east of Galway city where good land has facilitated a practice of sugar beet and potato growing. There is a strong, although localised, tradition of malting barley growing in south Galway where local merchants have acted as intermediaries with Guinness's brewery. The light sandy soils are favourable to this crop while it serves the requirements of rotation where sugar beet and potatoes are also grown.

It is noteworthy how undifferentiated the map is for the non-tillage areas, indicating that any tillage which is recorded in these areas is more likely to be potatoes than cereals.

Table 21: Percentage share of selected tillage crops in each region, 1991

Region	Wheat	Barley	Oats	Sugar Beet	Potatoes
Dublin	11.3	2.3	4.6	0.2	15.4
Mid-East	32.8	16.1	21.6	7.8	21.2
South-East	27.6	35.4	31.2	46.4	14.8
South-West	14.5	17.6	18.4	31.4	14.3
Mid-West	1.3	4.9	2.5	3.1	2.7
West	0.2	2.4	9.8	0.9	4.2
Border (west)	0.5	3.1	5.6	0.0	16.6
Border (east)	6.7	5.8	1.8	0.3	7.7
Midland	5.1	12.3	4.4	9.9	3.2
Ireland	100.0	100.0	100.0	100.0	100.0

Source: Census of Agriculture 1991.

Table 22: Selected cereal crops as percentage ot total cereals area, 1980, 1991 and 1997

Year	Wheat	Barley	Oats	Other Cereals
1980	11.9	82.0	5.5	0.6
1991	28.4	64.1	6.8	0.6
1997	30.3	61.2	6.6	1.8

Source: Agricultural Statistics 1980; Census of Agriculture 1991; Crops and Livestock Survey 1997.

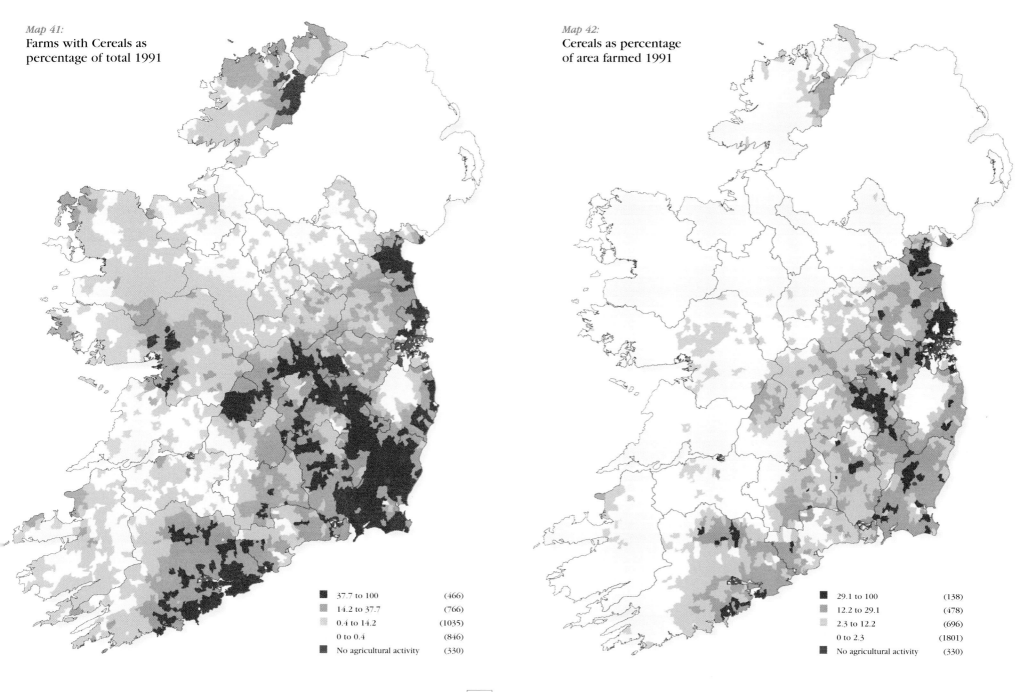

Map 41:
Farms with Cereals as percentage of total 1991

■	37.7 to 100	(466)
▓	14.2 to 37.7	(766)
░	0.4 to 14.2	(1035)
	0 to 0.4	(846)
■	No agricultural activity	(330)

Map 42:
Cereals as percentage of area farmed 1991

■	29.1 to 100	(138)
▓	12.2 to 29.1	(478)
░	2.3 to 12.2	(696)
	0 to 2.3	(1801)
■	No agricultural activity	(330)

Ireland has a cool-temperate maritime climate with mild, moist and changeable weather. Extremes of cold and heat are exceptions. Given that Ireland extends through only 4° of latitude and that no point on the island is more than 112 km from the moderating influence of the sea the climate tends to exhibit an "even rhythm"; one season merges unnoticeably with the next with rain being the only common element throughout. Ireland's climate tends to reflect its mid-latitude position which places it in the paths of the North Atlantic Drift and the frequent eastward passage of frontal depressions (Orme, 1970).

Despite its relatively small size and island nature Ireland exhibits internal climatic variation due primarily to its unique relief pattern (Figure 8). The breaks in the western mountain range at various points allow for variation in the extent to which maritime influences penetrate the interior of the country while at the same time ensuring that western areas experience variation in terms of exposure or shelter from Atlantic weather. In addition the east-west trending mountains in the south-west and south provide some defence from southerly airstreams. This coastal rim, completed in the north by the Antrim Plateau, tends to provide the interior with shelter and produces the spatial pattern of weather elements presented in the following maps (Sweeney, 1997).

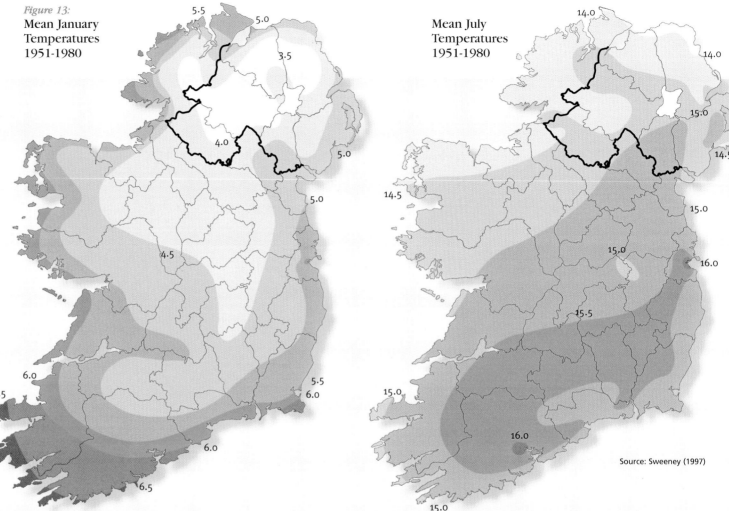

Figure 13:
Mean January Temperatures 1951-1980

Mean July Temperatures 1951-1980

Source: Sweeney (1997)

Temperature

Due primarily to the North Atlantic Drift the annual range of temperature in Ireland is small, ensuring that winter temperatures are typically 16° C above the latitudinal average (Sweeney, 1987/88). Figure 13 presents the mean January and July temperatures for the years 1951 to 1980. In January mean temperatures range from over 6.5° C in the extreme south-west to 3.5° C north of Lough Neagh in Northern Ireland.

Winter temperatures clearly run in a decreasing gradient from the south-west to the north-east. The warming effect of the sea is evident in the temperature gradient running parallel with the coast, with the coldest parts in the interior.

In July the mean temperature gradient runs in a north-west to south-east direction and ranges from 14° C on the northern coast to 16° C in the south and south-east. The range in summer temperatures is less than in winter with an obvious latitudinal influence between the south and north.

The implication of these temperature ranges is that Ireland enjoys an extensive frost-free period which allows for agricultural tasks to be conducted over a relatively large part of the year (Johnson, 1994). Air temperatures fall below freezing on only about 10 nights during a typical winter along the south, west and north-west coasts although frost may occur on up to 65 nights in the midlands (Sweeney, 1997).

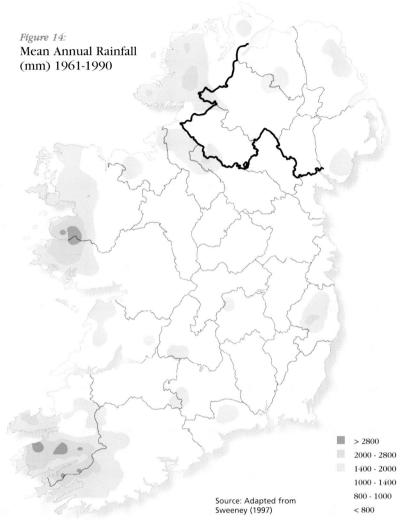

Figure 14:
Mean Annual Rainfall (mm) 1961-1990

> 2800
2000 - 2800
1400 - 2000
1000 - 1400
800 - 1000
< 800

Source: Adapted from Sweeney (1997)

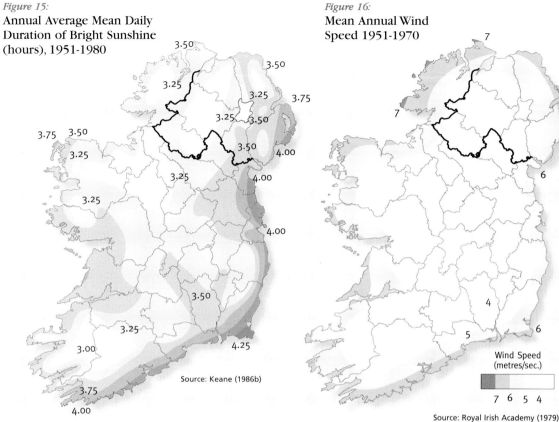

Figure 15:
Annual Average Mean Daily Duration of Bright Sunshine (hours), 1951-1980

3.50
3.50
3.25
3.25
3.75
3.25
3.50
3.75
3.50
3.50
3.25
4.00
3.25
4.00
3.25
4.00
3.50
3.25
3.00
4.25
3.75
4.00

Source: Keane (1986b)

Figure 16:
Mean Annual Wind Speed 1951-1970

7
7
6
4
5
6

Wind Speed (metres/sec.)

7 6 5 4

Source: Royal Irish Academy (1979)

Precipitation

Rainfall is probably the most important climatic variable influencing the location of agricultural enterprises in Ireland. Excessive moisture causes more problems than does drought due to the wetness of soils leading to problems of poaching by animals and damage by machinery, although in 'dry summers' soil moisture deficits may occur in eastern areas, especially where sandy soils prevail. The annual distribution of rainfall follows a west to east gradient with extensive parts of the mountainous areas of the west receiving over 1,600 mm annually compared to less than 800 mm around Dublin and northwards through county Louth. Sweeney (1997) highlights the close relationship between relief and precipitation levels with rain shadows evident to the east of the western mountain ranges and the Wicklow mountains. This west-east gradient is more related to differences in the duration of rainfall than to variation in intensity. The number of days with rain varies from approximately 240 in western locations to 150 in the east (Sweeney, 1997). Tillage farming is very much associated with the areas of lowest rainfall.

Sunshine

In terms of the average annual mean daily duration of bright sunshine there is a distinct south-east to north-west gradient with amounts decreasing to the north-west. Over the course of a year most locations average between 3.25 and 3.75 hours of bright sunshine per day, with amounts in excess of 4 hours found only along the east and south coasts. May and June are the sunniest months with the south-east receiving over 7 hours per day as compared to the north-west which obtains between 5 and 6 hours (Sweeney, 1997). This fact often means that, towards the end of the summer, insufficient sunshine hinders the ripening of crops for harvest.

Wind

The prevailing winds in Ireland are from the south-west although relief features provide a funnelling effect in many areas. North and western Ireland is one of the windiest locations in Europe due to its position along the main depression tracks in the north-eastern Atlantic (Sweeney, 1997). The extent to which the friction of land reduces the strength of the wind is evident from Figure 16 which illustrates that even a short distance inland winds abate quite substantially. Winds are seen to decrease from over 7 metres per second along the north-west coast to less than 4 metres per second in the interior south-east. Wind can be particularly damaging to trees and in exposed areas it can be a more serious inhibitor to plant growth than frost. While wind is generally regarded as a negative force, in moderation it also plays an important role in the harvesting of crops where it can, for example, aid the drying of hay. (Johnson, 1994).

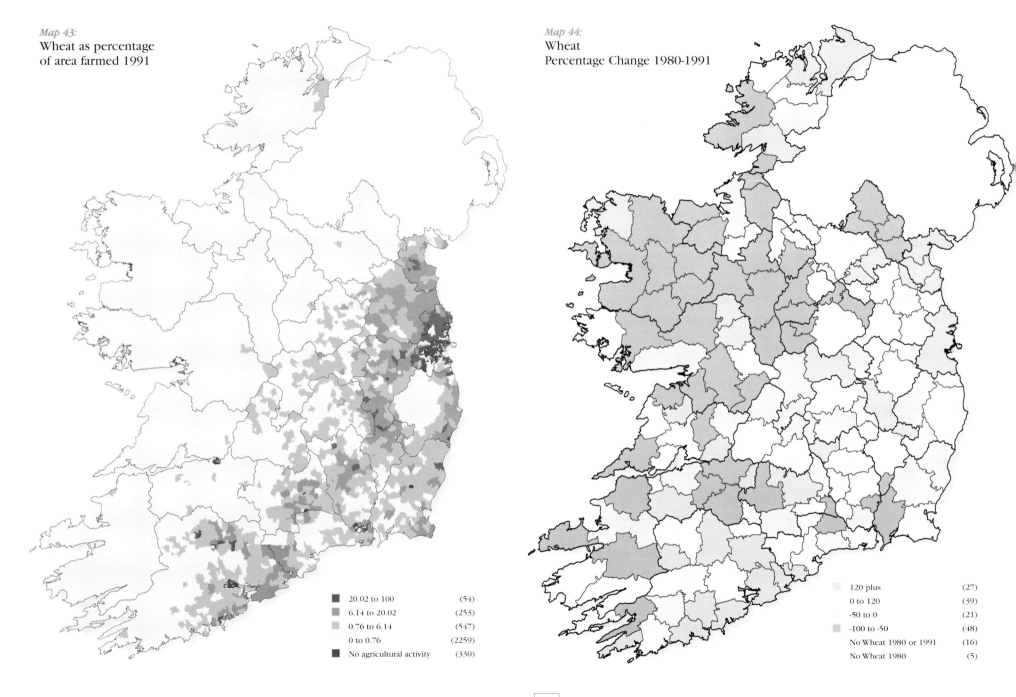

Map 43:
Wheat as percentage
of area farmed 1991

Map 44:
Wheat
Percentage Change 1980-1991

■	20.02 to 100	(54)
■	6.14 to 20.02	(253)
■	0.76 to 6.14	(547)
	0 to 0.76	(2259)
■	No agricultural activity	(330)

	120 plus	(27)
	0 to 120	(39)
	-50 to 0	(21)
	-100 to -50	(48)
	No Wheat 1980 or 1991	(16)
	No Wheat 1980	(5)

Wheat

Wheat in 1991 accounted for just under 30 per cent of the total area under cereals (Table 22). Some 85,650 hectares of wheat were grown on 4,580 farms. Of these, 44 per cent were classified as specialist tillage farms growing an average of 28 hectares.

Map 43 presents the percentage of the total area farmed occupied by wheat, which tends to be the most concentrated of all cereal crops due to its vulnerability to climatic conditions. It is most concentrated in the driest part of the State from Dublin to Dundalk where it gets an adequate supply of sunshine (Figure 15) to enable ripening of the crop (Gillmor, 1969a). Wheat is also quite intolerant of many soil conditions, especially acidic soils. From *Map 43*, north Dublin emerges as the strongest wheat district. Table 21 indicates that over 60 per cent of the total wheat crop is grown in the Mid-East and South-East regions. The Border (east) region has just under 7 per cent, mostly concentrated in Louth.

Between 1980 and 1991, the total area under wheat increased at an average annual rate of 5.6 per cent (Table 23). The increases are estimated to have continued through the 1990s, although at a much more modest average annual level of 1.6 per cent. Most of the increase has occurred in Dublin, the Mid-East and parts of both the South-West and Border (east) regions.

By contrast the greatest declines were in the West and Mid-West over both time periods, with the addition of the Border (west) over the 1991-97 period (Table 23). This is clearly confirmed by *Map 44,* with Mayo, Sligo, Leitrim, Roscommon and Galway showing declines in excess of 50 per cent, while the areas of increase are generally in the core areas of production. The interpretation of the data on *Map 44* must be undertaken with caution outside the main area of production as the actual area of cereal crops grown is quite insignificant in many districts.

Barley

Barley is the most widely grown cereal crop in the State (Table 22). In 1991 there were almost 193,400 hectares of barley grown, accounting for half of the total tilled area. The crop was grown on over 18,900 farms with an average area per farm of 10 hectares. However, cultivation is biased towards large farms with 44 per cent of the total area grown concentrated on approximately 3,800 specialist tillage farms, with an average area per farm of 22 hectares.

Just over two-fifths of the total area was grown in Wexford and Cork, with another one-third grown in Louth, Meath, Kildare, Offaly and Laois. A further 18 per cent of the total was grown in parts of Carlow, Kilkenny and South Tipperary. Beyond these areas there were localised concentrations in North Tipperary, north-east Donegal and east Galway.

Map 45 presents the detailed distribution of the barley crop within these areas.

Map 45:
Barley as percentage of area farmed 1991

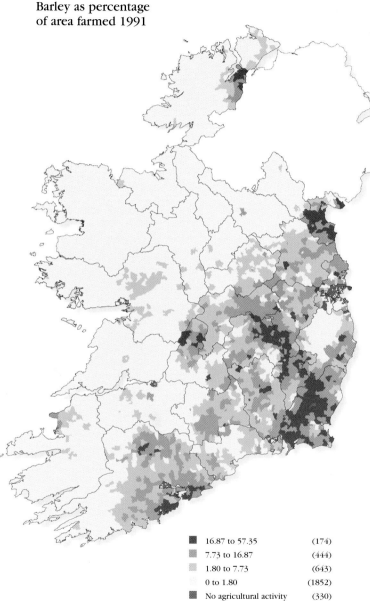

■ 16.87 to 57.35	(174)
■ 7.73 to 16.87	(444)
▫ 1.80 to 7.73	(643)
▫ 0 to 1.80	(1852)
■ No agricultural activity	(330)

The total barley crop tends to be classified under two main headings – malting barley and feeding barley. Malting barley, which is normally grown on contract, is broadly similar to wheat in terms of climatic and soil requirements, needing well-drained soils with a sufficient lime content. Traditionally, breweries and distilleries located adjacent to where the environmental requirements of malting barley were met, and, where the farmers had established the required skills to manage the crop.

The total area under barley declined by an average of 4.3 per cent annually over the period 1980-91 but the estimated annual declines for 1991-97 are much smaller at only 0.3 per cent (Table 23). Outside of Dublin, the largest declines were in the West, South-West and Border (west) regions. The largest declines over the 1990s occurred in the Border (west) region. *Map 46* demonstrates the 1980-91 trend in more detail with counties Mayo and Roscommon having the greatest declines in the west.

The decline is widespread, with the lowest declines in the core areas as suggested by *Map 45*. The areas of increase on the map need to be interpreted with caution due to the small number of hectares involved in each district.

Oats

Oats are the least important cereal crop with cultivation in 1991 confined to approximately 20,600 hectares on just over 5,000 farms, accounting for only 6.8 per cent of the total area of cereals grown (see Table 22). The traditional role of this crop was as feed for horses and its continued decline in western areas is related to the decline in the number of working horses (Horner *et al.*, 1984). Oats are less demanding than other cereal crops in terms of soil and climate conditions which facilitated a more dispersed pattern of growth into some very marginal areas such as north Donegal and north-west Mayo (*Map 47*). In fact, oats grow well in the relatively cooler moist conditions of the west and north which explains the crop's greater presence in Donegal and Galway (Gillmor, 1977). In 1991 the most important regions for oats were the South-East, Mid-East and South-West (Table 21). Oats have continued to maintain a surprisingly large presence in the West and Border (west) regions, which combined account for 15.4 per cent of the total crop.

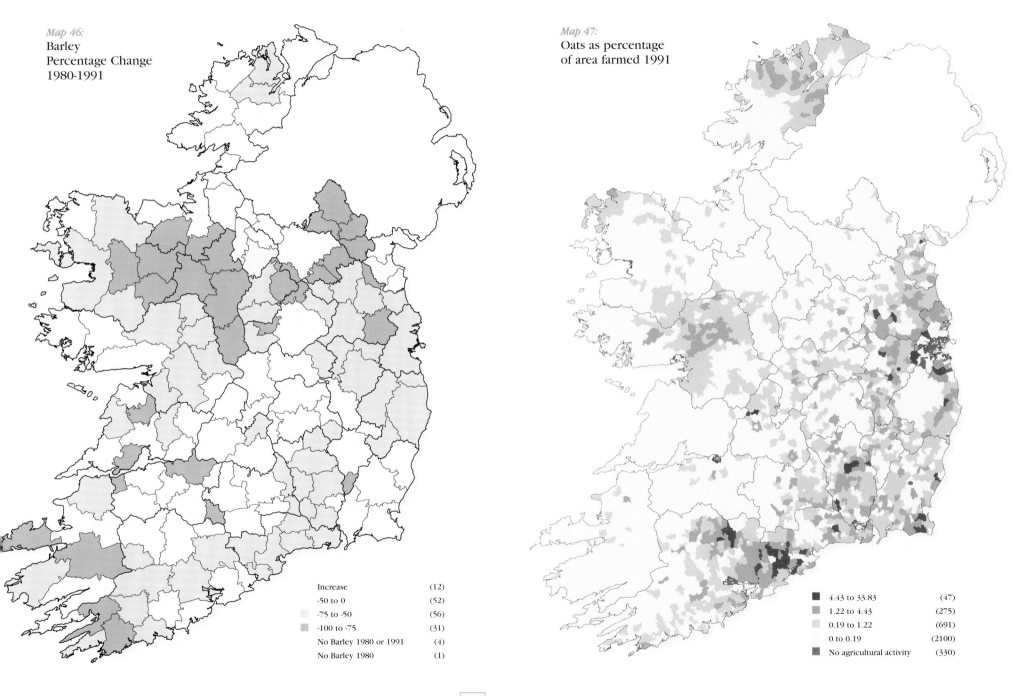

Map 46:
Barley
Percentage Change
1980-1991

Map 47:
Oats as percentage
of area farmed 1991

Increase	(12)
-50 to 0	(52)
-75 to -50	(56)
-100 to -75	(31)
No Barley 1980 or 1991	(4)
No Barley 1980	(1)

4.43 to 33.83	(47)
1.22 to 4.43	(275)
0.19 to 1.22	(691)
0 to 0.19	(2100)
No agricultural activity	(330)

Map 48:

Oats
Percentage Change 1980-1991

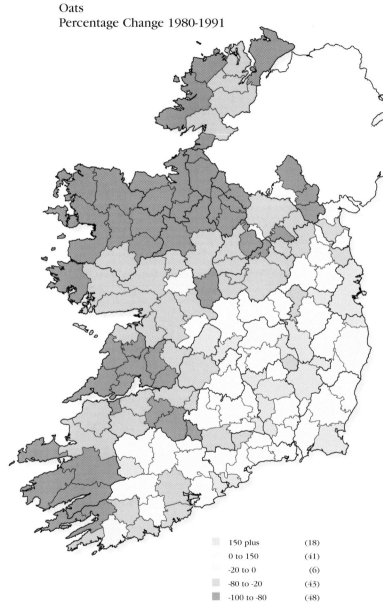

	150 plus	(18)
	0 to 150	(41)
	-20 to 0	(6)
	-80 to -20	(43)
	-100 to -80	(48)

Some striking regional contrasts in the pattern of change over the 1980s are shown on *Map 48*. Table 23 shows that the largest average annual regional declines were in the Border (west), West, Mid-West and Border (east) regions. Increases were confined to the core arable farming areas of the east and south, namely, the Dublin, South-East and Mid-East regions. The greatest increases occurred around Dublin, Kildare and Meath which could be related to the relatively high levels of bloodstock farming in these areas.

Table 23: Average annual percentage change in area under selected crops, 1980-1991 and 1991-1997

Region	Wheat		Oats		Barley		Sugar Beet		Potatoes		Total Crops[1]	
	80-91	91-97	80-91	91-97	80-91	91-97	80-91	91-97	80-91	91-97	80-91	91-97
Dublin	14.0	0.4	24.0	-2.3	-5.9	-1.1	-2.2	-	-0.6	2.0	-0.4	0.8
Mid-East	5.4	1.8	5.7	2.0	-5.2	-0.2	2.4	-1.3	-1.6	-1.9	-2.4	1.8
South-East	2.2	2.6	8.7	-2.1	-3.8	-0.7	-0.2	-1.2	-3.2	-2.8	-2.3	0.5
South-West	14.7	-0.2	0.6	0.2	-4.6	-0.4	0.3	0	-4.4	-2.9	-2.8	0.8
Mid-West	-0.9	-7.9	-4.3	2.0	-1.6	-0.3	2.0	-3.3	-6.9	-6.7	-2.4	-0.2
West	-5.8	-5.6	-6.1	-4.9	-5.5	-0.5	-6.6	-	-8.0	-5.6	-6.1	0.8
Border (west)	3.8	-1.1	-6.9	-0.2	-4.0	-1.9	-9.1	0	-4.8	-2.9	-4.6	-0.4
Border (east)	22.9	2.9	-4.4	13.0	-3.8	-0.6	-1.6	-	-3.9	0	-1.2	1.3
Midland	0.4	3.7	-0.7	-0.9	-3.6	1.3	1.7	3.5	-7.1	-2.4	-3.0	2.3
Ireland	5.6	1.6	-1.5	-0.8	-4.3	-0.3	0.1	-0.5	-4.6	-1.9	-2.7	1.0

Source: Agricultural Statistics 1980; Census of Agriculture 1991; Crops and Livestock Survey 1997.
[1] Includes fruit and horticulture.

Sugar Beet

In 1991 some 33,300 hectares of sugar beet were grown on just under 4,000 farms. Most of the crop is grown on specialist tillage farms and mixed crops and livestock farms. Together these two farm types account for 86 per cent of the total area grown.

The location of the crop is highly concentrated even within the main tillage areas (*Map 49*). This is as a result of its physical requirements, namely, deep well drained loam soils, high solar radiation receipts and compliance with a base temperature[7] of 7°C. In accordance with this, yields of sugar beet decrease with increased latitude, explaining its predominance in southern parts of the State (Keane, 1986b). Table 21 indicates that almost 78 per cent of the total crop is produced in the South-East and South-West regions while *Map 49* shows that most of this production occurs in Wexford, Carlow, Laois and Cork. The sugar beet processing plants are located in Carlow town and Mallow in north Cork. In the past there were also plants in Tuam (north Galway) and Thurles (north Tipperary). While some beet was grown in the hinterlands of these plants, Gillmor (1977) noted that their location was never actually very close to the main growing areas with transport costs being reduced through subsidies from the Irish Sugar Company.

Over the 1980-91 period cultivation of sugar beet in the West region declined by on average 6.6 per cent annually (Table 23), with this decline concentrated in east Mayo and east Galway. This was undoubtedly influenced by the closure of the sugar processing factory in Tuam and also by the fact that the conditions for growing the crop in these areas are less favourable. Many of the areas of increase shown on *Map 50* are districts in which only a small amount of the crop is grown.

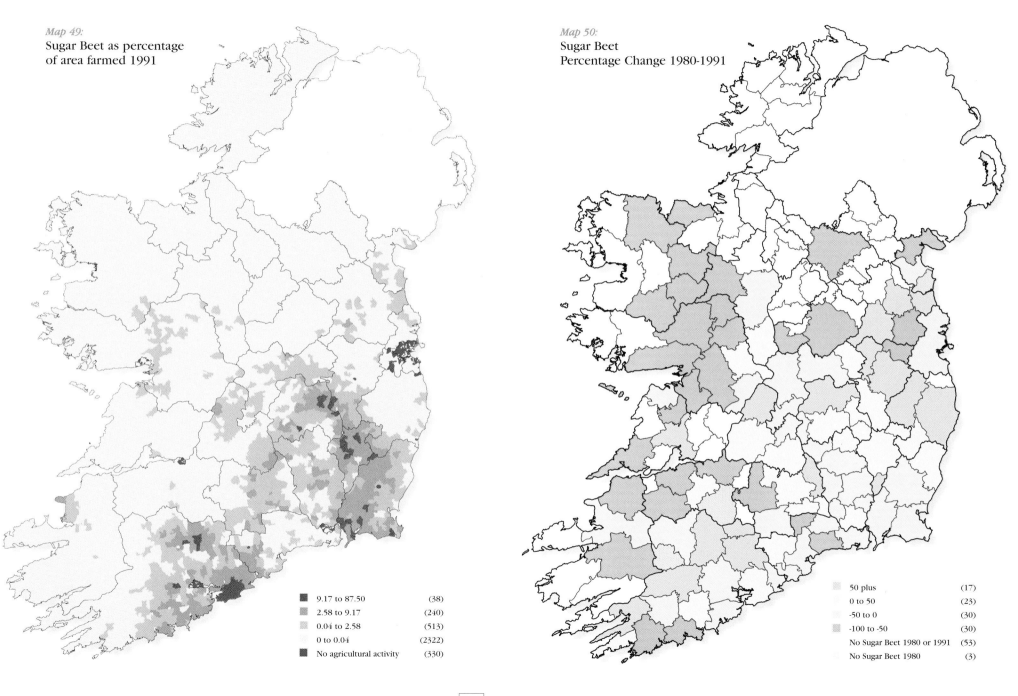

Map 49:
**Sugar Beet as percentage
of area farmed 1991**

Map 50:
**Sugar Beet
Percentage Change 1980-1991**

■ 9.17 to 87.50	(38)
■ 2.58 to 9.17	(240)
■ 0.04 to 2.58	(513)
■ 0 to 0.04	(2322)
■ No agricultural activity	(330)

50 plus	(17)
0 to 50	(23)
-50 to 0	(30)
-100 to -50	(30)
No Sugar Beet 1980 or 1991	(53)
No Sugar Beet 1980	(3)

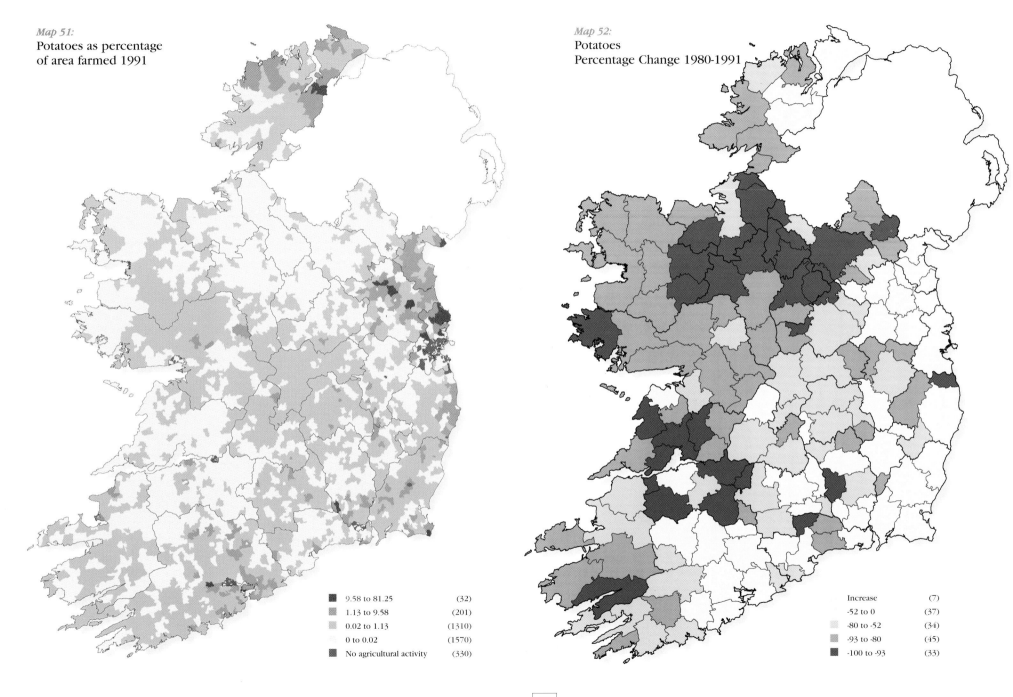

Map 51:
Potatoes as percentage
of area farmed 1991

Map 52:
Potatoes
Percentage Change 1980-1991

■	9.58 to 81.25	(32)
▨	1.13 to 9.58	(201)
▨	0.02 to 1.13	(1310)
□	0 to 0.02	(1570)
■	No agricultural activity	(330)

	Increase	(7)
	-52 to 0	(37)
	-80 to -52	(34)
	-93 to -80	(45)
	-100 to -93	(33)

Potatoes

In 1991 the total area of potatoes grown was just over 20,000 hectares on approximately 12,400 farms with an average area per farm of 1.7 hectares. However, like most other crops there has been a strong tendency towards specialisation and concentration so that by 1991 one-tenth of the growers accounted for 63 per cent of the total area under this crop. Potatoes have long been a traditional crop in Ireland. Indeed their continuing importance is quite well illustrated on *Map 51*. In contrast to other tillage crops which have a strong east and southern orientation, potatoes are grown much more widely across the State. The areas of highest concentration are in north Dublin, east Donegal and parts of counties Meath and Louth.

Potato growing is very suited to the Irish climate and soils, although excessive precipitation in the west can be problematic at harvest time, increasing the risk of disease (Gillmor, 1969b, 1977). Insufficient precipitation at certain times of the growing season can also pose disease risks but the biggest problem faced with potatoes is potato blight (Keane, 1986b). As is evidenced by the dispersed pattern of potato growth the crop is quite tolerant of different soil types. Commercial crops are grown mainly in north Dublin and in parts of Meath and Louth.

Beyond these eastern districts significant areas of potatoes are also grown commercially in east Donegal where the lower temperatures curtail the transmission of viral diseases making it very suitable for seed potato production. Seed potato growing is primarily confined to the north-west with most of the potatoes grown in other areas being for consumption and processing.

Table 23 shows that over the 1980s the area of potatoes declined in all regions with the largest average declines in the West, Midland and Mid-West regions. The general pattern has continued through the 1990s with declines in all regions except Dublin. The largest declines were in the Mid-West and West (Table 23). The estimated total area of potatoes in 1997 was approximately 23,400 hectares less than in 1980, representing an overall decline of 56 per cent.

From *Map 52* it can be seen that the areas which experienced the highest rates of decline between 1980 and 1991 were the poorest farming areas in Leitrim, Roscommon, Sligo and east Mayo. The areas of increase on the map must be viewed with caution due to the 'small numbers problem' by which large percentage increases can be derived from very small base figures. The general decline in the area under potatoes can be explained by increased specialisation at the level of the individual farm, the decline in farm labour, substitution away from potatoes in the human diet and an increase in the volume of imports.

Map 53:

Oilseed Rape as percentage of area farmed 1991

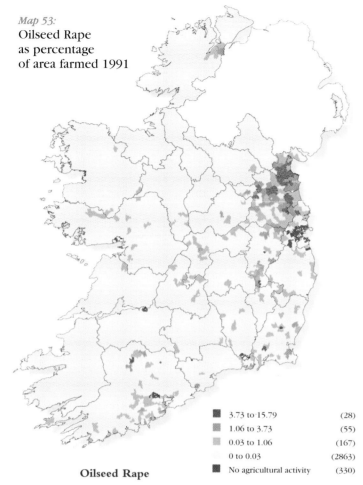

▪ 3.73 to 15.79	(28)
▪ 1.06 to 3.73	(55)
▪ 0.03 to 1.06	(167)
0 to 0.03	(2863)
▪ No agricultural activity	(330)

Oilseed Rape

Map 53 is one of the most striking because of the very high level of concentration of the oilseed rape crop. The total area grown in 1991 was just under 6,200 hectares on 576 farms. From Table 19, almost three-quarters of all oilseed rape production occurs in the Mid-East and Border (east) regions with two-thirds of the total area in Louth and Meath. This is largely as a result of climatic factors with the eastern parts of Louth and Meath receiving the lowest annual precipitation levels of any part of the State.

This crop also forms an important element in the rotation system with wheat and potatoes which are both significant in this area (see *Maps 43* and *51*). Traditionally, the crop was 'crushed' by a local processing company but it is now exported to the UK where it is used as the basis for vegetable oils and also as a protein component in animal feedstuffs.

Horticulture

Horticulture is generally taken to incorporate vegetable growing, fruit, flowers and nursery stock. Horticultural production tends to take place in a highly intensified fashion with high labour inputs. While it occupies a very small portion of the total agricultural area (0.14 per cent), in 1997 it accounted for 4 per cent of total agricultural output. Horticulture is a very complex sector with a wide range of different crops but data constraints limit analysis to the main categories used in the census – vegetables for sale and fruit for sale.

Table 24: Regional distribution of the area under vegetables and fruit, 1991

Region	Vegetables for sale (ha)	Fruit for sale (ha)	% of State total vegetables for sale (ha)	% of State total fruit for sale (ha)
Dublin	1,514	359	37.0	23.0
Mid-East	572	141	14.0	9.0
South-East	545	847	13.3	54.2
South-West	870	54	21.2	3.5
Mid-West	103	18	2.5	1.2
West	74	4	1.8	0.3
Border (west)	18	5	0.4	0.3
Border (east)	129	100	3.2	6.4
Midland	270	35	6.6	2.2
Ireland	4,095	1,563	100	100

Source: Census of Agriculture 1991.

Vegetables

Almost 4,100 hectares of vegetables for sale were grown on 1,100 farms in 1991 (Table 24). Proximity to markets is clearly very important with 67 per cent of the total area grown in counties Dublin, Meath and Cork (*Map 54*). In addition, these areas have suitable soils as well as a diminished risk of frost due to the influence of the sea (Gillmor, 1977). Improved transport and increased processing have resulted in vegetable growing becoming a possibility at relatively long distances away from the major urban centres as, for example, in parts of Offaly and Wexford. Other factors of local importance include the presence of processing plants as in south Kildare, or the sheltered conditions on sandy soils on the northern side of the Dingle peninsula where onions and, latterly, carrots have been cultivated.

Fruit

Apples and soft fruit such as strawberries, raspberries and gooseberries were grown on 1,563 hectares distributed over approximately 490 farms in 1991. The principal orchard areas have traditionally been located in north Dublin, south Kilkenny, Waterford and south Tipperary. These four counties account for over two-fifths of the total area grown (*Map 55*). Half of the total area under soft fruit is located in Wexford, especially around Enniscorthy. Another 20 per cent of the area under fruit is found in parts of Kilkenny and north Dublin.

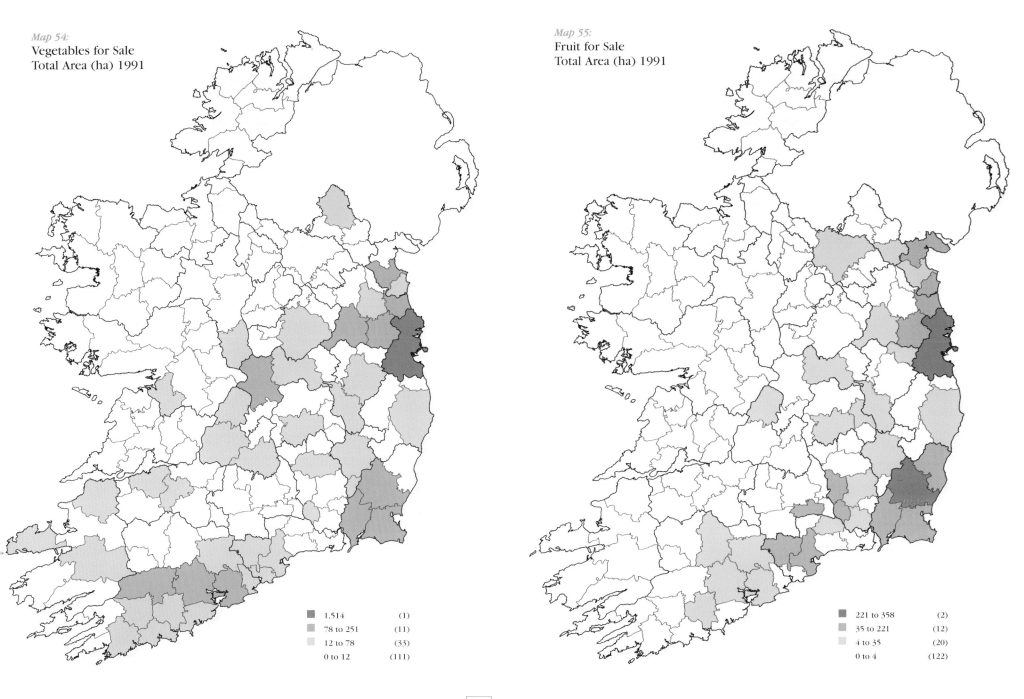

Map 54:
Vegetables for Sale
Total Area (ha) 1991

	1,514	(1)
	78 to 251	(11)
	12 to 78	(33)
	0 to 12	(111)

Map 55:
Fruit for Sale
Total Area (ha) 1991

	221 to 358	(2)
	35 to 221	(12)
	4 to 35	(20)
	0 to 4	(122)

Change in Total Tillage Area

Map 56 provides a summary of the change
in aggregate tillage farming over the 1980s.
The overwhelming impression is the widespread
decrease in tillage crops over all regions, with the
largest declines in the west and north-west.
The smallest declines were in the traditional tillage
areas with modest levels of increase in only four RDs.
The regional figures in Table 23 confirm the overall
decline in every region with the lowest average
annual declines in the Dublin (-0.4 per cent) and east
Border (-1.2 per cent) regions. The largest declines
occurred in the West (-6.1 per cent) and west Border
(-4.6 per cent) regions. This significant decline is in
response to many factors including reductions in
cereal prices on the part of the EU in order to curb
serious overproduction. The geography of the decline
emerges from the underlying trend towards
concentration, with production becoming more
confined to a smaller number of larger farms,
combined with specialisation in terms of the range of
crops produced. The estimated figures for 1991-97
show a turnaround of the decline with the total figure
increasing by one per cent annually, although, there
continued to be modest declines in two regions – the
Border (west) and Mid-West.

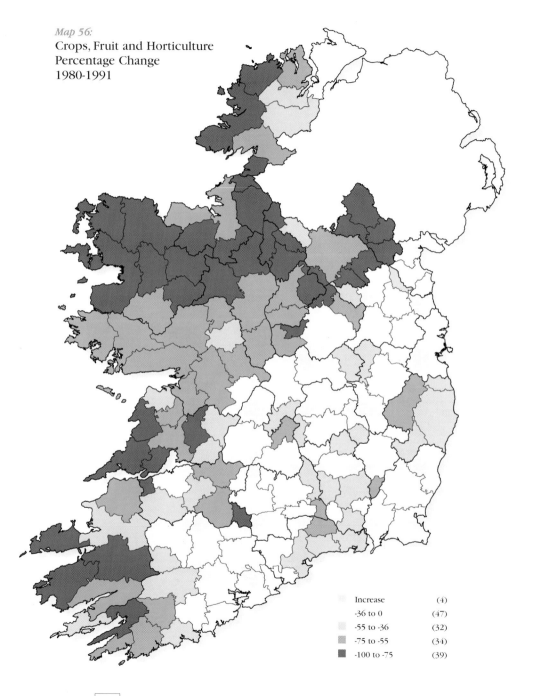

Map 56:
Crops, Fruit and Horticulture
Percentage Change
1980-1991

	Increase	(4)
	-36 to 0	(47)
	-55 to -36	(32)
	-75 to -55	(34)
	-100 to -75	(39)

Section Four

Livestock Production

Introduction

Livestock and livestock products accounted for over 87 per cent of the value of gross agricultural output in Ireland in 1997. This proportion has remained remarkably steady over time. The traditional orientation of Irish farming towards livestock enterprises can be explained by a number of factors, including climate, soil, topography, history, and by economic conditions which have ensured a market for livestock and livestock products in the UK and mainland Europe (Gillmor, 1977; Horner et al., 1984). The greatest contribution to the value of gross output came from the beef and dairying sectors, with beef traditionally making the larger contribution. However, in 1996 there was a change in this trend as the contribution of the beef sector fell below that of milk as a result of the BSE crisis and the subsequent collapse of foreign markets for Irish beef.

This section outlines the spatial distribution of the main types of livestock enterprises, together with the spatial changes that have occurred over the 1980s and between 1991 and 1997. The material will be presented under the general headings: dairying, suckler cows, beef, sheep, horses and ponies, pigs and poultry. This section also contains a summary of the data in standardised livestock units (LUs) allowing for comparison of the relative importance of the different livestock enterprises.

Dairying

Ireland enjoys very favourable climatic and soil conditions for dairying based on a long growing season with low costs of housing and winter feeding. Temperature is the most important climatic factor affecting milk production with optimum temperatures between 4°C and 21°C. Since most cows are housed over the winter low temperatures are rarely a problem in Ireland. Of greater significance could be excess precipitation in the summer months, leading to the poaching of grassland, and poor quality fodder production having effects that extend into the following winter (Keane, 1986b).

Table 25: Percentage distribution of State totals for selected livestock categories, 1991

Region	Dairy Cows[1]	Other Cows[2]	Other Cattle	Sheep
Dublin	0.5	0.4	0.7	0.9
Mid-East	7.4	7.0	8.9	14.2
South-East	20.7	12.8	18.3	20.0
South-West	31.9	13.0	17.7	12.7
Mid-West	16.9	13.5	13.8	4.2
West	5.9	23.2	15.6	24.6
Border (west)	2.8	12.1	5.8	12.2
Border (east)	7.4	7.7	7.2	3.5
Midland	6.6	10.3	11.9	7.5
Ireland	100	100	100	100

Source: Census of Agriculture 1991.
[1] Includes dairy heifers-in-calf.
[2] Includes other heifers-in-calf.

In 1991, dairy cows were enumerated on just under 50,000 farms, 29 per cent of the total. Average herd size on these farms was 27 cows. Dairying has become a very specialised type of farming so that by 1991 approximately 93 per cent of all dairy cows were enumerated on 42,000 specialist dairy farms.

Traditionally, there have been two main dairying regions in the State – the south-west and the north-east (which in fact extends into parts of Northern Ireland). While both of these regions are prominent on *Map 57* there are substantial differences between them in terms of the scale and intensity of milk production. The south-west dairying region includes north and east Kerry, almost all of Cork and Limerick and substantial parts of Tipperary, Waterford and Kilkenny, as well as south-west Clare. Regionally, almost 70 per cent of the dairy herd is located in the South-West, Mid-West and South-East regions (Table 25).

Of lesser importance is the Cavan-Monaghan area (east-Border region) which accounts for another 7.4 per cent of the State total. These figures can be contrasted with 2.8 per cent of the total herd located in the Border (west) and 5.9 per cent in the West regions. Most of the dairy herd in the West is found in north and east Mayo which forms part of the catchment of the North Connacht Farmers Co-Operative.

Table 26 shows that 45.2 per cent and 39.3 per cent of all farms in the South-West and Mid-West regions respectively are in the specialist dairying category; combined they account for almost 50 per cent of all specialist dairy farms in the State (Table 29).

Map 57:

Farms with Dairy Cows as percentage of total 1991

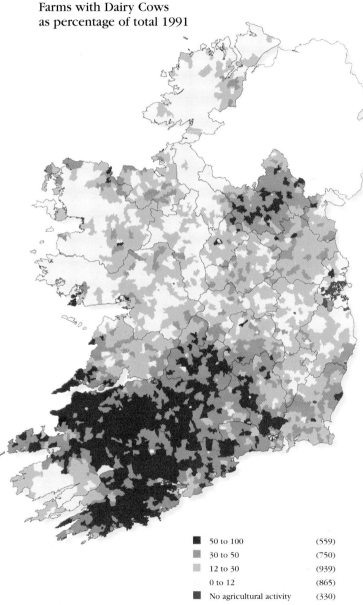

■ 50 to 100	(559)
▨ 30 to 50	(750)
▨ 12 to 30	(939)
0 to 12	(865)
■ No agricultural activity	(330)

Table 26: Percentage share of livestock farms in each region, 1991

Region	Specialist Dairy	Specialist Beef
Dublin	7.4*	21.0
Mid-East	16.9	31.7
South-East	31.0	25.7
South-West	45.2	29.2
Mid-West	39.3	45.5
West	9.8	51.9
Border (west)	8.5	51.0
Border (east)	30.6	44.3
Midland	16.9	54.2
Ireland	24.4	42.1

* 7.4% of all farms in Dublin are specialist dairy.
Source: Census of Agriculture 1991.

The areas represented by the top interval of *Map 57* have dairy cows on more than half of their farms. By contrast, in the lowest interval, covering most of the north and west, less than 12 per cent of all farms have dairy cows. This map does not present a measure of the relative importance of dairying to the farm, it merely indicates whether or not dairy cows are present. *Map 58*, on the other hand, illustrates the percentage of 'specialist' dairy farms in each district. It shows the location of the farms in which dairying accounts for more than two-thirds of the total farm standard gross margin. This presents a very similar pattern since 85 per cent of the farms with dairy cows are, in fact, specialist dairy farms. *Map 58* removes some of the smaller scale milk producers in east Galway, Roscommon and Donegal, where dairying is undertaken in combination with other farm enterprises such as sheep and cattle rearing.

Map 59 provides an alternative way of looking at the specialist dairy regions by considering the proportion of the total economic size (ESUs) of each DED accounted for by this enterprise. In the top interval over 65 per cent of the total gross margin of the DED is produced by specialist dairy farms. Again, the fact that both *Maps 58* and *59* show broadly similar patterns indicates that where dairying occurs, it is on a scale that makes it the most important farm enterprise.

Table 27: Change in number of dairy cows and dairy heifers-in-calf, 1980-1991 and 1991-1997

Region	Actual change 1980-91	Average annual % change 1980-91	Actual change 1991-97[1]	Average annual % change 1991-97[1]	Actual change 1980-97[1]	Total % change 1980-97[1]
Dublin	-1,000	-1.2	-200	-0.5	-1,200	-15.8
Mid-East	-10,400	-0.8	+3,700	0.6	-6,700	-5.7
South East	-47,000	-1.2	+16,600	0.9	-30,400	-8.7
South-West	-85,500	-1.4	+43,700	1.6	-41,800	-7.6
Mid-West	-73,600	-2.1	+9,800	0.7	-63,800	-20.0
West	-48,600	-3.3	+7,400	1.4	-41,200	-30.7
Border (west)	-25,000	-3.4	+1,600	0.7	-23,400	-35.3
Border (east)	-31,400	-2.1	+8,900	1.4	-22,500	-16.2
Midland	-20,700	-1.6	+4,300	0.7	-16,400	-13.9
Ireland	-343,200	-1.7	+95,800	1.1	-247,400	-13.7

Source: Agricultural Statistics 1980; Census of Agriculture 1991; Crops and Livestock Survey 1997.
[1] 1997 figures are estimates based on CSO annual crops and livestock survey.
Note: Increases between 1991 and 1997 are accounted for by a decline of 15,000 dairy cows and an increase of over 110,000 dairy heifers-in-calf.

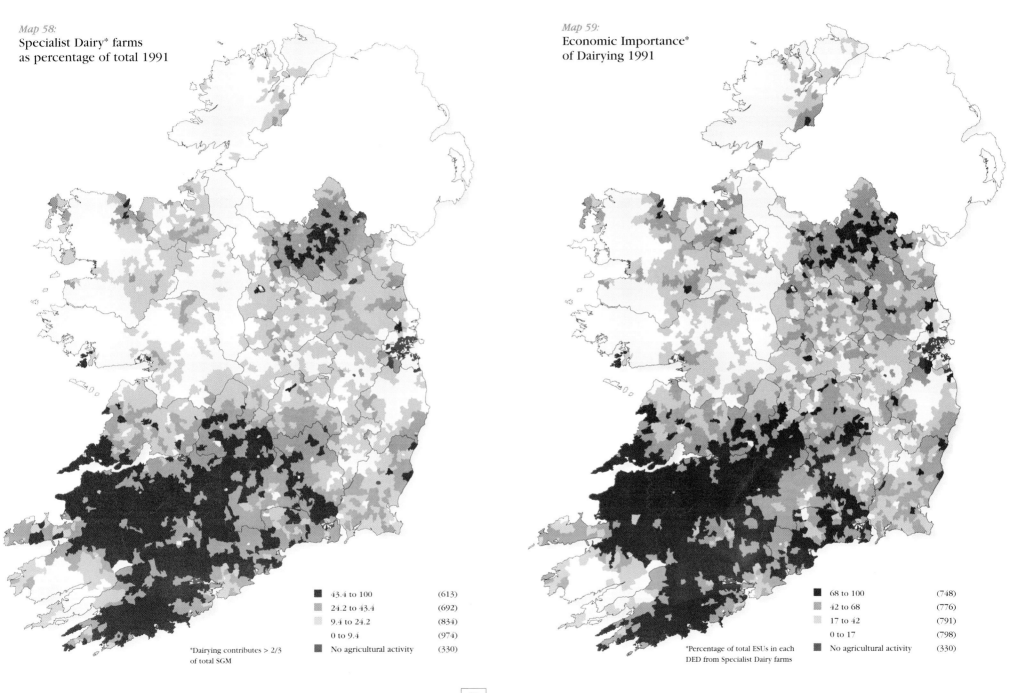

Map 58:
**Specialist Dairy* farms
as percentage of total 1991**

Map 59:
**Economic Importance*
of Dairying 1991**

■	43.4 to 100	(613)
■	24.2 to 43.4	(692)
■	9.4 to 24.2	(834)
	0 to 9.4	(974)
■	No agricultural activity	(330)

*Dairying contributes > 2/3
of total SGM

■	68 to 100	(748)
■	42 to 68	(776)
■	17 to 42	(791)
	0 to 17	(798)
■	No agricultural activity	(330)

*Percentage of total ESUs in each
DED from Specialist Dairy farms

Map 60:

Dairy Cows and Heifers-in-Calf Percentage Change 1980-1991

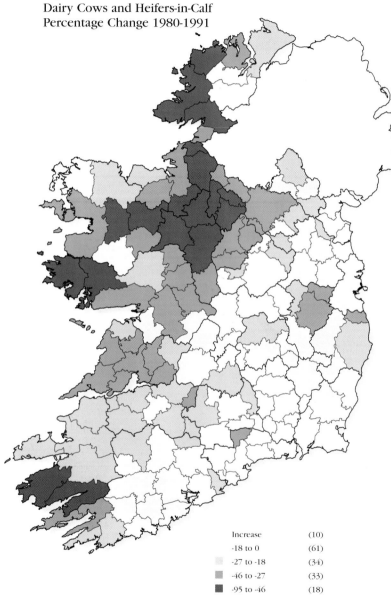

Increase	(10)
-18 to 0	(61)
-27 to -18	(34)
-46 to -27	(33)
-95 to -46	(18)

Change in Dairy Herds

There have been some quite dramatic changes in the number and distribution of dairy herds and animals, especially since the introduction of milk quotas in 1984. The percentage of farms with dairy cows declined from 41.4 per cent in 1983 to 28.8 per cent in 1991 while, over the same period, the average herd size increased by 50 per cent, from 18 to 27 cows. Table 27 shows that the largest absolute declines were in the core dairying regions in the South-West and Mid-West. However, the greatest relative declines were to the north and west of a line from Limerick to Cavan and particularly in Donegal, Leitrim, Roscommon, Mayo and west Galway. These are the areas with the smallest farms and the greatest structural problems. Furthermore, farmers in this region faced difficulties in meeting the high levels of investment required to comply with more exacting standards of production (Gillmor and Walsh, 1993). This fact is highlighted by Table 27 where the total dairy herd was seen to contract by on average 1.7 per cent per annum in the period 1980-91, amounting to a total reduction of over one-third of a million animals. The regions with the largest decreases were the Border (west), the West, the Mid-West and the Border (east). Again, the difference in scale of production between the north-east and the south-west is evident from the extent of their respective declines. The average annual rate of decline in the Border (east) was 2.1 per cent

while the decrease in the South-West was much smaller at 1.4 per cent. Caution is required in analysing the areas of increase on *Map 60*. In some RDs the percentage changes are actually very small, and in aggregate the actual change in the numbers was only 2,663 – which represented only 0.2 per cent of the total number of these livestock in the State in 1991. In addition, some of the districts which recorded increases are very small in size and have relatively small numbers of dairy livestock.

The data for 1991-97 indicate a reversal of the trend of the previous decade with an estimated average annual increase of 1.1 per cent in the size of the national herd of dairy cows and heifers-in-calf (Table 27). It is noteworthy that while there was an increase of 95,800 between in the total number of dairy cows and dairy heifers-in-calf between 1991 and 1997 the data conceal a decline of 15,000 in the number of dairy cows, which was offset by a very significant increase in the number of dairy heifers-in-calf.

The largest increases are to be found in the South-West, West and Border (east). A comparison of the gains and losses over the two periods reveals somewhat contrasting patterns of adjustment. For example, in the South-West and South-East where farms are on average larger in size, the increases in the 1991-97 period represented a very significant

replacement of the losses recorded for the 1980s
(51 per cent in the case of the South-West and 35 per
cent for the South-East). By contrast, in the Mid-West,
West and Border (west) where herd sizes are typically
less than the State average, the gains in the 1991-97
period amounted to only 13 per cent of the losses
recorded over the previous decade. Thus in the 1990s
the stronger dairying areas proved more capable
of offsetting the declines of the 1980s by retaining
replacement stock.

Other (Suckler) Cows

In 1991 cows other than those kept primarily
to produce milk for human consumption were kept
on 54 per cent of all farms in the State, of which
55 per cent were classified as specialist beef farms.
Most of these livestock are kept on small farms so that
the average number per farm in 1991 was only 8.8
cows. While 'other' or suckler cows are mainly
associated with beef farming, there are about 28 per
cent of specialist beef farms without cows (i.e., they
specialise in the finishing stages of this enterprise,
mostly on large farms).

However, a significant minority
of specialist dairy farms (10 per cent in
1991) also had some suckler cows.

In 1991 almost half of the total herd
of suckler cows was contained in the three
regions – Border (west), West and Mid-West
(Table 25). Substantial pockets were also
found in south-west Kerry, Wicklow and
isolated districts throughout Carlow,
Kilkenny and Laois. The lowest densities
were in Cork, Limerick, Tipperary South,
north Dublin and parts of Louth and Meath
(*Map 61*). This suggests that 'suckler' cows
tend to be associated, for the most part,
with those areas where the structural
impediments to farming are greatest.

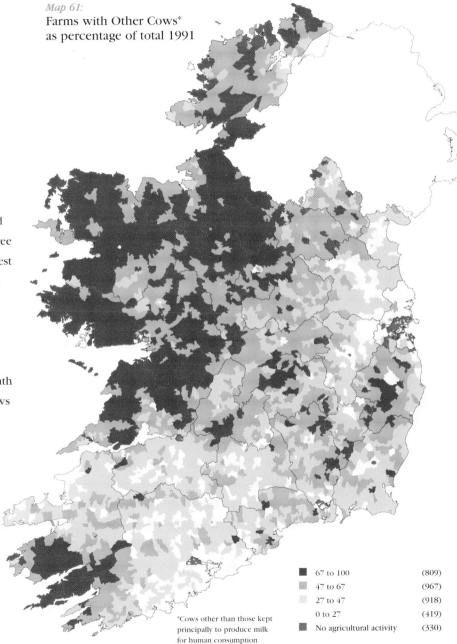

Map 61:
Farms with Other Cows*
as percentage of total 1991

■	67 to 100	(809)
■	47 to 67	(967)
■	27 to 47	(918)
□	0 to 27	(419)
■	No agricultural activity	(330)

*Cows other than those kept
principally to produce milk
for human consumption

Map 62:

Other Cows and Heifers-in-Calf Percentage Change 1980-1991

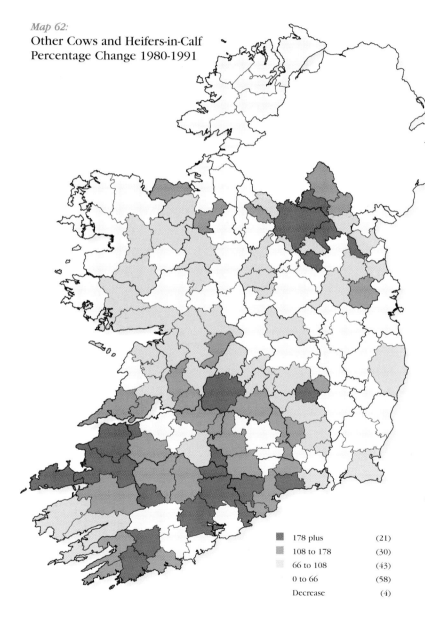

178 plus   (21)
108 to 178   (30)
66 to 108   (43)
0 to 66   (58)
Decrease   (4)

Change in number of Suckler Cows

There have been significant increases in the number of 'other' cows and in the number of farms on which they are kept. The percentage of farms with suckler cows increased from 33 per cent in 1983 to 54 per cent in 1991 and over the same period the average number per farm increased from 5.6 to 8.8.

Table 28 shows an average annual increase of 6.5 per cent over the period from 1980 to 1991 in the number of suckler cows, while the percentage was as large as 12.3 per cent in the South-West, 10.1 per cent in the Mid-West and 10.3 per cent in the Border (east). This trend is clearly evident from *Map 62* where the main areas of expansion were the traditional dairying areas of Munster and Cavan-Monaghan. This was due to substitution from dairy to suckler cows as a result of policy changes. The areas of smallest increase were those which had the highest numbers to begin with, especially Donegal, west Mayo and Roscommon. The only areas of actual decline were in Leitrim and south Roscommon.

From Table 28, the trend towards expansion in suckler cows is seen to have continued through the 1990s with the total herd increasing at an average annual rate of 8.3 per cent over the period 1991-97. The highest average annual increases were recorded in Dublin, followed by the South-West, the Midland and the Mid-West regions.

Since 1980 the largest absolute gains were in the West, in response to very significant declines in the number of dairy cows, and also in the traditional dairying regions of the South-West and Mid-West where substitution and intensification were important adjustments. Another notable feature was the relatively low level of increase in the Border (west) even though there was a very large decline in the number of dairy cows in this structurally weak region.

Table 28: Change in number of 'other cows' and 'other' heifers-in-calf, 1980-1991 and 1991-1997

Region	Actual increase 1980-91	Average annual % increase 1980-91	Actual increase 1991-97[1]	Average annual % increase 1991-97[1]	Actual increase 1980-97[1]	Total % increase 1980-97[1]
Dublin	1,200	4.2	3,100	13.6	4,300	165.4
Mid-East	23,400	5.7	24,400	6.7	47,800	127.1
South-East	46,200	6.5	53,600	8.0	99,800	153.5
South-West	64,700	12.3	67,800	10.1	132,500	277.8
Mid-West	61,800	10.1	66,200	9.4	128,000	230.2
West	72,600	5.1	88,900	7.4	161,500	126.0
Border (west)	26,200	3.0	38,100	6.1	64,300	81.6
Border (east)	35,400	10.3	36,700	9.2	72,100	231.1
Midland	30,600	4.8	52,900	9.9	83,500	143.2
Ireland	362,100	6.5	431,700	8.3	793,800	157.2

Source: Agricultural Statistics 1980; Census of Agriculture 1991; Crops and Livestock Survey 1997.
[1] 1997 figures are estimates based on CSO annual crops and livestock survey.

Beef Cattle

Traditionally, beef production has been of major importance to the Irish agricultural sector. While cattle rearing is the least profitable farming enterprise, due to its extensive nature and low returns per hectare, it has maintained its importance based on a range of factors. Gillmor (1977) suggests the role of 'tradition' as being of crucial significance to the survival of beef production in Ireland. Irish farmers have a long established knowledge of cattle and indeed attach a certain degree of 'prestige' to ownership of a good quality herd. Also of importance, and increasingly so in today's agricultural scene, is the low labour requirement making cattle a suitable enterprise for older as well as part-time farmers. Input costs are also relatively low and the physical and husbandry requirements of cattle are such as to allow their production on almost any type of land and on any size of farm (Gillmor, 1977).

Table 29: Percentage distribution of livestock farms, by region, 1991

Region	Specialist Dairy	Specialist Beef
Dublin	0.3*	0.5
Mid-East	4.7	5.1
South-East	15.2	7.3
South-West	30.7	11.5
Mid-West	19.0	12.7
West	9.2	28.2
Border (west)	4.2	14.4
Border (east)	10.5	8.8
Midland	6.2	11.5
Ireland	100	100

* 0.3% of all specialist dairy farms in the State are in the Dublin region.
Source: Census of Agriculture 1991.

While specialist beef farms exist in almost every DED in the country, *Map 63* indicates that the highest concentrations are found in Mayo, Sligo, Leitrim, north Roscommon and into the midlands through Longford, Westmeath and Offaly. High concentrations are also found in Galway, especially west of the city. There is also a strong orientation towards beef production in Clare. Those parts of the State which are least associated with beef production are the mainly tillage areas of the south-east, north Dublin and Cork.

Elsewhere, beef production maintains a presence to some extent but, particularly noteworthy is its relatively greater importance in the dairying region of the north-east as compared to the more intensive dairying region of the south-west. From Table 26 it can be seen that over half of all farms in each of the Midland, West and Border (west) regions are engaged in specialist beef production while between them these three regions account for over 54 per cent of all specialist beef farms in the State (Table 29).

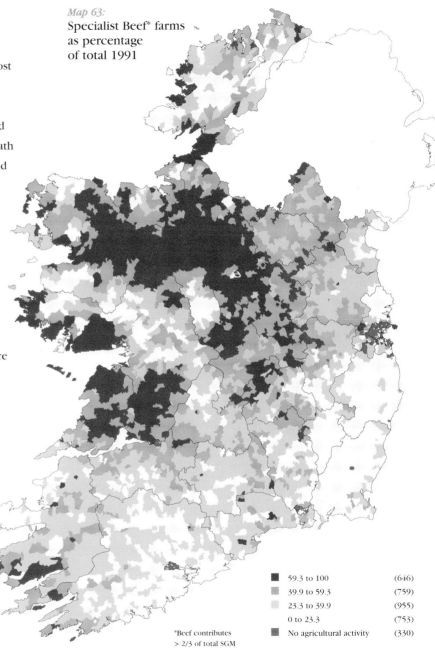

Map 63:
Specialist Beef* farms as percentage of total 1991

■ 59.3 to 100	(646)
▨ 39.9 to 59.3	(759)
▧ 23.3 to 39.9	(955)
□ 0 to 23.3	(753)
■ No agricultural activity	(330)

*Beef contributes > 2/3 of total SGM

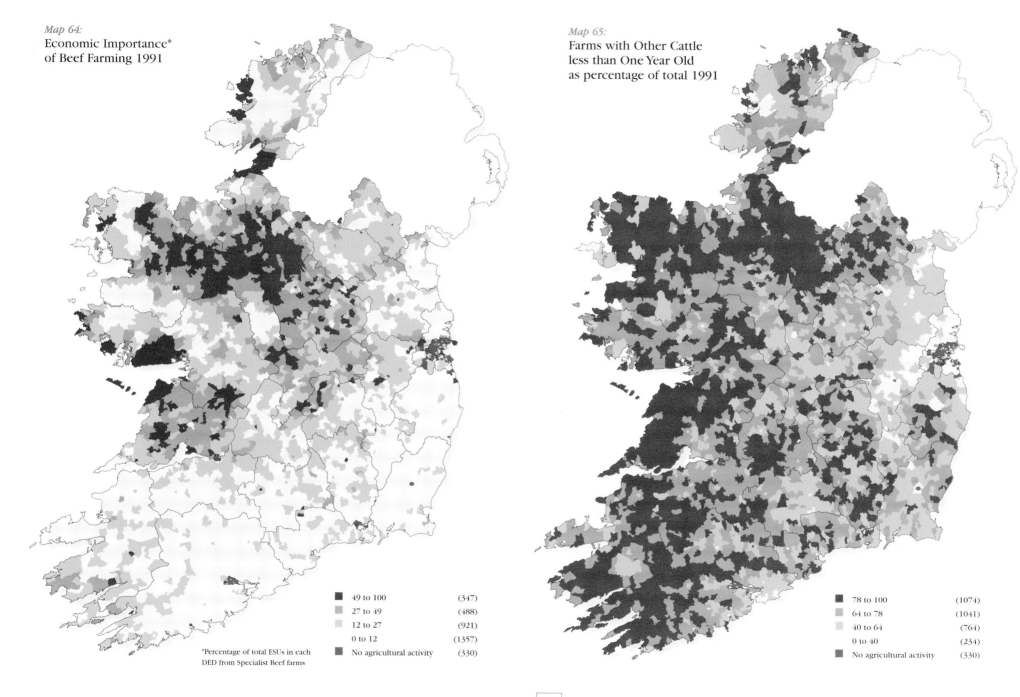

Map 64:
Economic Importance*
of Beef Farming 1991

Map 65:
Farms with Other Cattle
less than One Year Old
as percentage of total 1991

	49 to 100	(347)
	27 to 49	(488)
	12 to 27	(921)
	0 to 12	(1357)
	No agricultural activity	(330)

*Percentage of total ESUs in each
DED from Specialist Beef farms

	78 to 100	(1074)
	64 to 78	(1041)
	40 to 64	(764)
	0 to 40	(234)
	No agricultural activity	(330)

While *Map 63* provides a clear picture of the general location of specialist beef farms, *Map 64* shows the relative economic importance of this enterprise. The latter map is particularly important as it restricts the highest class interval to a much narrower band across north Connacht and also greatly diminishes the apparent significance of this enterprise in the midlands and Clare. The top interval highlights DEDs in which over 49 per cent of the total economic size is accounted for by specialist beef farms. That is to say, the map isolates those parts of the State where beef farming is of paramount importance. Again, the contrast between the importance of beef in the north-east as compared to the south-west is clearly apparent. Most of counties Cavan and Monaghan fall within the range where 12 to 27 per cent of the total economic size is accounted for by beef production, as opposed to less than 12 per cent over most of the south-west. Beef accounts for about one-quarter of total ESUs in each of the West, Midland and Border (west) regions. It is least important in the South-West, South-East and Mid-East/Dublin regions where it accounts respectively for 7 per cent, 8 per cent and 11 per cent of total ESUs.

Cattle Production and Rearing: Regional Movements and Specialisation

While beef enterprises are present in almost all parts of the State, there is a high level of regional specialisation within the beef sector. This variation is in response to such variables as physical conditions, farm size, farmer demographics and general farm economy factors (Gillmor, 1968). These regional differences reflect a movement of cattle around the country which has long marked cattle rearing in Ireland. Calves are produced in the dairying regions of the south and are ultimately finished in the grassland areas of the midlands and east. *Maps 65-75* allow for an analysis of this movement and some discussion of how movement patterns have changed in response to external influences on the sector since the 1980s.

The major source of calves has traditionally been the dairying region of the south-west, due in part to the fact that most of the milk produced on these farms is for processing. At an early age calves have tended to be marketed from the south-west and sold primarily to farmers in Connacht and the west midlands for rearing. As the cattle become older and approach the finishing stage the direction of their movement has tended to be generally eastwards onto larger farms with better quality grassland in the east midlands (Gillmor, 1969b; 1977).

This pattern of movement has largely continued although there have been some changes. These have been brought about as a result of diversification, particularly by dairy farmers, as they retain calves in response to the restrictions in dairying following the imposition of quotas in 1984. This trend is described in *Maps 71* to *75* while *Maps 65* to *70* illustrate the 1991 situation with regard to the geography of the various stages of the beef production cycle.

Other Cattle aged less than 1 year

Beef cattle aged less than one year were enumerated on 80 per cent of all farms with cattle in 1991. They are found extensively in the western half of the State particularly in the south-west, Clare, Mayo, Leitrim and parts of Sligo, Roscommon and Galway. They are also prominent in Laois, Kilkenny and in the dairying regions of Cavan and Monaghan (*Map 65*). The parts of the State with the smallest numbers of farms in this category are in the east, especially counties Louth, Meath, Kildare and Dublin.

Map 66 was produced following Gillmor (1969b) and presents the ratio of calves to cows. The lowest interval on this map indicates areas which are characterised by having fewer than one calf to every cow, indicating that an outflow of calves has taken place. Similarly, there are areas which have more than one calf to every cow showing an influx of calves. These areas are Connacht and particularly Offaly and parts of Westmeath, south Roscommon, east Galway and north Tipperary. Clearly the main areas of net out-migration are the dairy regions of the south-west and north-east as well as along the eastern seaboard. The general patterns identified by Gillmor (1969b) are still evident, although to a lesser extent, as will be highlighted in *Map 71*.

Other Cattle aged 1-2 years

Cattle aged 1-2 years (excluding heifers-in-calf) were recorded on 72 per cent of all farms with cattle in 1991. *Map 67* shows that there is a shift in the spatial extent of this older age group as compared to the younger category. There is a move away from the western extremities, a clear move from Leitrim and an inflow to the general Midland region. Table 30 further bears out this pattern with the Midland region having the highest percentage of farms with beef cattle aged 1-2 years, followed closely by the Mid-West and West. Again, Dublin and the Mid-East regions show up as having the lowest incidence of farms with this category of animal.

Table 30: Percentage of farms with 'other' cattle[1], 1991

Region	Other cattle less than 1 year	Other cattle 1-2 years	Other cattle greater than 2 years
Dublin	26.5	29.8	35.1
Mid-East	39.9	42.1	48.2
South-East	66.2	64.6	44.0
South-West	75.2	63.2	39.2
Mid-West	76.6	69.0	46.8
West	75.4	68.8	48.3
Border (west)	73.0	50.5	29.1
Border (east)	69.9	65.8	41.9
Midland	68.4	70.2	57.0
Ireland	71.2	63.9	44.0

Source: Derived from Census of Agriculture 1991.
[1] Excluding all cows and heifers-in-calf.

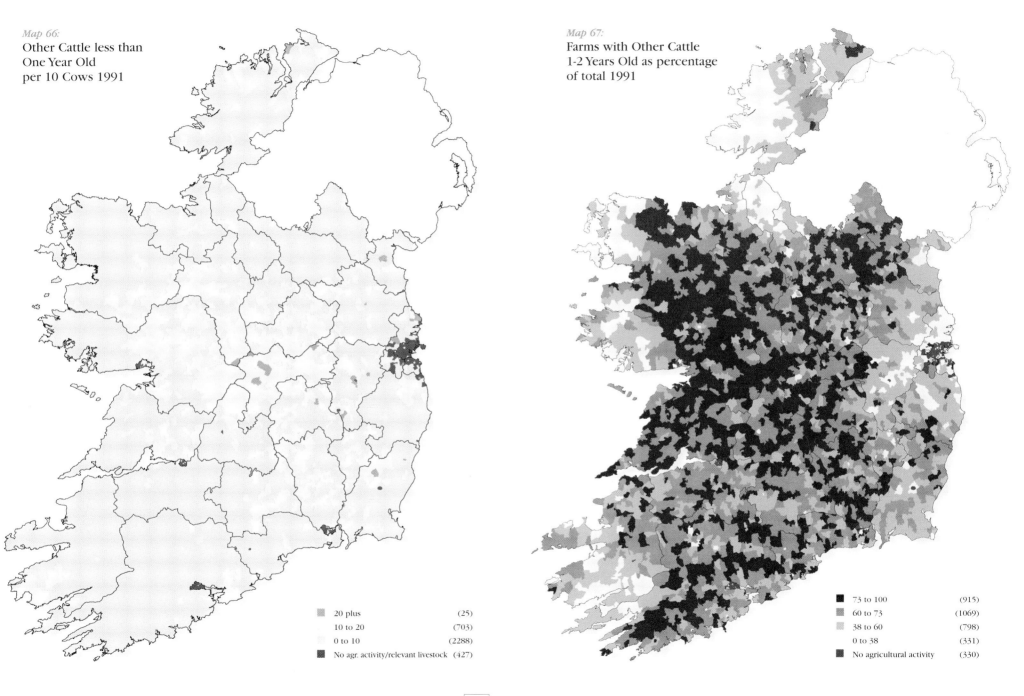

Map 66:
**Other Cattle less than
One Year Old
per 10 Cows 1991**

Map 67:
**Farms with Other Cattle
1-2 Years Old as percentage
of total 1991**

20 plus	(25)
10 to 20	(703)
0 to 10	(2288)
No agr. activity/relevant livestock	(427)

73 to 100	(915)
60 to 73	(1069)
38 to 60	(798)
0 to 38	(331)
No agricultural activity	(330)

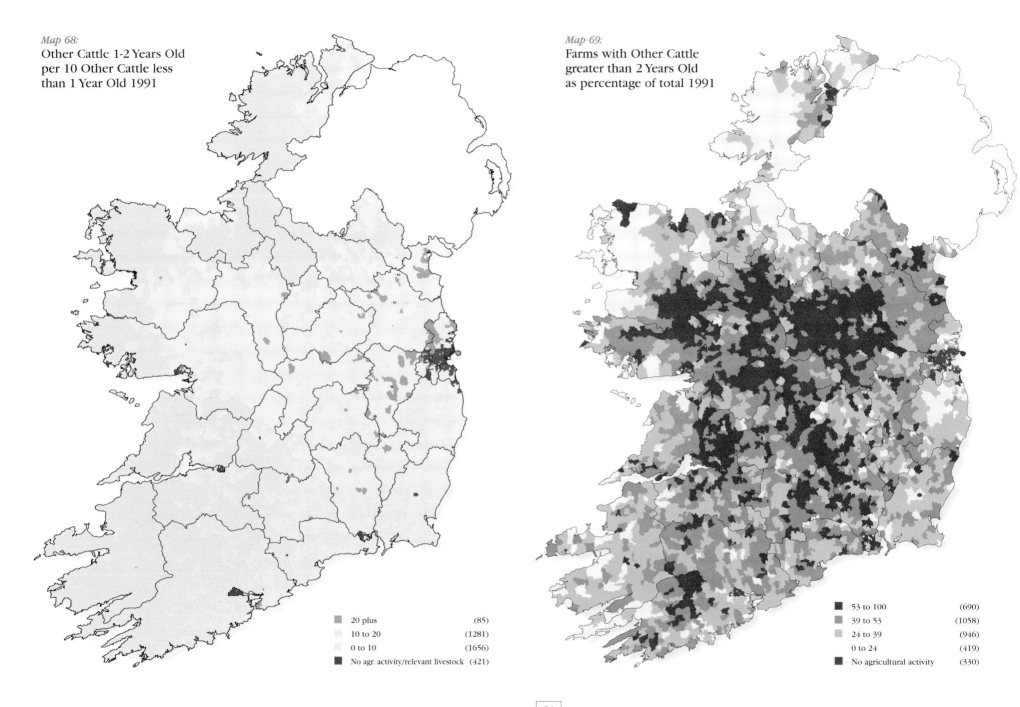

Map 68:
Other Cattle 1-2 Years Old per 10 Other Cattle less than 1 Year Old 1991

Map 69:
Farms with Other Cattle greater than 2 Years Old as percentage of total 1991

■	20 plus	(85)
	10 to 20	(1281)
	0 to 10	(1656)
■	No agr. activity/relevant livestock	(421)

■	53 to 100	(690)
■	39 to 53	(1058)
	24 to 39	(946)
	0 to 24	(419)
■	No agricultural activity	(330)

Map 68 presents the ratio of other cattle aged 1-2 years to those aged less than 1 year so as to assess the movements of the former age category. Again, the general eastward movement is evident with the main source areas being the south-west and along the west coast including extensive parts of Donegal, Leitrim and Sligo. The main destination area is east Connacht and the midlands, extending eastwards into Louth, Meath and Kildare.

Other Cattle aged greater than 2 years

Other cattle aged over two years were enumerated on 43 per cent of all farms with cattle in 1991. *Map 69* shows that the most important location for farms with beef cattle in this age group is the midlands. This is confirmed by Table 30 in which the Midland region is prominent with 57 per cent of all farms having beef cattle of this type. The West and Mid-West follow with 48.3 per cent and 46.8 per cent respectively.

Map 70 is the final in the series of maps illustrating the movement of beef cattle. It shows the influx onto the larger farms of the midlands and east as the cattle approach the final fattening stage. This map clearly demonstrates the role of counties Louth, Meath, Westmeath and Kildare as the core areas for finishing cattle. These tend to be the areas with the best quality grassland.

Changes in Beef Cattle Production and Cattle Movements

Maps 65 to *70* outline the spatial distribution of beef cattle production in Ireland and the basics of the geography of beef cattle movements as the animals mature. The following set of maps, presenting change in the different categories of cattle between 1980 and 1991, allows for some analysis of how cattle movements have changed in response to external policy influences over the 1980s.

Other Cattle aged less than 1 year: change 1980–1991

The most striking feature of change in this category is the high percentage increases in the south-western districts (*Map 71*). This suggests that the specialised dairy farmers in the region, who would previously have sold the majority of their calves north and eastwards, are now retaining them in greater numbers. Most likely this is a diversification measure due to the imposition of milk production quotas which curtailed expansion in dairying (Gillmor and Walsh, 1993). This can also be seen from Table 31 where the largest average annual percentage changes over the period occurred in the South-West region followed by the South-East and Mid-West. This pattern of retention of calves is also evident in the north-eastern dairying region although the percentage increase is smaller due to the fact that this area had a higher beef cattle component initially.

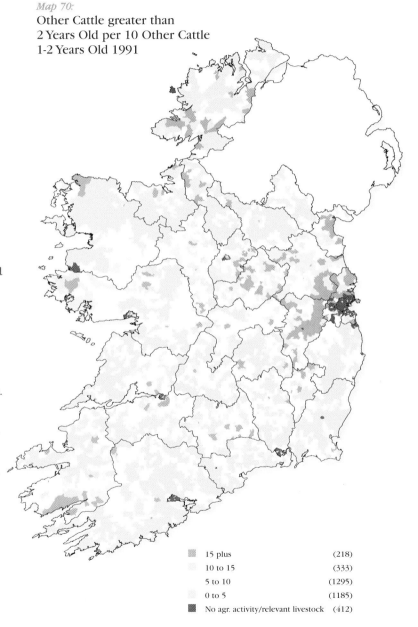

Map 70:
Other Cattle greater than
2 Years Old per 10 Other Cattle
1-2 Years Old 1991

▓	15 plus	(218)
▒	10 to 15	(333)
░	5 to 10	(1295)
░	0 to 5	(1185)
▓	No agr. activity/relevant livestock	(412)

Other areas of increase are in east and north Donegal, west Mayo, Dublin and along the eastern seaboard including Louth, Meath, Wicklow and Wexford. The areas of decrease are those which would traditionally have been the core districts for this category of beef cattle, that is Connacht and the midland counties of Westmeath and Offaly, and southwards through Kildare and Carlow. The largest declines were in the West and Border (west) regions. Obviously, the influx of under one year old cattle from the south to these latter areas has declined.

Table 31: Change in number of other cattle aged less than one year, 1980 -1991 and 1991-1997

Region	Actual change 1980-91	Average annual % change 1980-91	Actual change 1991-97[1]	Average annual % change 1991-97[1]	Actual change 1980-97[1]	Total % change 1980-97[1]
Dublin	0.0	0.0	-400	-1.0	-400	-5.9
Mid-East	+14,600	1.3	12,900	+1.8	27,500	26.6
South-East	+51,800	1.7	20,100	1.0	71,900	26.3
South-West	+68,200	2.0	40,900	1.8	109,100	36.0
Mid-West	+35,800	1.4	31,400	2.0	67,200	29.4
West	-21,700	-0.7	30,300	2.0	8,600	3.1
Border (west)	-2,300	-0.2	12,200	1.7	9,900	8.0
Border (east)	+8,700	0.7	13,900	1.8	22,600	19.1
Midland	-1,900	-0.1	15,800	1.5	13,900	8.0
Ireland	+153,300	0.9	177,000	1.7	330,300	20.5

Source: Agricultural Statistics 1980; Census of Agriculture 1991; Crops and Livestock Survey 1997.
[1]1997 figures are estimates based on CSO annual crops and livestock survey.

Table 32: Change in number of other cattle[1] aged 1-2 years, 1980 -1991 and 1991-1997

Region	Actual change 1980-91	Average annual % change 1980-91	Actual change 1991-97[2]	Average annual % change 1991-97[2]	Actual change 1980-97[2]	Total % change 1980-97[2]
Dublin	-140	-0.1	1,600	2.9	1,500	16.0
Mid-East	+7,800	0.5	11,800	1.4	19,600	15.0
South-East	+71,100	2.5	11,500	0.6	82,600	32.3
South-West	+69,300	2.8	12,900	0.7	82,200	37.1
Mid-West	+26,000	1.2	7,000	0.5	33,000	16.4
West	-36,500	-1.1	2,100	0.1	-34,400	-11.0
Border (west)	-31,900	-2.4	7,600	1.4	-24,300	-20.1
Border (east)	+11,400	0.9	-1,900	-0.3	9,500	8.2
Midland	+12,700	0.6	12,800	1.0	25,500	13.0
Ireland	+129,800	0.8	65,400	0.7	195,200	12.5

Source: Agricultural Statistics 1980; Census of Agriculture 1991; Crops and Livestock Survey 1997.
[1]Excludes all cows and heifers-in-calf.
[2]1997 figures are estimates based on CSO annual crops and livestock survey.

Other Cattle aged 1–2 years: change 1980–1991

Map 72 shows the same basic picture as for cattle aged under one year. Older cattle show numerical increases in those very areas where, historically, they would have been quite unimportant, while decreasing in number in the traditional western and north-western counties. This is evidenced in Table 32 where the largest increases occurred in the South-West followed by the South-East. The largest declines occurred in the Border (west) and West regions.

Other Cattle aged greater than 2 years: change 1980–1991

Cattle in this age category have become relatively less important in the 1980s (*Map 73*). Table 33 confirms this, showing declines in all regions. However, the lowest rates of decline are to be seen in the eastern parts of the State. This suggests that the established pattern of keeping older cattle in more eastern areas has in fact been reinforced during the 1980s. Many of the areas of increase on the map can be discounted due to the percentage increases occurring in RDs which are particularly small in area and in which large percentage changes occur from very small increases in actual numbers.

Table 33: Change in number of other cattle[1] aged greater than two years, 1980 -1991 and 1991-1997

Region	Actual change 1980-91	Average annual % change 1980-91	Actual change 1991-97[2]	Average annual % change 1991-97[2]	Actual change 1980-97[2]	Total % change 1980-97[2]
Dublin	-1,900	-0.9	-7,300	-6.9	-9,200	-47.2
Mid-East	-45,900	-2.2	-15,000	-1.7	-60,800	-31.5
South-East	-38,500	-1.6	-9,400	-0.9	-47,900	-21.6
South-West	-33,800	-1.7	1,900	0.2	-31,900	-17.9
Mid-West	-36,000	-1.9	500	0.1	-35,500	-20.3
West	-70,000	-2.6	200	0.0	-69,800	-28.4
Border (west)	-28,200	-3.1	-3,700	-1.2	-31,900	-38.9
Border (east)	-11,900	-1.2	-700	-0.2	-12,600	-14.5
Midland	-48,900	-2.1	-2,500	-0.3	-51,400	-24.3
Ireland	-314,900	-2.0	-36,000	-0.6	-351,000	-24.8

Source: Agricultural Statistics 1980; Census of Agriculture 1991; Crops and Livestock Survey 1997.
[1]Excludes all cows and heifers-in-calf.
[2]1997 figures are estimates based on CSO annual crops and livestock survey.

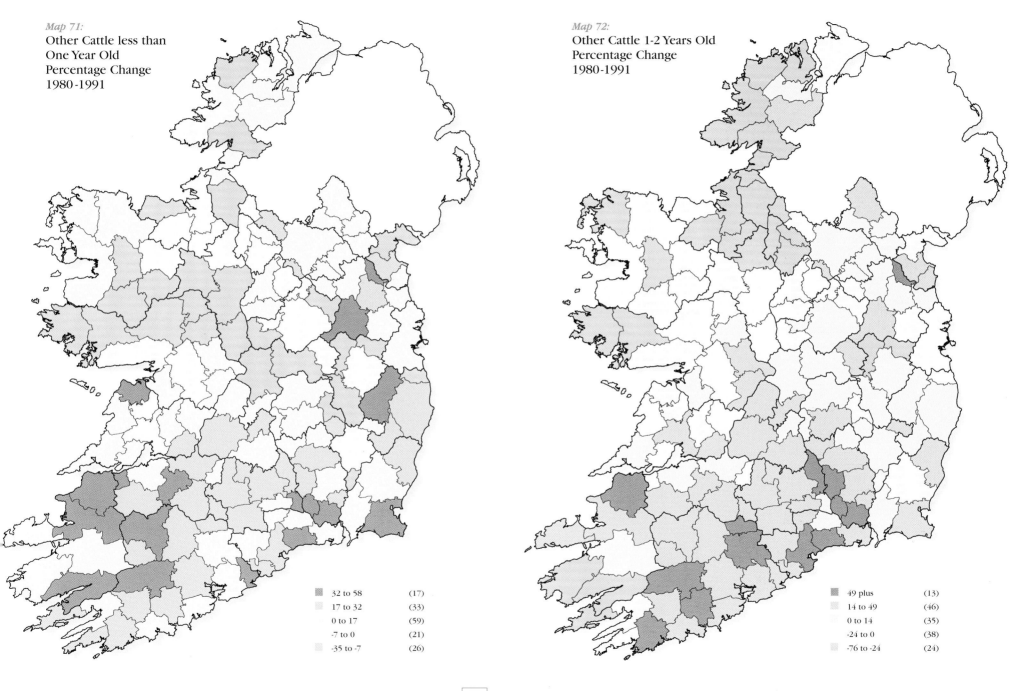

Map 71:

Other Cattle less than
One Year Old
Percentage Change
1980-1991

Map 72:

Other Cattle 1-2 Years Old
Percentage Change
1980-1991

32 to 58	(17)
17 to 32	(33)
0 to 17	(59)
-7 to 0	(21)
-35 to -7	(26)

49 plus	(13)
14 to 49	(46)
0 to 14	(35)
-24 to 0	(38)
-76 to -24	(24)

Table 34: Change in number of total other cattle[1], 1980-1991 and 1991-1997

Region	Actual change 1980-91	Average annual % change 1980-91	Actual change 1991-97[2]	Average annual % change 1991-97[2]	Actual change 1980-97[2]	Total % change 1980-97[2]
Dublin	-2,000	-0.5	-6,100	-3.0	-8,100	-22.7
Mid-East	-23,500	-0.5	9,800	0.4	-13,700	-3.2
South-East	+84,400	1.0	22,200	0.5	106,600	14.2
South-West	+103,700	1.3	55,700	1.2	159,400	22.7
Mid-West	+25,800	0.4	38,900	1.0	64,700	10.7
West	-128,100	-1.4	32,500	0.8	95,600	-11.4
Border (west)	-62,400	-1.7	16,100	1.0	-46,300	-14.2
Border (east)	+8,300	0.2	11,200	0.6	19,500	6.1
Midland	-38,100	-0.6	26,100	0.8	-12,000	-2.1
Ireland	-31,900	-0.1	206,400	0.8	174,500	3.8

Source: Agricultural Statistics 1980; Census of Agriculture 1991; Crops and Livestock Survey 1997.
[1]Excludes all cows and heifers-in-calf.
[2]1997 figures are estimates based on CSO annual crops and livestock survey.

Map 74 summarises the data of the previous three maps, and is therefore less prone to the problem of small numbers. Clearly there is a stark geographical pattern to the changes that have impacted on the beef sector over the 1980s. Table 34 shows that the areas of increase were the South-West, South-East and to a lesser extent the Mid-West and Border (east). The largest declines occurred in the Border (west) and the West. The increases are in the dairying regions while the large decreases are mainly in the traditional beef areas. The increases in the dairying region were encouraged by small-scale dairy producers availing of incentive schemes to expand suckler cow herds. In the 1990s increases have been recorded in all regions except Dublin with the largest gains in the South-West and Mid-West.

The turnaround in the areas that were in decline in the 1980s has been most marked in the Midland region where the recent gains amount to two-thirds of the losses in the 1980s. In the West and Border (west) regions the ratio of gains to losses is only about one-quarter.

Map 75 provides a synthesis of the changes for all types of cattle combined, including cows and heifers-in-calf. The extent of the overall decline in the north-west and parts of the midlands provides a striking confirmation of the attrition of the traditional cattle economy.

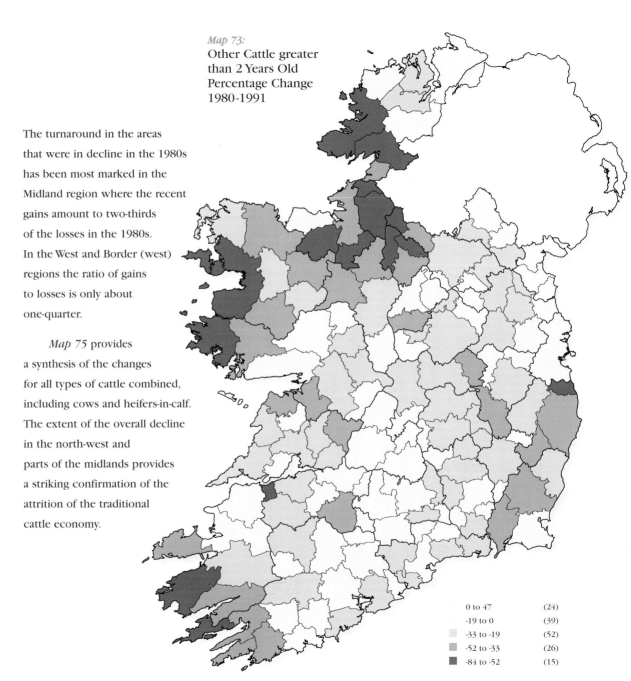

Map 73:
Other Cattle greater than 2 Years Old Percentage Change 1980-1991

0 to 47	(24)
-19 to 0	(39)
-33 to -19	(52)
-52 to -33	(26)
-84 to -52	(15)

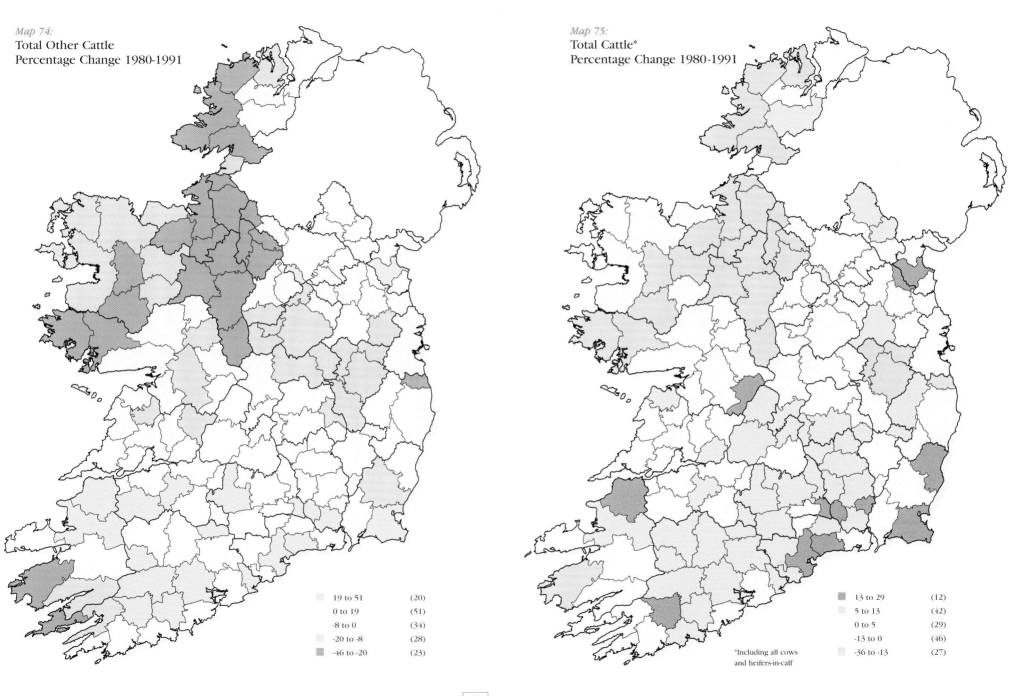

Map 74:
Total Other Cattle
Percentage Change 1980-1991

	19 to 51	(20)
	0 to 19	(51)
	-8 to 0	(34)
	-20 to -8	(28)
	-46 to -20	(23)

Map 75:
Total Cattle*
Percentage Change 1980-1991

	13 to 29	(12)
	5 to 13	(42)
	0 to 5	(29)
	-13 to 0	(46)
	-36 to -13	(27)

*Including all cows
and heifers-in-calf

Sheep

Traditionally, the sheep sector has been of lesser importance than cattle to Irish agriculture although there have been phases of expansion and reduction since the turn of the century. In 1997 sheep and lambs accounted for 5.9 per cent of the value of gross agricultural output. The spatial distribution of sheep has always borne a strong relationship to topography with sheep farming being particularly important in the mountainous regions. Sheep enjoy a comparative advantage in such areas due to their ability to withstand the harsher climate, the rugged terrain, and the generally poorer quality grazing land.

Of all lowland regions the extensive limestone parts of south-east Connacht are particularly suited to sheep due to the dry conditions which help to prevent diseases such as fluke and footrot. These problems have militated against sheep on poorly drained soils such as those around the Shannon estuary and in the drumlin belt where wet gleys and peat soils prevail (Keane, 1986b).

Sheep rearing is a more lucrative farm enterprise than some forms of cattle rearing, and sheep are also much less demanding in terms of housing requirements, feedstuffs and capital investments. However, traditionally they have not been able to totally displace beef farming due in large measure to farmer preferences for cattle and the fact that, particularly at lambing time, sheep require more attention (Gillmor, 1977). Throughout the 1970s lowland sheep were not favoured as farmers specialised in other enterprises such as dairying, beef production and tillage. This changed in the 1980s following the introduction of ewe premia which made sheep farming a more profitable enterprise. Numbers increased dramatically so that by 1991 the total number of sheep in Ireland (almost 9 million) was the highest for many decades (Gillmor and Walsh, 1993; CSO, 1997).

Table 35: Indicators of significance of sheep farming, 1991

Region	Percentage of farms with sheep	Specialist sheep farms as percentage of all farms	Perventage of Specialist sheep farms within the State	Percentage of total ESUs accounted for by sheep
Dublin	23.2	7.9*	0.8**	} 8
Mid-East	41.6	12.7	9.9	
South-East	67.7	8.6	11.7	4
South-West	21.1	6.6	12.3	4
Mid-West	18.1	1.7	2.3	1
West	42.6	11.5	29.9	16
Border (west)	40.8	19.0	25.8	24
Border (east)	18.7	3.8	3.6	3
Midland	40.0	3.6	3.7	3
Ireland	32.2	8.8	100	7

Source: Census of Agriculture 1991.
* 7.9% of all farms in Dublin are specialist sheep;
** 0.8% of all specialist sheep farms in the State are in Dublin.

The 1980-91 expansion in total numbers came about from an increase of almost 10,000 in the number of farms with sheep (from 45,000 in 1980) and an increase in average size of flock from 73 to 162. In contrast to the situation whereby a high proportion of specialist dairy farms have only dairy cows, sheep are grazed on a much larger number of farms than those that are categorised as specialist sheep. While sheep were grazed on almost 55,000 farms, less than 15,000 were specialist sheep farms. These specialist sheep farms accounted for 43 per cent of the total number of sheep and had an average flock of 254. Another 36 per cent of the total flock were recorded on 19,650 mixed grazing livestock farms (approximately two-thirds of all farms in this category).

Table 35 shows that 68 per cent of farms in the South-East have some sheep which can be contrasted with the significantly lower figures of less than 43 per cent in the West and 41 per cent in the Border (west). The relatively high incidence of farms with sheep in the South-East is due to the large numbers of specialist sheep farms on the uplands and the many mixed crops and livestock farms on the lowlands. In these areas grazing of breeding flocks has traditionally been complemented by autumn/winter feeding on cereal stubble and root crops such as turnips which are grown as a rotation crop in tillage farming.

The largest sheep flocks, with an average of 265 animals, are found on about half of the mixed crops and livestock farms, which are mostly located in the South-East. Sheep rearing occurs very infrequently on either specialist dairying (only on 17 per cent of these farms) or specialist beef farms (14 per cent). Together these two categories of farm account for only one-eighth of the total sheep flock.

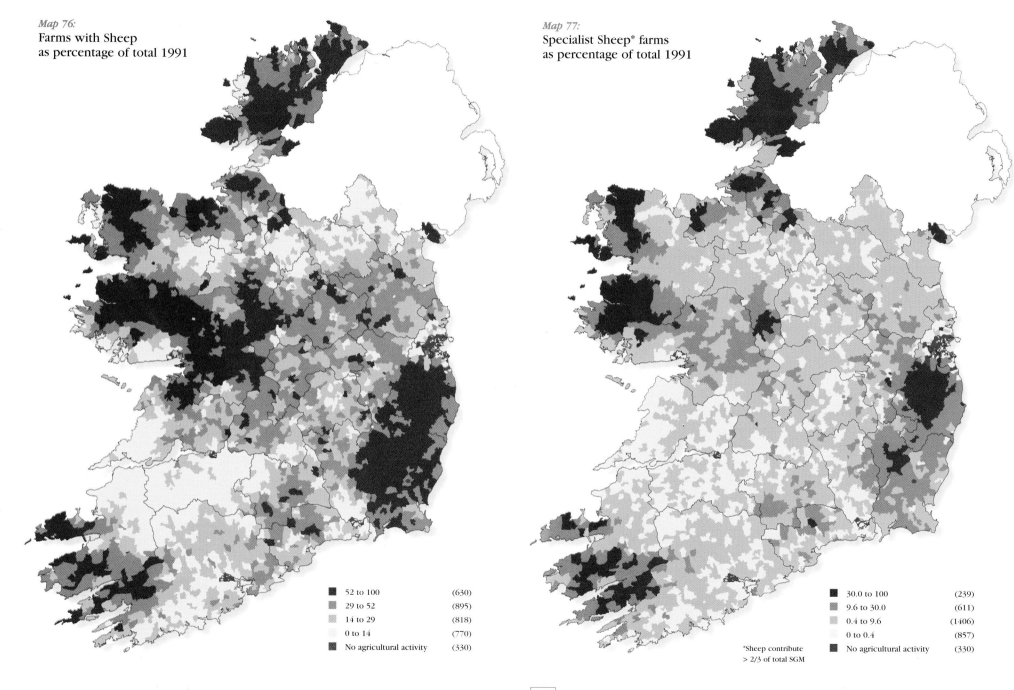

Map 76:
**Farms with Sheep
as percentage of total 1991**

Map 77:
**Specialist Sheep* farms
as percentage of total 1991**

■	52 to 100	(630)
■	29 to 52	(895)
■	14 to 29	(818)
■	0 to 14	(770)
■	No agricultural activity	(330)

■	30.0 to 100	(239)
■	9.6 to 30.0	(611)
■	0.4 to 9.6	(1406)
■	0 to 0.4	(857)
■	No agricultural activity	(330)

*Sheep contribute
> 2/3 of total SGM

The detailed spatial distribution of sheep is most evident in upland parts, namely the western mountain ranges and the Leinster Mountain Range (*Map 76*). Of these two areas, Leinster has the advantage in terms of having better quality grazing land. The most notable lowland area involved in sheep enterprises is the limestone countryside of east Galway and south Roscommon, although sheep do maintain a significant presence in the midlands where sequential grazing with cattle makes optimum use of grassland (Gillmor and Walsh, 1993). The areas most averse to sheep rearing are in the Munster dairying region and in a zone stretching from east Mayo through north Roscommon, south Leitrim and through the dairying region of Cavan/Monaghan. Poor drainage in the drumlin belt poses a particular disease risk for sheep while in the Cavan/Monaghan area the predominance of dairying militates against sheep farming. In the hinterland of the Shannon estuary, poorly drained land and the dominance of dairying have also resulted in very few farms rearing sheep.

Map 77, presenting the number of specialist sheep farms in each DED as a percentage of all farms, highlights a much more localised pattern. The highest numbers of specialist sheep farms are found mainly in the mountain areas. For example, the extensive lowland parts of east Galway are greatly reduced in their significance (when compared to *Map 76*).

The very limited range of farming possibilities for farmers in Donegal and Wicklow has resulted in the proportion of farms categorised as specialist sheep in these areas being over three times the average for the State. Table 35 shows that almost 56 per cent of all specialist sheep farms are in the West and Border (west) regions compared with only 7.3 per cent in the Midland and Border (east) regions.

Map 78 illustrates the economic importance of sheep to agricultural output and presents an even more restricted picture of areas where sheep are important. Throughout most of the uplands, at least half of total gross margins come from sheep enterprises. By contrast, sheep rearing makes a minor contribution to the total agricultural gross margin for most of the State.

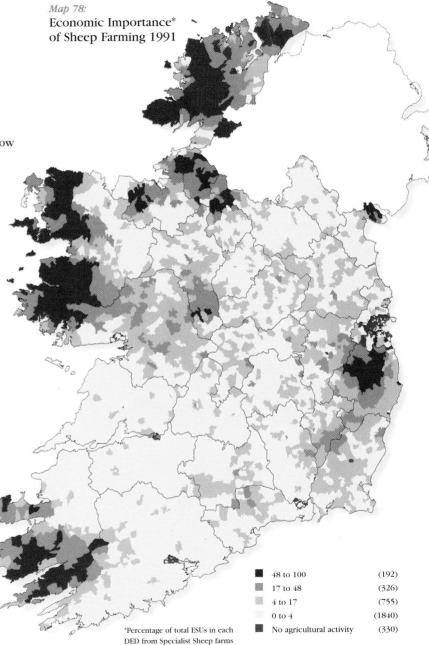

Map 78:
Economic Importance*
of Sheep Farming 1991

■	48 to 100	(192)
▨	17 to 48	(326)
▨	4 to 17	(755)
□	0 to 4	(1840)
■	No agricultural activity	(330)

*Percentage of total ESUs in each
DED from Specialist Sheep farms

Change in number of Sheep

The total number of sheep in the State almost trebled (overall increase of 170 per cent) between 1980 and 1991. As already indicated this was mainly in response to the inclusion of sheepmeat in the Common Market regime in 1980 and the introduction of premia payments to encourage expansion of the number of ewes (Gillmor and Walsh, 1993). The effect was to substantially improve prices to farmers, thus ensuring that this enterprise could emerge as a lucrative activity and show rapid and significant increase.

Map 79:
**Sheep
Percentage Change
1980-1991**

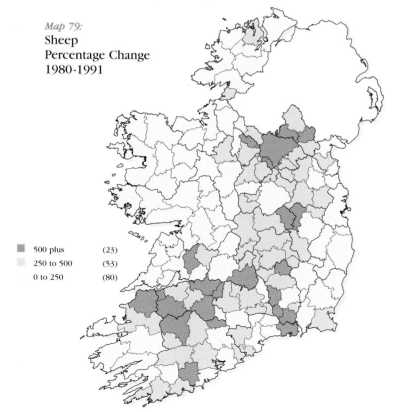

▓ 500 plus	(23)
▒ 250 to 500	(53)
□ 0 to 250	(80)

Table 36: Change in numbers of sheep, 1980-1991 and 1991-1997

Region	Actual change 1980-91	Average annual % change 1980-91	Actual change 1991-97[1]	Average annual % change 1991-97[1]	Actual change 1980-97[1]	Total % change 1980-97[1]
Dublin	51,800	14.5	-5,400	-1.1	46,400	143.2
Mid-East	838,200	17.8	-123,600	-1.6	714,600	167.0
South-East	1,186,400	18.3	-235,700	-2.2	950,700	161.4
South-West	713,500	15.6	-100,600	-1.5	612,900	146.9
Mid-West	272,200	24.0	-57,300	-2.6	214,900	208.4
West	1,158,400	10.2	-33,300	-0.3	1,125,100	109.4
Border (west)	642,100	13.1	-27,300	-0.4	614,800	138.1
Border (east)	229,000	24.1	-34,000	-1.8	195,000	225.4
Midland	505,200	28.4	-86,200	-2.2	419,000	259.8
Total	5,596,700	15.5	-703,300	-1.3	4,893,400	148.7

Source: Agricultural Statistics 1980; Census of Agriculture 1991; Crops and Livestock Survey 1997.
[1]1997 figures are estimates based on CSO annual crops and livestock survey.

Table 36 illustrates these huge increases with a national average annual increase of 15.5 per cent between 1980 and 1991, with significantly higher figures in the Midland (28.4 per cent), Border (east) (24.1 per cent) and Mid-West (24.0 per cent) regions. The lowest increases occurred in the West (10.2 per cent) and west Border (13.1 per cent) regions. *Map 79* clearly illustrates that the areas of lowest increase were those which already had the highest numbers before 1980, namely, the mountainous regions. The highest percentage increases occurred in the Midland region and in the traditional dairy regions of the south-west and north-east. The huge increases are a reflection of the scale of the movement towards sheep rearing from a low base as farmers became more aware of the profitability of lowland sheep farming and the potential earnings from subsidies.

From Table 36 it is evident that the increases of the 1980s were not carried over to the 1990s. The size of the total flock decreased by an average of 1.3 per cent annually between 1991 and 1997, with decreases evident in all regions due to the falling real prices paid to farmers. By far the largest absolute decline in the 1990s occurred in the South-East. Nevertheless, the region had the second highest net gain in sheep numbers over the longer period 1980-97. More recently the number of sheep on upland areas has been reduced through a culling programme aimed at lowering stocking rates.

Mixed Grazing Livestock

In 1991 there were approximately 30,600 farms in the mixed grazing livestock category, about 18 per cent of all farms. The most common type of livestock on these farms are suckler cows and 'other cattle' with large numbers of sheep and some dairy cows. While some farms of this type are found throughout most of the State the category is particularly strongly represented in the lowlands of east Galway and south Roscommon and also in parts of the South-East and Mid-East (Table 37). Given the weak association between this type of farming and dairying, the proportions shown on *Map 80* are especially low in parts of the south-west and north-east. Comparing *Maps 80* and *81* with *Maps 77* and *78*, it is clear that sheep enterprises occupy a very significant position in the agriculture of mixed grazing livestock areas. The association between sheep and cattle has long been recognised as typifying farming in east Galway (Freeman, 1945; Gillmor 1967).

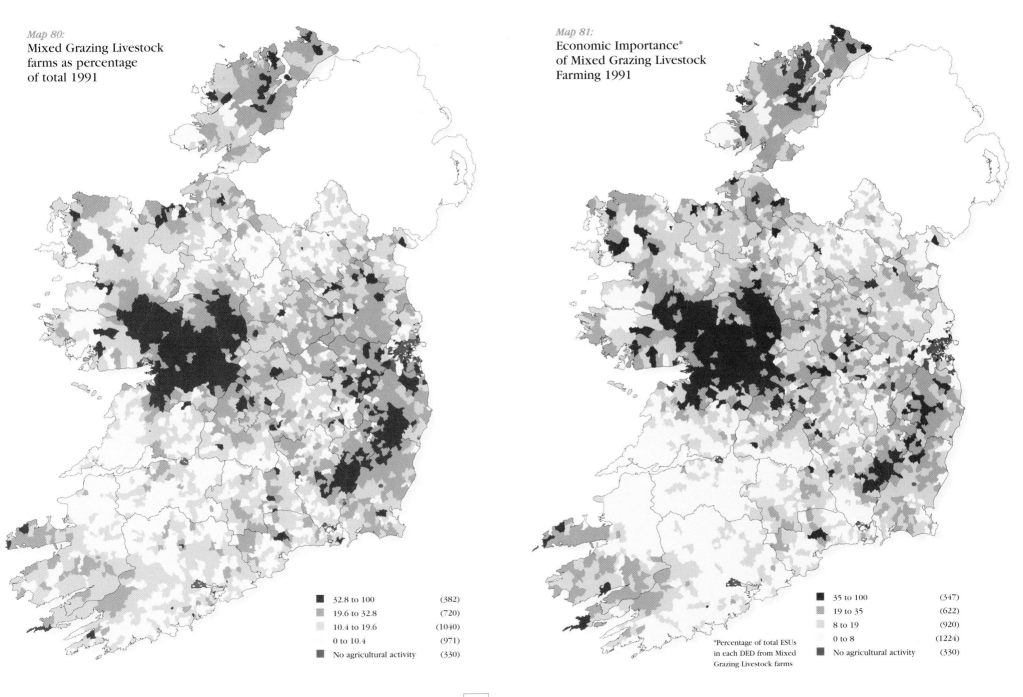

Map 80:
Mixed Grazing Livestock
farms as percentage
of total 1991

Map 81:
Economic Importance*
of Mixed Grazing Livestock
Farming 1991

■	32.8 to 100	(382)
▨	19.6 to 32.8	(720)
▨	10.4 to 19.6	(1040)
□	0 to 10.4	(971)
▨	No agricultural activity	(330)

■	35 to 100	(347)
▨	19 to 35	(622)
▨	8 to 19	(920)
□	0 to 8	(1224)
▨	No agricultural activity	(330)

*Percentage of total ESUs
in each DED from Mixed
Grazing Livestock farms

Mixed Crops and Livestock

In 1991 there were just over 4,300 farms in the mixed crops and livestock category. Cereals and sugar beet are the main crops while sheep and cattle are the most common types of livestock. This categorisation has a very distinctive geography (*Map 82*) which, to a large extent, can be related to the very favourable physical conditions for agriculture and the presence of large farms (Table 38).

There is an almost complete absence of this categorisation north and west of a line from Cork to Dundalk, where less than one per cent of the total economic size of each DED falls within the mixed crops and livestock combination, except in a very small number of districts in north-east Donegal (*Map 83*). Livestock enterprises in these areas are attractive due to the ready supply of winter feed from fodder crops and the straw from some cereals.

Table 37: Indicators of significance of mixed grazing livestock farming, 1991

Region	Mixed Grazing Livestock farms as % of all farms	% of all Mixed Grazing Livestock farms within State	% of total ESUs accounted for by Mixed Grazing Livestock farms
Dublin	20.7*	1.0**	} 14
Mid-East	24.3	9.2	
South-East	18.7	12.5	13
South-West	11.8	10.8	6
Mid-West	11.1	7.3	7
West	25.5	32.5	32
Border (west)	18.1	12.0	20
Border (east)	13.1	6.1	9
Midland	17.2	8.6	16
Ireland	17.9	100	13

Source: Census of Agriculture 1991.
* 20.7% of all farms in Dublin are mixed grazing livestock.
** 1.0% of all mixed grazing livestock farms in the State are in Dublin.

Table 38: Indicators of significance of mixed crops and livestock farming, 1991

Region	Mixed Crops and Livestock farms as % of all farms	% of all Mixed Crops and Livestock farms within State	% of total ESUs accounted for by Mixed Crops and Livestock farms
Dublin	5.0*	1.7**	} 8
Mid-East	4.7	12.8	
South-East	7.4	34.9	9
South-West	2.4	16.0	3
Mid-West	0.8	3.8	1
West	0.4	3.5	1
Border (west)	1.5	7.2	3
Border (east)	2.1	7.0	4
Midland	3.7	13.1	5
Ireland	2.5	100	5

Source: Census of Agriculture 1991.
* 5.0% of all farms in Dublin are mixed crops and livestock.
** 1.7% of all mixed crops and livestock farms in the State are in Dublin.

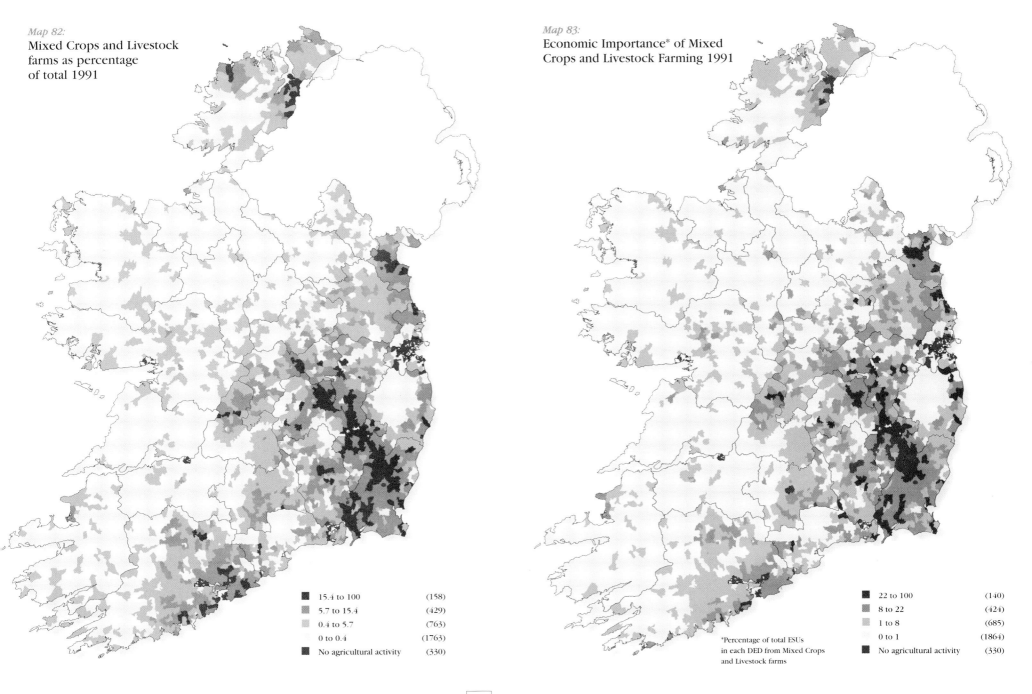

Map 82:
**Mixed Crops and Livestock
farms as percentage
of total 1991**

Map 83:
**Economic Importance* of Mixed
Crops and Livestock Farming 1991**

■ 15.4 to 100	(158)
▨ 5.7 to 15.4	(429)
▨ 0.4 to 5.7	(763)
□ 0 to 0.4	(1763)
■ No agricultural activity	(330)

■ 22 to 100	(140)
▨ 8 to 22	(424)
▨ 1 to 8	(685)
□ 0 to 1	(1864)
■ No agricultural activity	(330)

*Percentage of total ESUs
in each DED from Mixed Crops
and Livestock farms

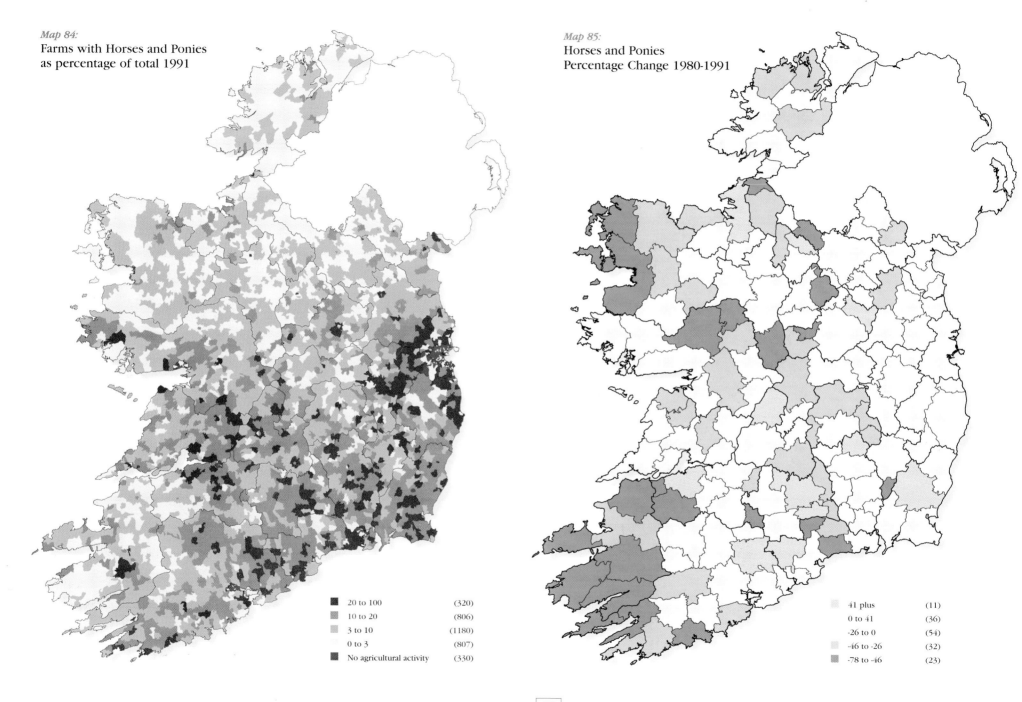

Map 84:

**Farms with Horses and Ponies
as percentage of total 1991**

■	20 to 100	(320)
■	10 to 20	(806)
■	3 to 10	(1180)
■	0 to 3	(807)
■	No agricultural activity	(330)

Map 85:

**Horses and Ponies
Percentage Change 1980-1991**

■	41 plus	(11)
■	0 to 41	(36)
■	-26 to 0	(54)
■	-46 to -26	(32)
■	-78 to -46	(23)

Horses and Ponies

Ireland has a long established international reputation for the quality of its horses and for its considerable achievements in equestrian sport. Equine quality is largely accredited to physical factors such as climate, soils and topography. Good quality grass all year round, aided by fairly evenly distributed rainfall throughout the year, as well as flat plains with suitable ground, offer an ideal environment for horses. In addition to these physical factors, the long tradition of horse rearing in association with keeping agricultural work horses has resulted in a considerable reserve of knowledge and management skills which have helped towards making Ireland a world leader in the thoroughbred industry (Gillmor, 1977).

In 1991 just over 63,100 horses and ponies were enumerated on 13,600 farms. The highest incidence of these farms is in Dublin, followed by the South-East, the Mid-East and the Mid-West regions (Table 39). *Map 84* allows for their exact location to be pinpointed, with north Kildare and south Meath identifiable as the core areas. Other counties that have a substantial complement of horses are Wicklow, Wexford, Kilkenny, Waterford, Tipperary, east Cork and around Limerick city. Regionally, the South-East and the Mid-East account for the largest percentages with 24.9 per cent and 19.4 per cent respectively.

Kildare has the highest percentage of thoroughbred horses (16.1 per cent of the total) with the largest concentration around the Curragh, the principal training centre. Cork and Tipperary South follow with 13.9 per cent and 11.3 per cent of the State total respectively. Between them, the South-East and the Mid-East regions account for over 57 per cent of all thoroughbred horses (Table 39). While horses for agricultural work were found on many of the small and medium size farms of the western regions up to the 1970s, by 1991 they were virtually absent from these areas as a result of the adoption of mechanisation (Walsh, 1992).

Change in number of Horses and Ponies

Over recent decades the total number of horses and ponies declined, principally due to the demise of horses for agricultural work (*Map 85*). These declines would have been significantly greater but for the fact that as the number of 'working horses' was declining, the number of horses kept for recreational purposes increased. While horses were kept on 50 per cent of all holdings in the State in 1960, the figure declined to just 8 per cent of farms in 1991 (Table 39). There have been significant increases in the West and Border regions in the 1990s (Table 40) which are probably associated with the availability of grant aid to encourage farm diversification from conventional to alternative farm enterprises.

Table 39: Indicators of significance of horses and ponies, 1991

Region	% of all farms with horses and ponies	Total horses and ponies	Total thorough-bred 1991	% of total horses in each region	% thorough-bred horses
Dublin	17.2	1,764	517	2.8	2.1
Mid-East	12.3	12,218	7,041	19.4	28.2
South-East	13.4	15,698	7,254	24.9	29.0
South-West	8.1	9,264	3,688	14.7	14.7
Mid-West	10.4	8,614	2,817	13.6	11.3
West	5.8	6,181	1,022	9.8	4.1
Border (west)	3.9	2,364	395	3.7	1.6
Border (east)	4.8	2,349	552	3.7	2.2
Midland	7.3	4,662	1,720	7.4	6.9
Ireland	8.0	63,114	25,006	100.0	100.0

Source: Census of Agriculture 1991.

Table 40: Change in number of horses and ponies, 1980-1991 and 1991-1997

Region	Actual change 1980-91	Average annual % change 1980-91	Actual change 1991-97[1]	Average annual % change 1991-97[1]	Actual change 1980-97[1]	Total % change 1980-97[1]
Dublin	-500	-2.0	100	0.9	-400	-17.4
Mid-East	300	0.2	-100	-0.1	200	1.7
South-East	1,100	0.7	0	0	1,100	7.5
South-West	-1,700	-1.5	1,300	2.5	-400	-3.6
Mid-West	-700	-1.9	1,100	3.6	400	4.3
West	-2,500	-2.7	2,700	7.7	200	2.3
Border (west)	-100	-0.4	1,400	9.7	1,300	52.0
Border (east)	-200	-0.7	1,100	8.0	900	36.0
Midland	-1,100	-0.7	900	2.1	-200	-3.4
Ireland	-5,400	-0.7	8,800	2.3	3,400	5.0

Source: Agricultural Statistics 1980; Census of Agriculture 1991; Crops and Livestock Survey 1997.
[1] 1997 figures are estimates based on CSO annual crops and livestock survey.

Pigs

In 1997 pigs contributed 7.7 per cent of the value of gross agricultural output. Traditionally, pig rearing took place on a very small scale on a large number of farms. In many cases a farm household may have had only one or two sows (Gillmor, 1977). This has changed dramatically as profitable pig production now requires a large number of animals and has come to be a highly specialised activity dominated by a small number of very large producers. In 1973 the average size of herd was 29 animals, by 1983 this had increased to 114 and by 1997 it was 846, indicating the extent of the 'industrialisation' associated with pig production (CSO, 1999b).

Pig rearing is now confined to approximately 2,000 farms, of which one-fifth account for 91 per cent of the total number of animals. From Table 41 it can be seen that the largest numbers of pigs are found in the South-East region which has over 21 per cent of the total herd while the South-West and the Border (east) regions follow with 20 per cent each. On a county basis the highest numbers are located in counties Cork and Cavan each of which has 16 per cent of the total (*Map 86*). The total number of pigs has increased in all regions since 1980 (Table 42), although declines have been recorded in some counties (*Map 87*).

Table 41: Distribution of pigs and poultry, 1991

Region	Total pigs	Total poultry	Percentage of State total pigs	Percentage of State total poultry
Dublin	9,045	37,008	0.7	0.3
Mid-East	88,011	648,272	6.8	5.4
South-East	276,128	1,212,584	21.2	10.1
South-West	260,669	912,792	20.0	7.6
Mid-West	89,740	1,430,837	6.9	11.9
West	45,246	613,656	3.5	5.1
Border (west)	44,062	111,750	3.4	0.9
Border (east)	260,432	6,804,176	20.0	56.5
Midland	230,362	281,764	17.7	2.3
Ireland	1,303,695	12,052,839	100	100

Source: Census of Agriculture 1991.

Table 42: Change in number of pigs, 1980-1991 and 1991-1997

Region	Actual change 1980-91	% change 1980-91	Actual change 1991-97[1]	% change 1991-97[1]	Actual change 1980-97[1]	% change 1980-97[1]
Mid-East & Dublin	37,800	63.9	-8,400	-8.7	29,400	49.7
South-East	22,400	8.8	94,100	34.1	116,500	45.9
South-West	33,100	14.5	159,400	61.1	192,500	84.6
Mid-West	17,800	24.8	8,300	9.3	26,100	36.3
West	7,800	20.9	16,400	36.3	24,200	64.7
Border	41,500	15.8	113,800	37.4	155,300	59.1
Midland	112,700	95.8	12,400	5.4	125,100	106.3
Ireland	273,200	26.5	395,800	30.4	669,000	64.9

Source: Agricultural Statistics 1980; Census of Agriculture 1991; Crops and Livestock Survey 1997.
[1] 1997 figures are estimates based on CSO annual crops and livestock survey.

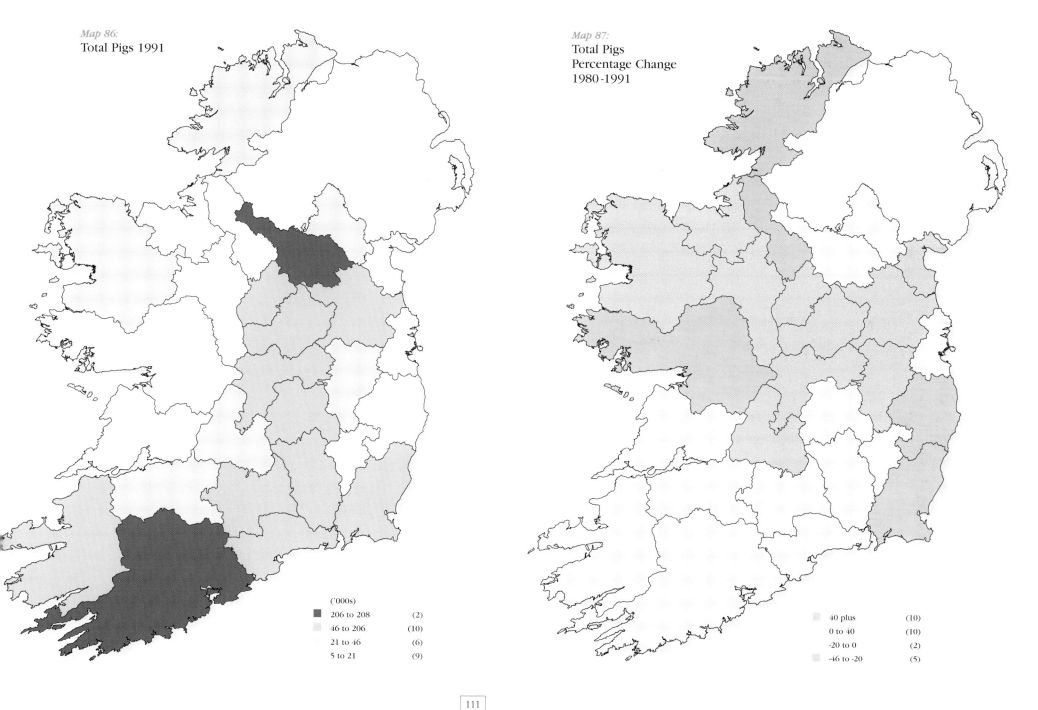

Map 86:
Total Pigs 1991

Map 87:
Total Pigs
Percentage Change
1980-1991

('000s)

■	206 to 208	(2)
░	46 to 206	(10)
	21 to 46	(6)
	5 to 21	(9)

░	40 plus	(10)
	0 to 40	(10)
	-20 to 0	(2)
░	-46 to -20	(5)

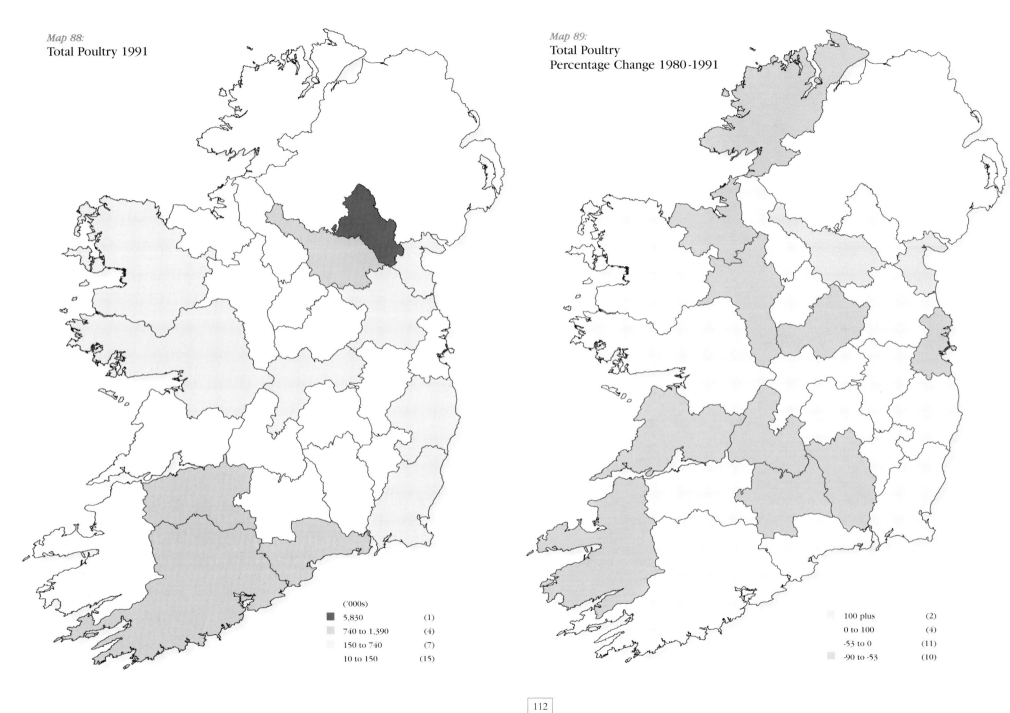

Map 88:
Total Poultry 1991

Map 89:
Total Poultry
Percentage Change 1980-1991

('000s)

■	5,830	(1)
▦	740 to 1,390	(4)
	150 to 740	(7)
	10 to 150	(15)

	100 plus	(2)
	0 to 100	(4)
	-53 to 0	(11)
▦	-90 to -53	(10)

Poultry

Traditionally, poultry were kept on a free-range basis on many farms throughout the State. They had a particular association with small farms on which they provided a much needed additional source of income. Changes in the organisational structure of poultry production have resulted in this enterprise becoming highly specialised and concentrated. In 1991 poultry were kept on just over 26,600 farms with an average flock size of 453 birds. However, approximately 720 large units, with an average flock size of over 11,200 birds, accounted for two-thirds of the total. About 30 per cent of the flocks are on specialist dairy farms, and another 20 per cent are on mixed grazing livestock farms.

Table 41 shows that over 56 per cent of the total flock is located in the Border (east) region. At county level, almost half of the total is in Monaghan (*Map 88*). This trend towards concentration is well illustrated in Table 43 which shows increases of over 87 per cent in poultry numbers between 1980 and 1991 in the Border region while decreases were recorded in almost every other region. The trend since 1991 indicates significant decline in the West and Midland regions while concentration continues in the Border region and also in the Mid-West after some decline there in the 1980s.

Table 43: Change in number of poultry, 1980-1991 and 1991-1997

Region	Actual change 1980-91	Percentage change 1980-91	Actual change 1991-97	Percentage change 1991-97	Actual change 1980-97	Percentage change 1980-97
Dublin & Mid-East	-355,500	-34.2	44,500	6.5	-311,000	-29.9
South-East	-7,400	-0.6	260,800	21.5	253,400	20.8
South-West	-124,500	-12.0	262,700	28.8	138,200	13.3
Mid-West	-407,700	-22.2	605,600	42.3	197,900	10.8
West	+66,800	12.2	-127,800	-20.8	-61,000	-11.2
Border	3,222,100	87.2	532,100	7.7	3,754,200	101.6
Midland	-244,000	-46.4	-198,400	-70.4	-442,400	-84.1
Ireland	2,149,500	21.7	1,379,700	11.4	3,529,200	35.6

Source: Agricultural Statistics 1980; Census of Agriculture 1991; Crops and Livestock Survey 1997.

Map 90:

Total Livestock Units per 100 ha Grassland* 1991

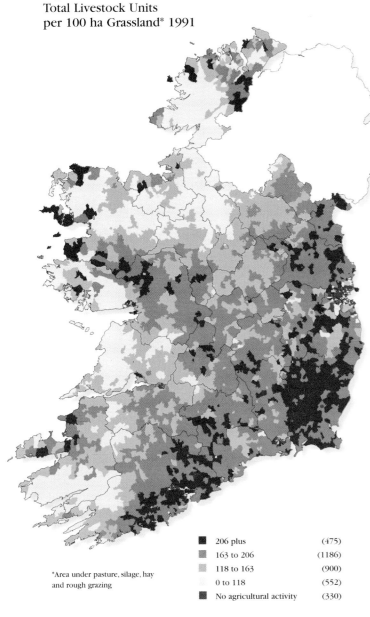

■	206 plus	(475)
■	163 to 206	(1186)
▨	118 to 163	(900)
▫	0 to 118	(552)
■	No agricultural activity	(330)

*Area under pasture, silage, hay and rough grazing

Livestock Units (LUs)

In order to make meaningful comparisons of trends in different categories of livestock it has become normal to convert their actual numbers into standard units termed Livestock Units (LUs). A system of coefficients suited to Irish conditions was initially devised by Attwood and Heavey (1964) based on the dry matter intake and body weight of different categories of livestock. The coefficients used here are as follows: bulls and cows 1.0; other cattle over 2 years 1.0; heifers-in-calf 0.7; other cattle 1-2 years 0.67; other cattle under 1 year 0.33; rams and ewes 0.2; other sheep over 1 year 0.16; other sheep under 1 year 0.1; all horses 1.0 (Horner *et al.*, 1984).

Table 44: Density of LUs and percentage share of total LUs accounted for by principal livestock categories, 1991

Region	Total LUs per 1,000 ha grassland[1]	Percentage share of total LUs				
		Dairy cows & heifers-in-calf	Other cows, heifers-in-calf, bulls	Total other cattle	Total sheep	Horses and ponies
Dublin	1859	12.3	7.4	51.0	25.8	3.5
Mid-East	1908	15.9	9.4	42.8	30.0	1.9
South-East	1955	24.3	9.5	42.3	22.6	1.3
South-West	1597	37.2	9.7	37.7	14.6	0.8
Mid-West	1467	29.8	15.0	47.0	7.2	1.0
West	1510	7.8	18.6	41.6	31.4	0.6
Border (west)	1206	8.5	22.4	32.7	35.8	0.6
Border (east)	1640	24.7	15.8	47.4	11.6	0.5
Midland	1659	14.5	13.7	55.3	15.8	0.7
Ireland	1618	22.0	13.4	42.9	21.0	0.7

Source: Derived from Census of Agriculture 1991.

In 1991 there were approximately 6.5 million LUs in the State (Table 45). Of this total almost 43 per cent were accounted for by beef cattle, 22 per cent by dairy cattle, 21 per cent by sheep and over 13 per cent by suckler cows, heifers-in-calf and bulls. The distribution of LU densities per 1,000 hectares of grassland in 1991 varied considerably from 1,206 in the Border (west) to 1,956 in the South-East region (Table 44). Dairy cattle are important in the South-West, South-East and Mid-West regions while suckler cows are most significant in the West region. Sheep farming is also very prominent in the West and South-East regions.

At district level the variation in livestock unit densities is much greater (*Map 90*) and is strongly related to variations in land quality. There are three main areas of high intensity grazing – Carlow, Wexford and contiguous parts of Kilkenny in the south-east; Meath and Louth; and Cork, Tipperary South and west Waterford. A less extensive, yet remarkable, area of intensive grazing is located around north and east county Galway which is largely the result of intensive sheep grazing. The relatively high densities of LUs in some dispersed districts in western counties may be associated with the availability of commonage which has not been included in calculating the ratios for this map.

Map 91 presents the percentage of the total LUs accounted for by the dairy herd. It demonstrates the same basic pattern but with a certain amount of contraction around the margins when compared to *Maps 57* and *58*. This indicates the decrease in intensity with increasing distance away from the core areas of production. This is particularly evident in Clare, north Tipperary, Kilkenny and Waterford. The smaller contribution of dairying to the overall livestock economy in Cavan and Monaghan is also evident.

The relative importance of suckler cows shown on *Map 92* differs somewhat with the pattern depicted on *Map 61*. *Map 92* identifies more clearly the areas where this type of livestock is most significant – parts of north Clare, west Galway, Leitrim, south Sligo and north-east Mayo. *Map 93* isolates those parts of the Midland and West regions where 'other cattle' account for more than half of the livestock units. The map complements the distribution of sheep as measured in livestock units (*Map 94*). *Map 91* and *94* highlight the spatial segregation of sheep and dairy farming.

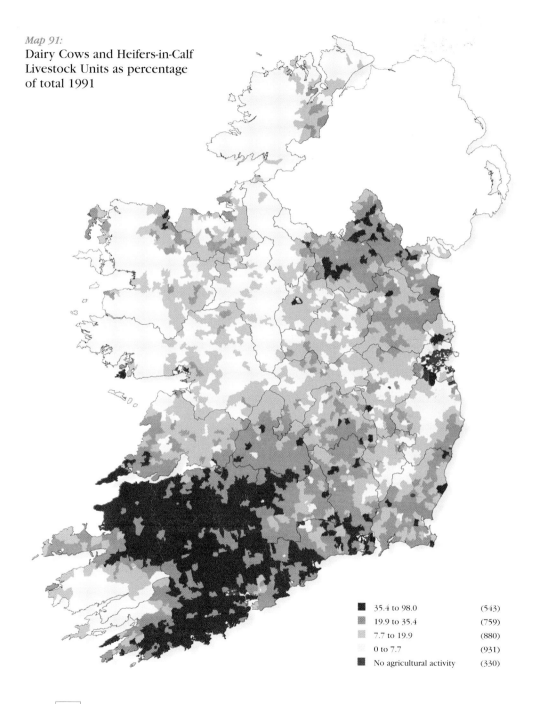

Map 91:
Dairy Cows and Heifers-in-Calf
Livestock Units as percentage
of total 1991

■	35.4 to 98.0	(543)
▨	19.9 to 35.4	(759)
▨	7.7 to 19.9	(880)
░	0 to 7.7	(931)
■	No agricultural activity	(330)

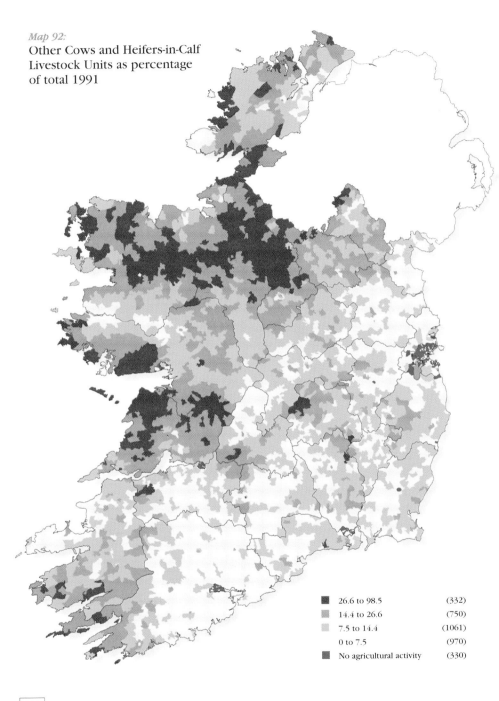

Map 92:

Other Cows and Heifers-in-Calf Livestock Units as percentage of total 1991

■ 26.6 to 98.5	(332)
14.4 to 26.6	(750)
7.5 to 14.4	(1061)
0 to 7.5	(970)
■ No agricultural activity	(330)

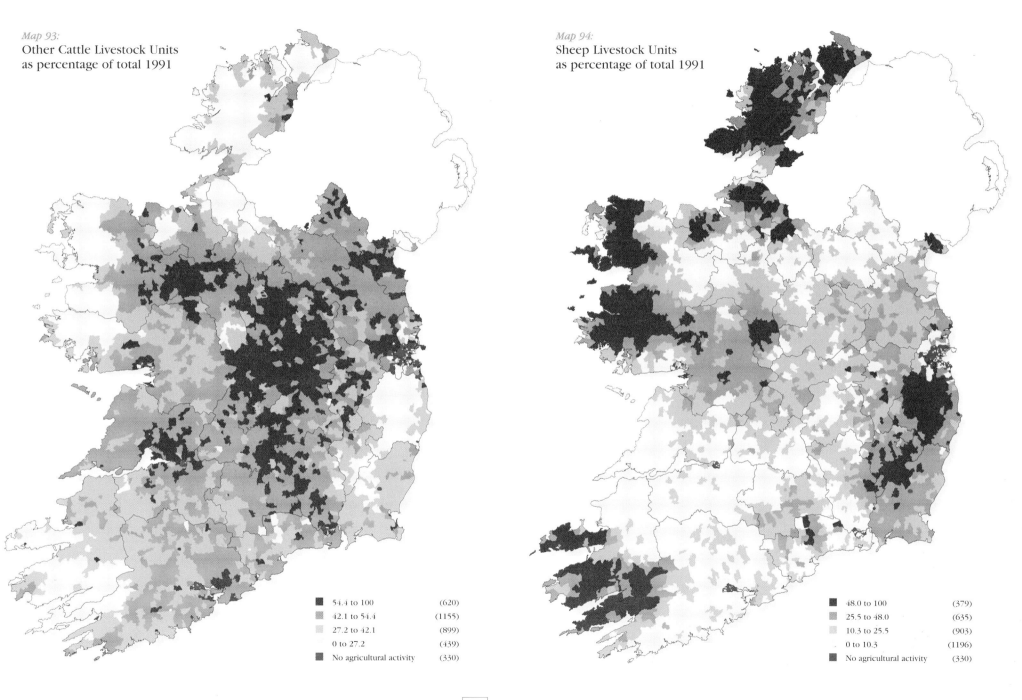

Map 93:
**Other Cattle Livestock Units
as percentage of total 1991**

Map 94:
**Sheep Livestock Units
as percentage of total 1991**

■	54.4 to 100	(620)
▨	42.1 to 54.4	(1155)
▨	27.2 to 42.1	(899)
	0 to 27.2	(439)
■	No agricultural activity	(330)

■	48.0 to 100	(379)
▨	25.5 to 48.0	(635)
▨	10.3 to 25.5	(903)
	0 to 10.3	(1196)
■	No agricultural activity	(330)

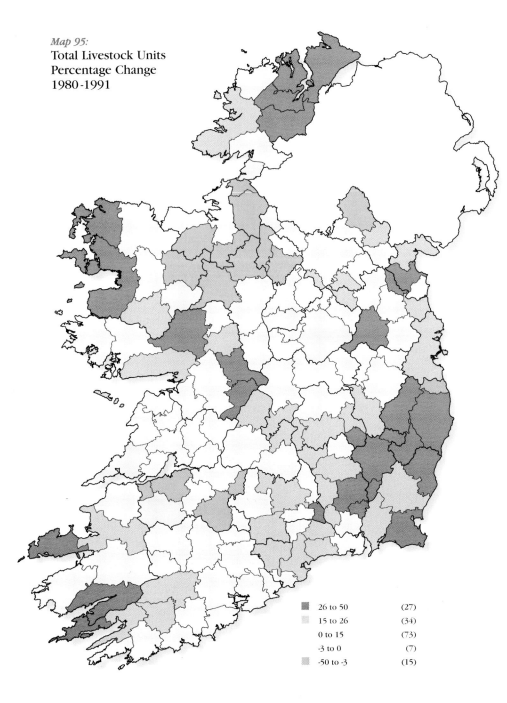

Map 95:
Total Livestock Units Percentage Change 1980-1991

Table 45: Number of livestock units, 1991 and changes, 1980-1991 and 1991-1997

Region	Total LUs 1991	Actual change 1980-91	Average Annual % change 1980-91	Actual change 1991-97[2]	Average Annual % change 1991-97	Actual change 1980-97[2]	Total % change 1980-97[2]
Dublin	51,200	5,900	1.2	-4,700	-1.5	1,200	2.6
Mid-East	651,600	110,046	1.8	6,300	0.2	116,346	21.5
South-East	1,205,000	218,456	2.0	36,600	0.5	255,056	25.9
South-West	1,224,200	138,548	1.2	110,100	1.5	248,648	22.9
Mid-West	806,300	30,757	0.4	77,600	1.6	108,357	14.0
West	1,070,000	103,056	1.0	106,200	1.7	209,256	21.6
Border (west)	469,300	50,568	1.1	43,700	1.6	94,268	22.5
Border (east)	425,900	40,606	1.0	41,800	1.6	82,406	21.4
Midland	650,100	49,615	0.8	53,700	1.4	103,315	17.2
Ireland	6,553,900	747,542	1.2	471,200	1.2	1,218,742	21.0

Source: Derived from Agricultural Statistics 1980; Census of Agriculture 1991; Crops and Livestock Survey 1997.

[1] Grassland includes pasture, hay, silage and rough grazing (commonage not included).

[2] 1997 figures are estimated based on CSO annual crops and livestock survey.

Change in Livestock Units

Table 45 indicates that there has been a steady expansion in the number of LUs, with average annual increases of 1.2 per cent between 1980 and 1991 and again over the period 1991-97. Over the 1980s, decline was evident in the contribution of dairy cattle, beef cattle and horses, with the largest decline in the dairying component. This was very strongly counteracted by huge increases in the contribution of sheep and suckler cows (Table 46). Between 1991 and 1997 the only decline was in the contribution of sheep with the suckler herd continuing to show an increase (Table 46).

■ 26 to 50	(27)
░ 15 to 26	(34)
0 to 15	(73)
-3 to 0	(7)
▨ -50 to -3	(15)

Table 46: Average annual percentage change in total LUs by type of livestock, 1980-1991 and 1991-1997

Region	Dairy Cows[1]		Other Cows[2]		'Other' Cattle		Sheep		Horses and Ponies	
	1980-91	1991-97	1980-91	1991-97	1980-91	1991-97	1980-91	1991-97	1980-91	1991-97
Dublin	-1.2	-0.8	4.3	13.6	0.6	-4.1	14.2	-1.5	-2.0	0.9
Mid-East	-0.7	0.3	5.9	6.8	-1.0	-0.2	18.2	-1.5	0.2	-0.1
South-East	-1.1	0.6	6.7	7.7	0.5	0.2	18.8	-2.0	0.7	0.0
South-West	-1.3	1.1	12.5	9.3	0.7	0.9	15.6	-1.2	-1.4	2.3
Mid-West	-2.0	0.3	10.3	8.9	-0.2	0.7	24.5	-2.4	-0.7	2.1
West	-3.3	1.1	5.3	7.2	-1.7	0.4	10.6	0.0	-2.6	7.3
Border (west)	-3.4	0.3	3.1	5.9	-2.2	0.6	12.8	-0.1	-0.4	9.7
Border (east)	-2.0	1.0	10.6	9.1	-0.1	0.2	24.6	-1.7	-0.7	8.0
Midland	-1.5	0.4	5.0	9.6	-0.9	0.5	29.3	-2.0	-1.7	3.2
Ireland	-1.7	0.7	6.8	8.0	-0.5	0.4	15.7	-1.1	-0.7	2.3

[1] Includes dairy heifers-in-calf.
[2] Includes 'other' heifers-in-calf and bulls.
Source: Derived from Agricultural Statistics 1980; Census of Agriculture 1991; Crops and Livestock Survey 1997.

The largest increases over the 1980s occurred in the South-East and the Mid-East, mostly due to increases in the numbers of sheep and to a lesser extent by expansion in the suckler cow herd. Table 46 highlights the poor performance of the Border (west) and West regions given that these areas also experienced a reduction in tillage over this period. In these regions the rates of decline in dairy and beef cattle were over three times the State average, while the increases in suckler cows and other beef animals were significantly below the increases for other regions. This is corroborated by *Map 95* which illustrates the extensive area of decline in the north-west. This provides clear evidence of the extent of disengagement from farming in this area.

Over the period from 1991-97 the increase was not as large, with the Dublin region actually showing a decline of 1.5 per cent (Table 45). This was due to decreases in dairy cattle, beef cattle and sheep with the increases in suckler cows and horses not sufficient to counteract the overall trend towards less intensive livestock farming in this region. Some of the decline in Dublin's agricultural activity is, of course, also attributable to the loss of agricultural land to urban use.

The West and Border (west) regions have performed relatively better over the 1991-97 period due to higher levels of expansion than was the case in other regions.

While beef enterprises are present

in almost all parts of the State,

there is a high level of regional specialisation

within the beef sector.

Section Five

Selected Agricultural
Policy Measures

Introduction

The earlier sections have been concerned mainly with farm structure, land use, livestock and cropping systems, and with demonstrating how these features are spatially patterned throughout the Republic. It was pointed out that geographical variations are accounted for by many factors: the distribution of the basic resources of climate and soil suitability; historical circumstances which influenced the distribution of people on land holdings; economic and technological forces driving the trend towards larger production units; the expansion of opportunities for alternative employment to farming; changes in demographic structures, especially those related to the depletion or renewal of the human resource; and cultural factors disposing farmers in different regions to follow different practices in managing farms and transferring land. The impact of policy measures was also noted, for example, in dictating decline in dairy cow numbers, and expansion in sheep production.

In this section the focus is more explicitly on the influence of policy measures on the geographical variations in land use and in farmer behaviour. However, for a number of the policy measures of interest it was not possible for the administrative bodies concerned to make available the required statistical information for the small area units of DED or RD. Consequently, the coverage of themes in this section is, unavoidably, not as complete as desired. In the restrictive policy context for commercial farming over recent years it would, for example, be informative to map the trends in farm investment – even if this is now mostly for the management of farm wastes. Such a map would show where commercial farming is most likely to be sustained. Similarly, given the thrust of the 1992 CAP reforms it would be of interest to trace in detail the spatial patterning of diversification from conventional agricultural production to different alternative enterprises.

Despite the constraints imposed by data limitations, it is suggested that the information provided here will usefully supplement the census data already presented. The policy measures covered concern farm development, income transfer measures, an agri-environmental scheme, early retirement for farmers, afforestation, and, to a more limited extent, indicators of investment for alternative enterprises.

Farm Development: Farm Improvement Programme (FIP)

In 1986 the Farm Improvement Programme (FIP) was initiated to implement an EC regulation supporting farm development. The FIP grant-aided full-time farmers in carrying out an 'improvement plan' for between two and six years. Aid under the programme covered investments in land improvement, certain farm buildings, fixed assets and mobile equipment.

Between 1986 and 1994, over 36,000 farmers participated in the programme, of whom approximately 50 per cent were in the western counties. Participants in these western counties tended to be younger farmers with larger farms on which the FIP is deemed to have helped maintain viability and improved working conditions (Leavy *et al.*, 1998). From *Map 96* the largest investments were made in some of the smaller scale dairying districts of Monaghan/Cavan, north Kerry, mid-west Cork and Kilkenny. It is likely that the large commercial farms had already completed programmes of investment under an earlier scheme and were, therefore, deemed ineligible for the FIP. Investments were generally low in the more marginal farming districts in the west, north-west and midland areas.

Transfer Payments to Farmers

Public policies provide financial support to farmers under two broad headings: market-based transfers and non-market or 'direct' payments. Commodity price supports – especially for milk – have traditionally been the main type of market-based payment. Gradually, over the years and especially since the 1992 CAP reform, the emphasis in policy supports has been shifting towards the direct supplementation of farm incomes.

Estimates of the volume of market-based income transfers[8] were made for 1995. The resulting geographical variation is strongly influenced by the fact that the payments are related to volume of production and as such accrue in larger quantities to the more commercially oriented farms in the State.

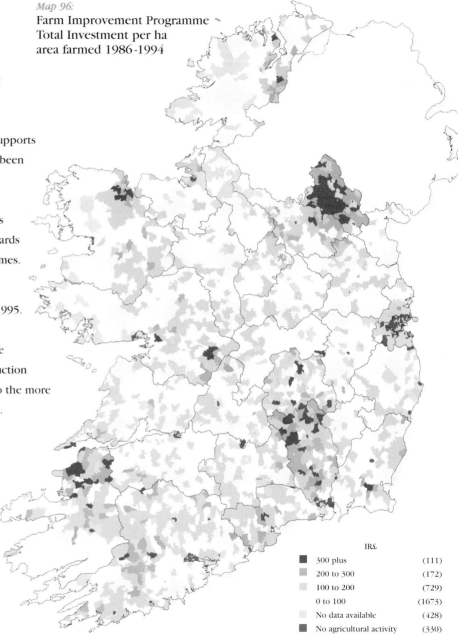

Map 96:
Farm Improvement Programme Total Investment per ha area farmed 1986-1994

IR£

■	300 plus	(111)
▩	200 to 300	(172)
▢	100 to 200	(729)
	0 to 100	(1673)
	No data available	(428)
■	No agricultural activity	(330)

The total amount of price supports paid in 1995 amounted to almost £750 million. These payments were strongly concentrated in the dairying regions with 38 per cent of the total going to farmers in the South-West and Mid-West, compared to just over 25 per cent of all direct payments. Average payments per hectare of area farmed and per annual work unit are particularly low in the Border (west) and West regions (Table 47).

The detailed distribution of these payments, summarised on *Map 97*, draws a contrast between the two dairying regions and the more marginal districts in the west, north-west and south-west, along with the upland areas in Wicklow and the intensive arable areas in north Dublin where some of the crops grown are ineligible for assistance.

Table 47: Estimated price supports per farm, per ha and per AWU, 1995

Region	Total price supports (IR£)	Price supports per farm (IR£)	Price supports per ha AAU (IR£)	Price supports per AWU (IR£)
Dublin	3,196,171	2115.3	64.9	1124.6
Mid-East	62,362,025	5362.6	149.0	3466.7
South-East	138,421,798	6793.0	186.1	3877.9
South-West	176,162,656	6251.8	210.4	3839.2
Mid-West	108,563,827	5410.3	192.7	3607.5
West	82,888,819	2127.3	115.3	1548.7
Border (west)	33,591,857	1657.4	83.8	1344.3
Border (east)	50,780,992	3547.6	180.4	2542.1
Midland	92,050,297	6027.8	214.8	4047.9
Ireland	748,018,442	4385.2	168.4	2948.1

Source: Based on data supplied by Department of Agriculture and Food.

Direct non-market payments were originally introduced in the 1970s to provide livestock 'headage' allowances to support farming in disadvantaged areas, which now comprise 75 per cent of the Republic (see Figure 5). An additional category of direct payments – 'premia' payments – was subsequently provided for certain types of livestock and crops in all regions to compensate farmers for actual or expected reductions in price supports. Additional to these were payments for specific schemes (environmental protection, early retirement of farmers and supports for the establishment of younger farmers). Compensatory allowances are modulated to give higher levels of support for livestock numbers below specified levels and are subject to a maximum per farm (Department of Agriculture and Food, 1999). Premia payments per farm are unlimited (provided eligibility conditions are met).

As a result of the 1992 CAP reform direct income transfers now make significant contributions to farm incomes. Prior to the reform and, excluding payments for specific schemes, they accounted for about 30 per cent of Family Farm Income (FFI) on the average farm in the State. By 1996 this proportion had doubled although the relative contributions differed substantially across types of farm. On specialist dairy farms direct payments represented 16 per cent of FFI but constituted all of FFI on cattle-rearing and 'mainly sheep' farms (Frawley, 1998a).

It will be understood, therefore, that the incidence of non-market income transfers is highest in the regions of cattle and sheep production. This is illustrated clearly in *Map 98* (in which payment for specific schemes is excluded). This form of income support is particularly important in the general Connacht area and in the 'mixed crops and livestock' farms of the south-east. While these payments are not very significant in the mainly dairying counties of the south-west they are of greater importance to income support in the north-eastern dairying region, where there tends to be a greater variety of farm types.

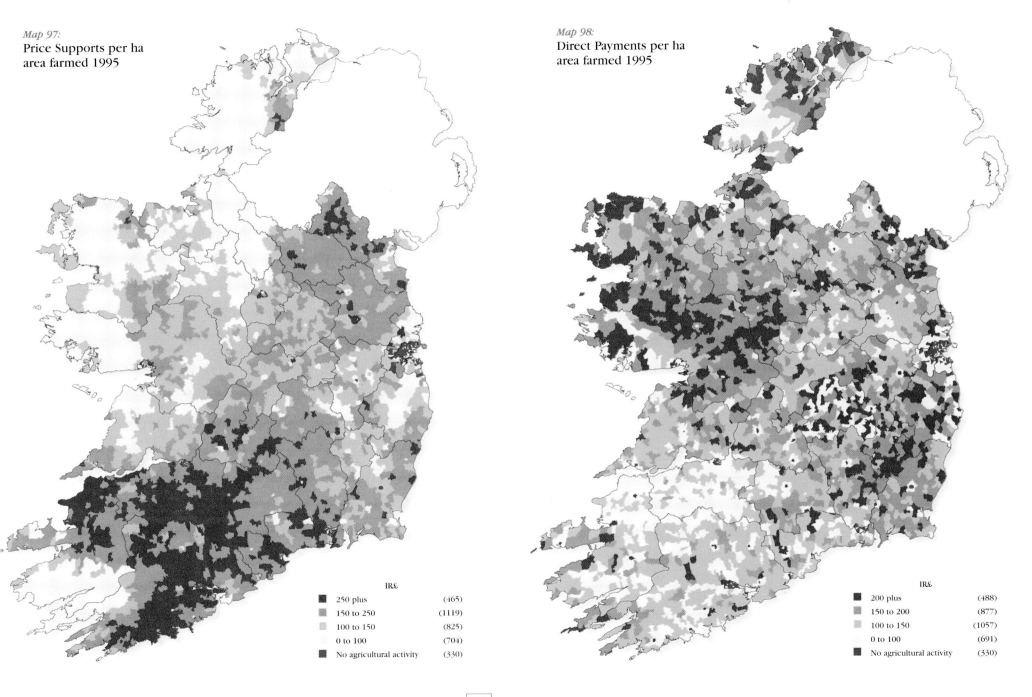

Map 97:
Price Supports per ha area farmed 1995

Map 98:
Direct Payments per ha area farmed 1995

IR£

■	250 plus	(465)
■	150 to 250	(1119)
■	100 to 150	(825)
□	0 to 100	(704)
■	No agricultural activity	(330)

IR£

■	200 plus	(488)
■	150 to 200	(877)
■	100 to 150	(1057)
□	0 to 100	(691)
■	No agricultural activity	(330)

In 1995 the total amount of direct payments to farmers was just over £700 million. In the absence of data on the actual number of farms in receipt of payments one can only estimate average levels of payment by reference to the total number of farms in each region. On this basis the average payment per farm ranged from between £3,100 and £3,300 in the West and Border regions to over £6,200 in the Mid-East region, with an exceptionally high level of almost £12,000 in Dublin. The magnitude of the payments per farm was strongly influenced by the dominant types of farming in each region and to a lesser extent by farm size, as is evident from the estimates of payments per hectare of area farmed. The lowest payments of this type occurred in the South-West and Mid-West regions.

The level of payments per annual work unit ranged between £2,200 and £2,500 in the western regions, while in the east and south-east they were much larger. The contribution of these payments to family farm income has been estimated by Teagasc to be 48 per cent for all farms in 1995. However, it varied from only 11 per cent on dairying farms to 65 per cent on tillage farms. On farms with cattle systems the contribution represented 80 per cent of family farm income while on mainly sheep farms it was in excess of 100 per cent (Power and Roche, 1996).

Table 48: Direct payments per farm, per ha and per AWU, 1995

Regions	Total direct payments (IR£)	Direct payments per farm (IR£)	Direct payments per ha AAU (IR£)	Direct payments per AWU (IR£)
Dublin	17,718,610	11,726.4	360.0	6,234.6
Mid-East	72,369,527	6,223.2	172.9	4,023.0
South-East	118,525,216	5,816.6	159.4	3,320.5
South-West	104,734,078	3,716.9	125.1	2,282.5
Mid-West	73,011,098	3,638.5	129.6	2,426.1
West	127,443,646	3,270.8	177.3	2,381.1
Border (west)	62,679,906	3,092.6	156.4	2,508.4
Border (east)	46,325,228	3,236.4	164.6	2,319.0
Midland	77,812,956	5,095.5	181.6	3,421.9
Ireland	700,620,266	4,107.3	157.7	2,761.3

Source: Based on data supplied by Department of Agriculture and Food.

The aggregate level of payments per farm (direct payments plus price supports) was approximately £8,500 in 1995. There is a wide range between regions from over £11,100 per farm in the South-East, Mid-East and Midland regions to only £4,750 in the Border (west) and approximately £5,400 in the West region. *Map 99* presents the total income support paid to farmers in the form of direct payments and price supports. The highest level of support went to the relatively better off farming regions, namely the dairying and arable regions. The lowest levels of support were recorded along the west coast and in Connacht generally. Thus, the total system of payments tends to reflect and reinforce existing sources of differentiation between the weaker and stronger farming regions.

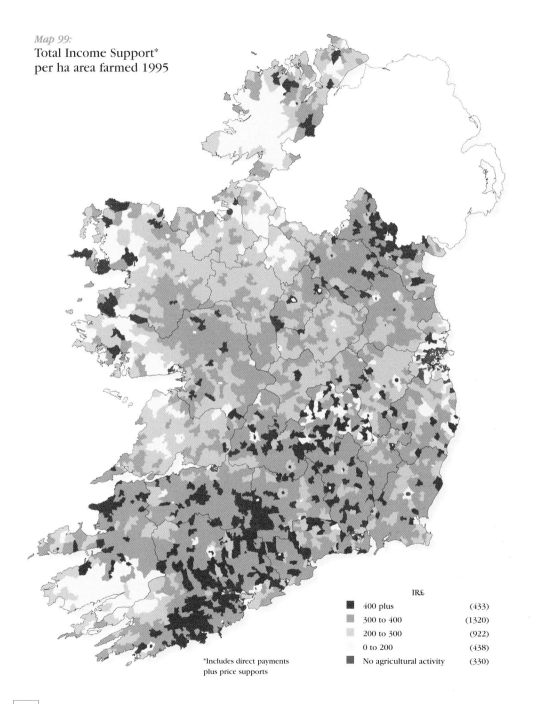

Map 99:
Total Income Support*
per ha area farmed 1995

IR£

- ■ 400 plus (433)
- ▨ 300 to 400 (1320)
- ▨ 200 to 300 (922)
- □ 0 to 200 (438)
- ■ No agricultural activity (330)

*Includes direct payments plus price supports

Rural Environment Protection Scheme (REPS)
The 1992 CAP reform included a provision to
introduce agri-environmental programmes in the EU.
In response Ireland initiated the Rural Environment
Protection Scheme (REPS) in 1994 which contains
financial incentives to improve the quality and visual
appearance of the rural environment through, among
other actions, the protection of endangered wildlife,
flora and fauna. REPS is a voluntary scheme providing
for payments to any farmer who agrees to implement
a plan for the management of land, farm waste and the
protection of flora, fauna and wildlife habitats.
Supplementary measures have specific environmental
aims such as the preservation of National Heritage
Areas, reduction of overgrazing and promotion of
organic farming.

**Table 49: Participation in Rural Environment Protection
Scheme, 1994-1999**

Regions	Total farms in REPS	% of farms in REPS	Total area in REPS (ha)	% of AAU in REPS
Dublin	124	8.2	4,312	8.0
Mid-East	2,199	19.0	77,199	16.8
South-East	3,815	18.8	155,670	19.9
South-West	4,741	16.8	232,935	25.1
Mid-West	4,722	23.6	173,760	30.4
West	11,836	30.4	441,037	49.8
Border (west)	5,131	25.4	227,564	48.9
Border (east)	2,794	19.7	74,377	25.7
Midland	4,792	31.4	156,229	36.2
Ireland	40,154	23.6	1,543,087	31.7

Source: Based on data supplied by Department of Agriculture and Food.

By early 1999, over 40,000 farmers were in
receipt of payments from REPS. While the number
of participants in REPS represents just under one-
quarter of all farms they account for almost one-third
of the total area farmed (Table 49). *Maps 100* and *101*
show that the adoption of the scheme has been
highest in those districts where farmers are mainly
involved in extensive grazing such as in Connacht,
Ulster, the midland counties, as well as in south Kerry
and west Cork. Some coastal areas of high natural
amenity also feature prominently. Over half of the area
farmed throughout most of the western districts in
Galway, Mayo and Donegal is included in the REPS
programme, compared with less than one-sixth
throughout much of the east and south.

Commins and Frawley (1998) have established
that participants are generally those with larger than
the national average farm size but in areas of low
farming intensity. Leavy (1997) suggests that low-
income and small-scale farmers are inhibited by the
capital costs of compliance with the scheme while the
intensive and mainly dairy farmers do not find the
incentives attractive enough, or consider the eligibility
conditions too restrictive.

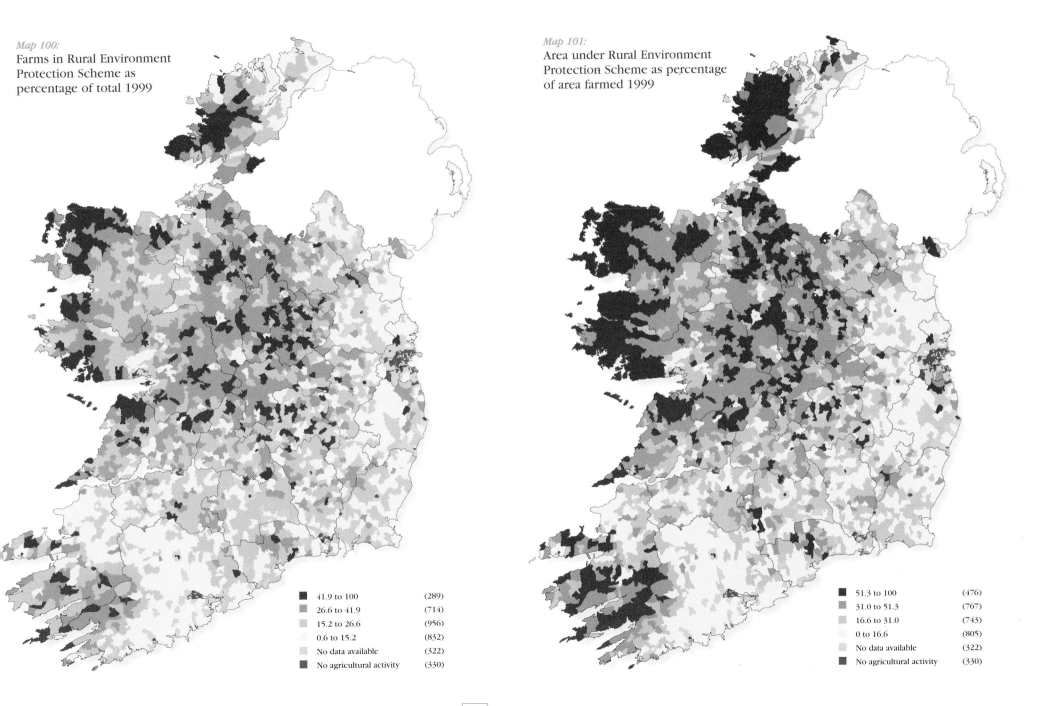

Map 100:
Farms in Rural Environment
Protection Scheme as
percentage of total 1999

Map 101:
Area under Rural Environment
Protection Scheme as percentage
of area farmed 1999

■	41.9 to 100	(289)
■	26.6 to 41.9	(714)
■	15.2 to 26.6	(956)
	0.6 to 15.2	(832)
	No data available	(322)
■	No agricultural activity	(330)

■	51.3 to 100	(476)
■	31.0 to 51.3	(767)
■	16.6 to 31.0	(743)
	0 to 16.6	(805)
	No data available	(322)
■	No agricultural activity	(330)

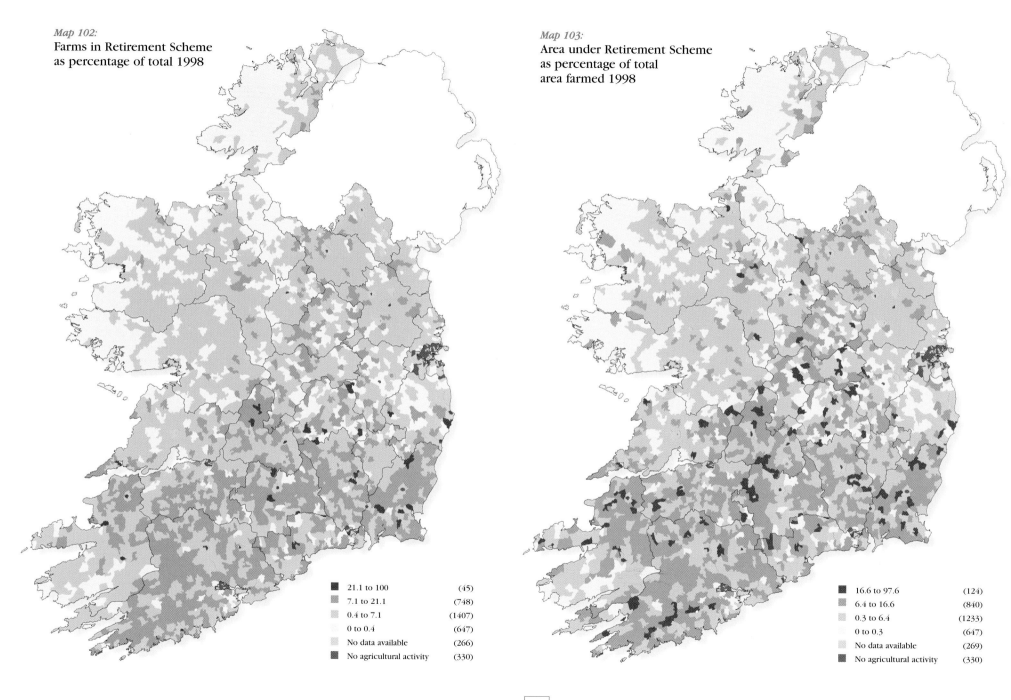

Map 102:
Farms in Retirement Scheme
as percentage of total 1998

Map 103:
Area under Retirement Scheme
as percentage of total
area farmed 1998

■	21.1 to 100	(45)
	7.1 to 21.1	(748)
	0.4 to 7.1	(1407)
	0 to 0.4	(647)
	No data available	(266)
■	No agricultural activity	(330)

■	16.6 to 97.6	(124)
	6.4 to 16.6	(840)
	0.3 to 6.4	(1233)
	0 to 0.3	(647)
	No data available	(269)
■	No agricultural activity	(330)

Table 50: Participation in Farmer Retirement Scheme, 1994-1998

Region	Number of Retirements	Per cent of Farms
Dublin	46	3.0
Mid-East	508	4.4
South-East	1,672	8.2
South-West	1,904	6.8
Mid-West	1,214	6.1
West	684	1.8
Border (west)	244	1.2
Border (east)	464	3.2
Midland	704	4.6
Total	7,440	4.4

Source: Based on data supplied by Department of Agriculture and Food.

Farmer Retirement Scheme (FRS)

Introduced in the context of the 1992 CAP reform, the Farmer Retirement Scheme (FRS) provides payments to farmers who opt for retirement between the ages of 55 and 66 years. To qualify, applicants must have practised farming as a main occupation for the preceding 10 years. They must also retire from farming definitively and transfer their holdings to qualified (trained) young farmers. A requirement is that the holding must be enlarged by a minimum of 5 hectares of AAU or 10 per cent of the transferor's holding, whichever is the greater.

By the end of 1998, over 7,400 farmers had accepted the FRS. *Maps 102* and *103* show that there has been quite widespread interest in this scheme, except for the coastal areas of Galway, Mayo and Donegal, together with Leitrim. While the incidence of its adoption is not notably high in any area it is clear that the percentages of farmers retiring under the scheme are highest in the southern regions. From Table 50 it can be seen that the proportion of farms participating in the scheme is six times greater in the South-East than in the Border (west). In the commercial farming areas there are likely to be relatively more qualified transferees, while it will also be recalled from *Map 10* that land mobility through lifetime transfers is more common in the south and east than in other parts of the State. Typically, between 6 and 16 per cent of the area farmed has been transferred under the Retirement Scheme in the southern districts.

Afforestation

Forestry has traditionally been of minor importance as a land use in the Republic of Ireland. This is due to a range of factors which include the small average farm size making it difficult for farmers to relinquish important agricultural land, the costs associated with establishment, as well as the long-term nature of the investment. These factors, together with the inertia inherent in agriculture in Ireland and the lack of a forestry tradition, ensured that forestry never developed as an accepted 'agricultural activity' (Gillmor, 1992).

Up until the early 1980s most afforestation was undertaken by the State. There are many possible reasons for the State 'monopoly' but clearly the substantial initial expense and the long-term returns made it more amenable to public sector investment than to private investors or farmers. From the early 1980s, however, not only was there an increase in overall levels of afforestation but there were also substantial increases in the levels of private planting. The stimulus for the increased level of private afforestation came largely from public policy. Specifically, the EC Agricultural Development Programme for the west of Ireland (known as 'the Western Package') paid grants to farmers for the afforestation of marginal agricultural land while, the 1987 Programme for National Recovery and the 1989-93 Forestry Operational Programme

Table 51: Forestry planting, 1982-1996

Region	State planting (ha)	% of total State planting	Private planting (ha)	% of total private planting	Total State & private planting (ha)	% of total planting
Dublin	250.9	0.3	557.7	0.5	808.6	0.4
Mid-East	5,009.1	5.5	5,468.6	5.2	10,477.7	5.3
South-East	12,613.7	13.8	10,503.3	10.0	23,117.0	11.7
South-West	12,607.2	13.7	20,567.1	19.6	33,174.3	16.9
Mid-West	13,677.1	14.9	15,512.4	14.8	29,189.4	14.8
West	24,693.9	26.9	22,058.8	21.0	46,752.7	23.8
Border (west)	12,938.8	14.1	18,305.6	17.4	31,244.4	15.9
Border (east)	2,013.1	2.2	2,488.6	2.4	4,501.7	2.3
Midland	7,892.8	8.6	9,592.1	9.1	17,484.9	8.9
Ireland	91,696.5	100	105,054.2	100	196,750.7	100

Source: Irish Timber Growers Association (1998).

provided further incentives for private planting and extended the incentives for afforestation from the west to the entire State (Gillmor, 1992; Hannan and Commins, 1993). The range of incentives has been continued under the Operational Programme for Agriculture, Rural Development and Forestry for the period 1994-99.

Map 104 shows the total area planted between 1982 and 1996. Clearly, there is an orientation towards the western half of the State, especially counties Donegal, Leitrim, Mayo and Clare. This is primarily due to forestry's association with agriculturally marginal land as well as to the incentive schemes of the early 1980s which promoted forestry in these western areas. Table 51 shows that the West region experienced the highest levels of planting – both State and private – with significantly lower figures recorded in Dublin, the Border (east), Mid-East and Midland regions.

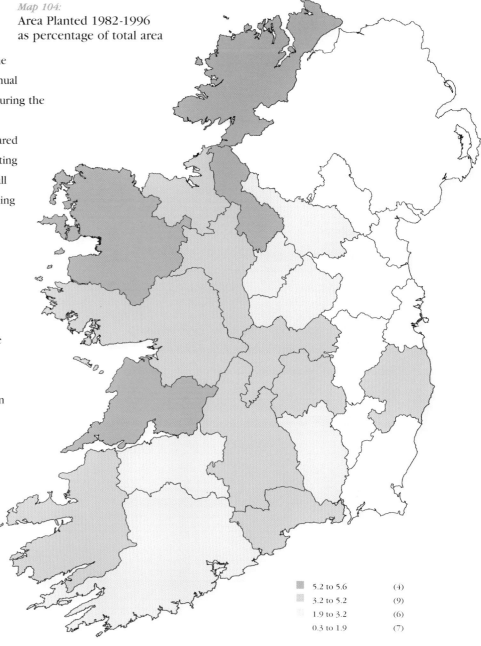

Map 104:
Area Planted 1982-1996
as percentage of total area

Forestry now accounts for one of the major shifts in Ireland's land use with annual planting rates of about 20,000 hectares during the mid-1990s. State policy aims to have 15 per cent of land under forestry, compared to just 8 per cent at present. Private planting now accounts for almost 80 per cent of all annual planting, of which the overwhelming proportion is undertaken by farmers. Between 1990 and 1996 the largest area planted was in the South-West followed by the West and Border (west) of which 78 per cent, 64 per cent and 66 per cent respectively was undertaken by farmers. Planting by non-farmers is relatively more important in the West, Border (west) and Border (east) regions but is much less important overall, accounting for less than 27 per cent of all private planting in the State between 1990 and 1996. Following the introduction of REPS there has been a slowdown in the rate of private afforestation due to the higher costs of acquiring land for planting.

5.2 to 5.6   (4)
3.2 to 5.2   (9)
1.9 to 3.2   (6)
0.3 to 1.9   (7)

133

Despite the increases in private afforestation it continues to be found on a very small proportion of farms. In 1991 only 4.5 per cent of all farms in the State had private forestry with this figure varying regionally from 6.5 per cent in the South-East to as little as 1.7 per cent in Dublin (Table 52).

Map 105 presents the total area of private planting over the period 1982 to 1996. The western counties again have the highest levels of private planting, although prior to the CAP reform of 1992 commercial farmers in the south and east showed a greater response to existing afforestation incentives than did the smaller-scale farmers of the north and west. This was complemented by the more active involvement of forestry companies in the latter areas (Hannan and Commins, 1993).

While forestry continues to be attractive to some of the more commercial farming counties it has also been making a more significant impact among farmers in the west and north-west. In fact since 1992 a high proportion of private planting has taken place in western counties (and in Wicklow) where more agriculturally marginal land is available (Commins and Frawley, 1998).

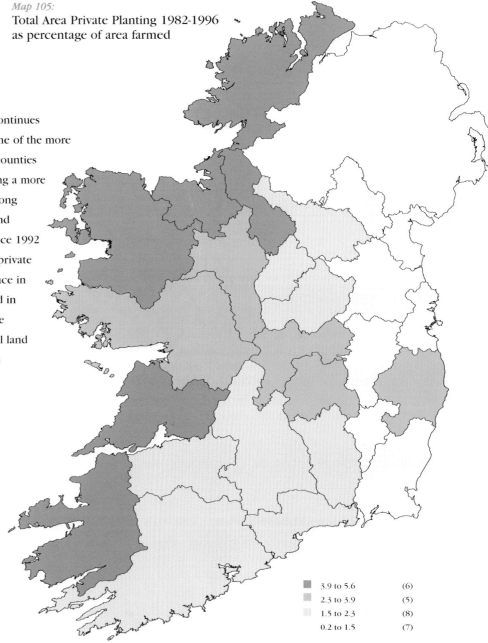

Map 105:
Total Area Private Planting 1982-1996
as percentage of area farmed

- 3.9 to 5.6 (6)
- 2.3 to 3.9 (5)
- 1.5 to 2.3 (8)
- 0.2 to 1.5 (7)

Table 52: Private forestry planting 1990-1996

Region	Farmers (ha)	% of total planting by farmers	Non-Farmers (ha)	% of total planting by non-farmers	Total (ha)	% of total farms with private planting
Dublin	249.1	49.9	249.7	50.1	498.8	1.7
Mid-East	3,949.0	76.1	1,238.4	23.9	5,187.4	4.5
South-East[1]	8,167.7	85.3	1,411.0	14.7	9,578.7	6.5
South-West	13,201.6	77.8	3,759.3	22.2	16,960.9	5.2
Mid-West[1]	8,667.0	70.2	3,668.5	29.8	12,338.5	5.6
West	9,858.3	63.9	5,563.0	36.1	15,421.3	3.4
Border (west)	9,811.5	66.3	4,992.4	33.7	14,803.9	4.6
Border (east)	1,194.6	69.2	532.4	30.8	1,727.1	1.4
Midland	7,597.3	84.8	1,366.3	15.2	8,963.6	5.6
Ireland	62,696.1	73.3	22,781.0	26.7	85,480.2	4.5

[1] The figures for Tipperary North and South Riding were derived on the basis of the proportion of area farmed in each.
Source: Irish Timber Growers Association (1998).

Diversification from Conventional Production

For more than a decade EU and Irish policies have advocated the need to diversify farm production and incentives have been increased accordingly. The options proposed include (apart from forestry): agri-tourism, alternative crops and livestock such as organic products, sport horses, deer farming and speciality food production.

In general, progress with diversification has been relatively slow (Cawley *et al.*, 1995). At the 1991 census approximately 2,000 farms reported having 'gainful non-agricultural activity', over half of which involved farm tourism and recreational activities. In 1996 there were an estimated 550 deer farms in the State. Currently, fewer than 1,000 farms are engaged in organic production or in rearing sport horses.

There is no comprehensive database on farm diversification; several grant-giving agencies are involved at different levels of public administration. Information is available, however, on the number of grants paid for housing and handling facilities for alternative enterprises over the four years 1995 to 1998. The average annual number was about 740. These grants are available under the 1994 Operational Programme for Agriculture, Rural Development and Forestry and are provided for farmers (and other rural dwellers) to enable them to develop housing/handling facilities for horses, deer, goats and other alternative enterprises.

In the four years 1995 to 1998 the number of grants paid was 2,967, or about 18 per 1,000 farms over two hectares in 1991. Table 53 shows that while there is a high level of variation between regions in the take-up of these grants, the variation in average size of grant is much less. The overall take-up of grants of this type is quite low at approximately two per cent. The highest adoption rates are in the Mid-East and South-East where there is a tradition of strong commercial farming. Adoption is also high in the West where, traditionally, the provision of livestock housing was limited and frequently of poor quality. By contrast, adoption is low on the more extensive cattle grazing Midland farms and on the intensive dairy farms of the South-West and Mid-West.

The average grant approved per farm typically ranges between £7,500 and £8,300, except in the South-West where the average grant was only £6,568, suggesting that the payments are mainly for small-scale projects.

Table 53: Housing and handling grants for alternative enterprises, 1995-1998

Region	Number of grants	Total cost (£000s)	Grants per 1,000 farms[1] 1991	Average grant per participating farm (IR£)
Dublin	26	210.3	19	8,088
Mid-East	318	2,635.5	28	8,288
South-East	495	3,620.9	25	7,315
South-West	279	1,832.5	10	6,568
Mid-West	246	1,809.1	13	7,354
West	907	6,926.0	24	7,636
Border (west)	261	2,083.7	13	7,984
Border (east)	268	2,144.6	19	8,002
Midland	167	1,288.8	11	7,717
Ireland	2,967	22,551.4	18	7,601

[1]Over 2 hectares.
Source: Derived from data provided by Department of Agriculture and Food.

Private 85,479 ha

Public 46,332 ha

Total 131,811 ha

Land Areas Planted 1990 -1996 (ha)

Private planting now accounts for almost 80 per cent of all annual planting, of which the overwhelming proportion is undertaken by farmers.

Land Areas Planted 1982-96 (ha)

Tota

Priv.

Pub

82 83 84 85 86 87 88 89 90 91 92 93 94 95 96

Section Six

Overview and Outlook

Objectives and Contents

The main objective of this atlas is to provide a detailed visual representation of the geographical variations in the contemporary agricultural economy of the Republic of Ireland. A second objective is to place the geography of Irish agriculture within the context of the transition from an expansionist era for conventional agricultural production to a more restrictive regime dictated by reforms in the EU's Common Agricultural Policy. There are two major but intertwined components in the atlas. One is a series of maps, based mostly on some 3,000 small area units; the second is a commentary on the maps supplemented by tabulations of the relevant statistical data, aggregated to regional level. The themes covered include: farm size and farm fragmentation, land tenure and methods of farm land acquisition, characteristics of the farm labour force, farm mechanisation, farm productivity, land use, livestock systems and cropping patterns, and the responses by land holders to selected agricultural policy measures.

The main database used was the 1991 Census of Agriculture – the latest available to date. Information was to hand for 3,113 District Electoral Divisions in the State reporting agricultural activity at census date. Changes during 1980 to 1991 were mapped for larger area units – 156 Rural Districts. Where data availability from post-1991 official surveys permitted, trends to 1997 were taken into account in the accompanying statistical tables for the regions. Statistics provided by public administration sources were also used.

The 1991 Census of Agriculture collected data for the first time under a number of headings. It was possible, therefore, to include some new maps in the atlas such as those relating to farm fragmentation, patterns of farm land transfer, part-time farming, and types of farming systems as classified by Eurostat and the Central Statistics Office. The public administration data provided by the Department of Agriculture and Food also allowed for the inclusion of new maps in this atlas, e.g., on the take-up rates for selected agricultural policy measures.

Significant Trends

Considered in sequence, the various maps depicting a series of individual aspects of the Republic's farming economy present a picture of quite complex geographical differentiation across local areas. However, at more aggregated territorial levels, and taking a number of maps together, there are general patterns worthy of note. At the broadest spatial scale – a division marked roughly by a line from Limerick to Dundalk – there are striking contrasts between the west and north-west and the south and east in the use of land resources. This is, perhaps, not surprising but what is of significance is that the boundary has been shifting southwards and the divergence in agricultural activity between those two parts of the State has increased. North of the dividing line there have been major reductions in tillage, dairying and beef cattle farming which have not been offset by expansion in other conventional lines of production (*Maps 56, 60 and 73*).

However, the rates of adoption of agri-environmental farming (the Rural Environmental Protection Scheme) have been highest in the low intensity grazing areas of Connacht, Ulster and the midland counties. In recent years afforestation has also made comparatively strong progress north of the Limerick/Dundalk line, especially in Donegal, Leitrim, Mayo and Clare (*Map 104*). Tree planting by non-farmers (e.g. by forestry companies) is relatively more important in the west and north-west than in other regions (Table 52).

The disengagement from more intensive and conventional land uses is associated with particular features of the farm labour force – an older age structure, late transmission of family holdings and high percentages of farm holders who are farming on a part-time basis or who are not economically active at all. The number of smaller farm holdings has also declined at a more rapid rate in the north-west than in other regions (*Map 6*).

In the eastern and southern counties there are clear indicators of a commercial farming culture, which is, in fact, gaining in strength in some more localised areas. Compared to the remainder of the State the incidence of full-time farming is higher, there is a greater degree of mechanisation, farmers are more disposed to early retirement and to the earlier transfer of their holdings, a higher percentage of agricultural land is rented, and there is a more active market in farm land.

In regard to the geographical patterns of change for the main enterprises, milk production has become more concentrated in the core dairying regions of the south and north-east. The degree of spatial concentration in tillage is even more pronounced. In the case of cattle the pattern of change has been somewhat diffuse as increases have taken place in the mainly dairying regions of the State where, in the context of the imposition of milk quotas, small-scale dairy producers availed of incentives to expand non-dairy cattle numbers. While the traditional pattern of cattle movements from the dairying regions of the south to the pasture lands of the east have been maintained there is also evidence of greater retention of younger cattle in the southern counties. Sheep numbers almost trebled during the 1980s with the highest percentage increases occurring from a low baseline position in the midlands and in the dairying regions of the mid-west and north-east.

In the 1990s, however, these same areas, together with the south-east, experienced the greater proportionate declines as sheep farming has tended to retreat to the more traditional sheep producing areas.

Irish Farming Regions – A Generalised Picture

The individual maps presented in this atlas portray a variegated and complex geographical pattern. For simplification purposes, however, it is possible to produce one generalised map of the Republic's main agricultural regions. This is achieved through well-known statistical procedures for reducing large numbers of interrelated variables to a relatively small number of key factors which can serve as surrogates for the original set. Spatial units can then be clustered on the basis of their similarity or difference on these basic factors[9].

To apply these procedures to the map database, an initial set of over 50 variables (e.g. farm size, type of enterprise, mechanisation levels) were selected and reduced to eight underlying factors. Using these as a basis for clustering the census districts, a composite map of agricultural regions for 1991 was produced (*Map 106*). It presents a concise but generalised summary that broadly reflects the spatial distribution of the main farming systems.

Future Outlook

In considering the future outlook for the agricultural regions of the Republic of Ireland it is necessary to take two considerations into account.

Firstly, this atlas has been compiled on the basis of data which pertain to a transitional stage in Irish agriculture. By way of context to the mapping work in the atlas it was suggested (in Section One) that Ireland is an illustrative case of the longer-term dynamics of change in the agricultural sector of modern economies. The patterns and trends depicted in the maps and statistical tables for the 1980s and 1990s represent a short, but significant, phase in the longer-term trajectory of agricultural restructuring and modernisation. The adjustments taking place are an outcome of economic and technological forces and, typically, incorporate a number of features: enlargement of farm business scale, labour outflow, concentration of production, polarisation of farm incomes, greater reliance on non-farm incomes and on various forms of public subsidisation and, the closer integration of agricultural practices with broader rural economic, social and environmental objectives. The contemporary adjustments have been characterised as a transition from a 'productivist' to a 'post-productivist' era in farming.

Secondly, future adjustments will take place in the context of the policy environment that will be established following the 1999 CAP agreement and the subsequent World Trade Organisation negotiations. These are unlikely to alter significantly the longer-term pathway of adjustments in the farm sector. Projections of the impact of the CAP Berlin agreement (Donnellan *et al.,* 1999) indicate that by 2007 the Republic will experience reductions in the value of its agricultural output, a further decline in the number of dairy farms and dairy cow numbers, a consequent fall in beef output, a reduction in the size of the sheep flock and a much reduced population dependent on the land. There will also be a significant increase in the contribution of direct payments to total farm income.

Taking these two considerations into account, it seems plausible to posit the following general scenario for Irish agriculture over the next decade. There will be a core of commercial farms operating competitively in a market environment dominated by world farm commodity prices. These will be mainly the larger-scale milk producers in the core dairying areas, especially in the south-west. In other words, the smaller-scale producers on the fringes of these areas will be increasingly vulnerable to economic forces. The second tier will depend heavily on direct payments, legitimised on the basis that land holders provide 'public goods', especially by managing the environment, or because their farms are in disadvantaged areas.

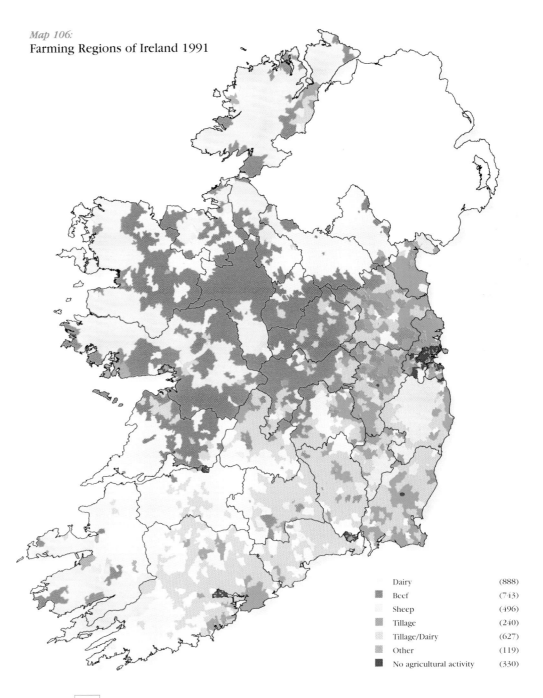

Map 106:
Farming Regions of Ireland 1991

	Dairy	(888)
	Beef	(743)
	Sheep	(496)
	Tillage	(240)
	Tillage/Dairy	(627)
	Other	(119)
	No agricultural activity	(330)

Where non-farm job opportunities are available this tier will overlap very much with a relatively large part-time farming category. Farms of this kind will predominate in the less-favoured areas of the west, north-west and midlands but are likely to become increasingly common throughout the south and east. A third and much smaller category will diversify into non-conventional lines of production – tree farming, alternative livestock and crop enterprises, organic farming, and agri-tourism. These are likely to be as geographically dispersed as resources and market opportunities permit. Overall, this scenario will accentuate the pattern of geographical differences identified in this atlas, and especially the increasing divergance in farming activity and land use between the west and north-west and the south and east.

Such an outlook for the Republic's agriculture will have significant negative implications for the widely held policy aspirations to maintain viable rural communities. Clearly, agricultural policies alone will not realise these aspirations. There is an urgent need, therefore, for a rural development policy which takes account of the dynamics of change within agriculture and which seeks to provide solutions based on more comprehensive approaches to local and regional development.

This is to reiterate the call for integrated policies for rural development proposed in recent reports from the National Economic and Social Council (1994), the Government-appointed Rural Development Policy Advisory Group (1997), and the Economic and Social Research Institute (Fitzgerald *et al.,* 1999).

The implications of the continuing transition in agriculture will need to be considered in the context of a detailed strategy for *spatial* development, giving adequate recognition to the roles of farmers, both as competitive food producers and as natural resource managers. An understanding of the individual and composite geographical patterns and trends portrayed and described in this atlas will contribute to the process of preparing regional and rural development strategies. These will need to acknowledge the complex adjustments taking place within the agricultural economy, the diversity and varied potential of agricultural resources throughout the State, and the linkages between urban centres and their rural hinterlands.

ENDNOTES

[1] *European Size Units are a measure of business scale on a farm where the Standard Gross Margins (SGMs) of all enterprises are aggregated. One ESU is equivalent to 1,200 ECU of SGM.*

[2] *A holding is technically defined as "all land used wholly or partly for agricultural or livestock production, that is operated, directed, or managed by one person (the holder), alone or with the assistance of others without regard to title, size or location and may be in one or more pieces if they are in the same neighbourhood and are known to be operated as a single holding or property" (Horner et al., 1984: 44).*

[3] *The data presented here on the farm labour force are taken primarily from the Census of Agriculture. These differ slightly from those contained in the Census of Population due to definitional differences. In the Census of Agriculture a 'farm holder' or 'family farm operator' was identified for each farm. This individual was usually the owner of the farm. In the Census of Population the categorisation of a farmer comes from the occupation code and includes retired farmers. For this reason over 26 per cent of Census of Population farmers are over 65 years compared to less than 23 per cent of Census of Agriculture farmers or farm holders.*

[4] *An individual is classified as a 'sole occupation' farmer if he/she has no other occupation from which an income is derived. Farmwork is regarded as the 'major occupation' if it takes up the greater portion of the individual's time or as a 'subsidiary occupation' if the time spent on gainful non-farming activity (including paid farmwork on other farms) exceeds that spent on farmwork.*

[5] *A farm is considered 'specialist' in a particular enterprise if that enterprise accounts for two-thirds or more of the total SGM for the farm.*

[6] *Pasture here refers to rotation less than 5 years and permanent pasture.*

[7] *The base temperature refers to the temperature below which no growth takes place.*

[8] *Estimates provided by A. Leavy, Rural Economy Research Centre, Teagasc.*

[9] *These procedures are factor analysis (principal components) and cluster analysis (see Johnston, 1978).*

BIBLIOGRAPHY

Aalen, F.H.A., Whelan, K. and Stout, M. (1997) (eds.) *Atlas of the Irish Rural Landscape*, Cork University Press, Cork.

Attwood, E.A. and Heavey, J.F. (1964) Determination of grazing livestock units, *Irish Journal of Agricultural Research*, 3, 249-251.

Cawley, M., Gillmor, D.A., Leavy, A. and McDonagh, P. (1995) *Farm Diversification: Studies Relating to the West of Ireland*, Teagasc, Dublin.

CEC [Commission of the European Communities] (1998) *Towards a Common Agricultural and Rural Policy for Europe*, European Economy – Reports and Studies, No. 5, Brussels.

CEU [Council of the European Union] (1999) *Presidency Conclusion: Berlin European Council*, 24 and 25 March, S/N 100/99, Brussels.

Central Statistics Office (1983) *Agricultural Statistics, June 1980*, Stationery Office, Dublin.

Central Statistics Office (1994) *Census of Agriculture - June 1991*: Detailed Results, Stationery Office, Dublin.

Central Statistics Office (1997) *Farming since the Famine: Irish Farm Statistics 1847-1996*, Stationery Office, Dublin.

Central Statistics Office (1998a) *Demographic, Social and Economic Situation of the Farming Community in 1991*, Stationery Office, Dublin.

Central Statistics Office (1998b) *Crops and Livestock Survey - June 1997*, Statistical Release, CSO, Cork.

Central Statistics Office (1998c) *Agricultural Labour Input 1997*, Statistical Release, CSO, Cork.

Central Statistics Office (1999a) *Agricultural Labour Input 1998*, Statistical Release, CSO, Cork.

Central Statistics Office (1999b) *Size of Herd - December 1997*, Statistical Release, CSO, Cork.

Central Statistics Office, Various Years, *Irish Statistical Bulletin*, Stationery Office, Dublin.

Collins, J.F. and Cummins, T. (eds.) *Agroclimatic Atlas of Ireland*, AGMET, Dublin.

Commins, P. (1990) Restructuring agriculture in advanced societies; transformation crisis and responses, in Marsden, T., Lowe, P. and Whatmore, S. (eds.) *Rural Restructuring: Global Processes and their Responses*, David Fulton Publishers, London.

Commins, P. (1993) *The Impact of Land Re-distribution in Ireland 1923-1974*, The Michael Dillon Memorial Lecture, Dublin, 3 December.

Commins, P. (1996) Agricultural production and the future of small-scale farming, in, Curtin, C., Haase, T., and Tovey, H. (eds.) *Poverty in Rural Ireland: A Political Economy Perspective*, Oak Tree Press, Dublin.

Commins, P. (1999) *Structural Change in the Agricultural and Rural Economy*, Teagasc, Dublin.

Commins, P. and Kelleher, C. (1973) *Farm Inheritance and Succession*, Macra na Feirme, Dublin.

Commins, P. and Keane M. (1994) Developing the rural economy: problems, progress and prospects, in, *New Approaches to Rural Development*, National Economic and Social Council, Dublin.

Commins, P. and Frawley, J. P. (1998) *Rural Land Use, Regional and Rural Development*, paper to National Conference of Regional Studies Association (Irish Branch), Dublin, 27 March.

Commins, P. and McHugh, C. (1998) *Farming and Rural Viability*, paper to RDS Autumn Conference, 3 November .

Conway, A.G. (1986) Land leasing – findings of a study in the west region of the Republic of Ireland, *Irish Journal of Agricultural Economics and Rural Sociology*, 11, 1-18.

Cox, P.G. (1976) Fertiliser use on rented land, *Irish Journal of Agricultural Economics and Rural Sociology, 6, 147-154.*

Crotty, Raymond D. (1966) *Irish Agricultural Production : Its Volume and Structure*, Cork University Press, Cork.

Cuff, D.J. and Mattson, M.T. (1982) *Thematic Maps: Their Design and Production*, Methuen, New York.

Department of Agriculture and Food (1999) *Schemes and Services 1999*, Department of Agriculture and Food, Dublin.

Dickinson, G.C. (1973) *Statistical Mapping and the Presentation of Statistics*, Second Edition, Arnold, London.

Donnellan, T., Binfield, J. and McQuinn, K. (1999) *Impact of the Berlin Agreement on Irish Agriculture*, Teagasc, Dublin.

Duffy, P.J. (1983) Rural Settlement Change in the Republic of Ireland - a Preliminary Discussion. *Geoforum*, 14 (2), 185-191.

Duffy, P.J. (1986) Planning Problems in the Countryside, in, Breathnach P. and Cawley, M.E. (eds.) *Change and Development in Rural Ireland*, Geographical Society of Ireland, Special Publication No. 1, Maynooth.

Duffy, P.J. (1997) Recent housing change in Kilclone, county Meath, in, Aalen, F.H.A., Whelan, K. and Stout, M. (eds.) *Atlas of the Irish Rural Landscape*, Cork University Press, Cork.

Evans, I.S. (1977) The selection of class intervals, *Transactions of the Institute of British Geographers*, 2 (1) 98-124.

Fitzgerald, D. (1984) Monthly and annual averages of rainfall for Ireland 1951-1980, *Climatological Note No. 7*, Meteorological Service, Dublin.

Fitzgerald, D. and Forrestal, F. (1996) Monthly and annual averages of rainfall for Ireland 1961-1990, *Climatological Note No. 10*, Meteorological Service, Dublin.

Fitzgerald, J., Kearney, I., Morgenroth, E. and Smyth, D. (1999) *National Investment Priorities for the Period 2000-2006*, Economic and Social Research Institute, Dublin.

Frawley, J.P. and Commins, P. (1996) *The Changing Structure of Irish Farming - Trends and Prospects*, Teagasc, Dublin.

Frawley, J.P. (1998a) *The Impact of Direct Payments at Farm Level: A County Study*, Teagasc, Dublin.

Frawley, J.P. (1998b) *The European Model of Agriculture and Sustainable Farm Development: Implications for Ireland*, paper to Annual Conference of Agricultural Economics Society of Ireland, Dublin, 15 October.

Freeman, T.W. (1945) The agricultural regions and rural population of Ireland, *Irish Geography*, 1, 21-30.

Freeman, T.W. (1950) *Ireland - Its Physical, Historical, Social and Economic Geography*, Methuen, London.

Gardiner, M.J. (1979) Soils, in, Gillmor, D.A. (ed.) *Irish Resources and Land Use*, Institute of Public Administration, Dublin.

Gardiner, M.J. and Radford, T. (1980) *Soil Associations of Ireland and their Land Use Potential*, An Foras Talúntais, Dublin.

Gardiner, M.J. (1981) The value of the soil survey in rural development, *Agricultural Record*, 41, 2 25-34.

Gillmor, D.A. (1967) The agricultural regions of the Republic of Ireland, *Irish Geography*, 5, 245-261.

Gillmor, D.A. (1968) The changing location of fowl production in the Republic of Ireland, *Irish Geography*, 5, 485-91.

Gillmor, D.A. (1969a) Spatial distribution of tillage and its component crops in the Republic of Ireland, *Irish Journal of Agricultural Economics and Rural Sociology*, 2, 135-70.

Gillmor, D.A. (1969b) Cattle Movements in the Republic of Ireland, *Transactions of the Institute of British Geographers*, 46, 143-154.

Gillmor, D.A. (1972) Aspects of agricultural change in the Republic of Ireland during the 1960s, *Irish Geography*, 6, 492-8.

Gillmor, D.A. (1977) *Agriculture in the Republic of Ireland*, Akadémiai Kiadó, Budapest.

Gillmor, D.A. (1979) (ed.) *Irish Resources and Land Use*, Institute of Public Administration, Dublin.

Gillmor, D.A. (1987) Concentration of enterprises and spatial changes in the agriculture of the Republic of Ireland, *Transactions of the Institute of British Geographers*, 12, 204-216.

Gillmor, D.A. (1989) Agricultural development, in, Carter, R.W.G. and Parker, A.J. (eds.) *Ireland - A Contemporary Geographical Perspective*. Routledge, London.

Gillmor, D.A. (1991) Land ownership and farm size in the Republic of Ireland - stability and change, in Brunet, P. (ed.) *Rural France and Great Britain,* Centre de Recherches sur l'Evolution de la Vie Rurale, Université de Caen, Caen.

Gillmor, D.A. (1992) The upsurge in private afforestation in the Republic of Ireland, *Irish Geography*, 25, 89-97.

Gillmor, D.A. and Walsh, J.A. (1993) County-level variations in agricultural adjustment in Ireland in the 1980s, *Geographical Viewpoint,* 21, 25-44.

Hannan, D. and Commins, P. (1993) *Factors Affecting Land Availability for Afforestation,* Economic and Social Research Institute, Dublin.

Heavey, J., Roche, M. and Burke, T. (1998) *National Farm Survey 1997,* Teagasc, Dublin.

Herries Davies, G.L. and Stephens, N. (1978) *The Geomorphology of the British Isles - Ireland*, Methuen, London.

Horner A.A., Walsh J.A. and Williams J.A. (1984) *Agriculture in Ireland: A Census Atlas,* Department of Geography, University College Dublin.

Ilberry, B., Chiotti, Q. and Rickard, T. (1997) *Agricultural Restructuring and Sustainability,* CAB International, New York.

Inter-departmental Committee on Land Structure Reform (1978), *Inter-departmental Committee on Land Structure Reform - Final Report*, Stationery Office, Dublin.

Irish Timber Growers Association (1998) *1998 Forestry Yearbook*, Irish Timber Growers Association, Dublin.

Jenks, G.F. and Caspall, F.C. (1971) Error on choroplethic maps: definition, measurement, reduction, *Annals, Association of American Geographers,* 61 (2), 217-245.

Johnson, J.H. (1994) *The Human Geography of Ireland*, Wiley, Chichester.

Johnston, R.J. (1978) *Multivariate Statistical Analysis in Geography*, Longman, London.

Keane, D. (1985) Air temperature in Ireland 1951-1980: monthly, seasonal and annual mean and extreme values, *Climatological Note No. 8*, Meteorological Service, Dublin.

Keane, D. (1986a) Monthly, seasonal and annual mean and extreme values of duration of bright sunshine in Ireland 1951-1980, *Climatological Note No. 9,* Meteorological Service, Dublin.

Keane, T. (1986b) *Climate, Weather and Irish Agriculture*. AGMET, Dublin.

Kelly, P.W. (1982) *Agricultural Land-Tenure and Transfer*, Socio-Economic Research Series, 1, An Foras Talúntais, Dublin.

Leavy, A. (1997) The Rural Environment Protection Scheme, *Farm and Food*, 7 (7), 12-15.

Leavy, A. (1998) *Impact of New Agricultural Policies*, Teagasc, Dublin.

Leavy, A., McDonagh, P. and Commins, P. (1997) Farm development - the impact of the Farm Improvement Programme, *Farm and Food*, 7 (3), 21-22.

Leavy, A., McDonagh, P. and Commins, P. (1998) *An Economic Assessment of the Farm Improvement Programme*, Rural Economy Research Series No. 4, Teagasc, Dublin.

Lee J. and Diamond, S. (1972) *The Potential of Irish Land for Livestock Production*, Soil Survey Bulletin No. 26, An Foras Talúntais, Dublin.

Lee, J and Gardiner, M.J. (1974) The nature, extent and distribution of difficult land areas in Ireland, *Farm and Food Research*, 5, 28-31.

Lee, J. (1991) Soil mapping and land evaluation research in Ireland, in Hodgson, J.M. (ed.) *Soil Survey - A Basis for European Soil Protection*, Soil and Groundwater Research Report 1, Commission of the European Communities, Luxembourg.

Lee, J. (1994) A Biophysical evaluation of Ireland and Scotland for crop production in Fenton A. and Gillmor D.A. (eds.) *Rural Land Use on the Atlantic Periphery of Europe: Scotland and Ireland,* Royal Irish Academy, Dublin.

Macra na Feirme (1992), *Land Transfer Survey*, Macra na Feirme, Dublin.

MapInfo (1998) *MapInfo Professional, Users Guide.* MapInfo, New York.

McDonagh, P., Leavy, A. and Commins, P. (1998) The Farm Improvement Programme: A Survey of Participants in Western Counties, Teagasc, Dublin, (Unpublished).

McDonagh, P. and Commins, P. (1999) Globalization and rural development: demographic revitalisation, entrepreneurs and small business formation in the west of Ireland, in, Kasimis C. and Papadopoulos A.G. (eds.), *Local Responses to Global Integration*, Ashgate, Aldershot.

McDonagh, P., Commins, P. and Leavy, A. (1999) *Development Programmes and Policy Measures in Western Counties*, Teagasc, Dublin.

Mitchell, F. and Ryan, M. (1997) *Reading the Irish Landscape,* Revised Edition, Town House and Country House, Dublin.

Monmonier, M. (1991) *How to Lie with Maps*, University of Chicago Press, Chicago and London.

NESC (1994) *New Approaches to Rural Development*, Report No. 97, National Economic and Social Council, Stationery Office, Dublin.

Orme, A.R. (1970) *The World's Landscapes - Ireland*, Longman, London.

Phelan, J.F. (1987) *An analysis of factors associated with decisions related to property and management transfer on Irish farms,* unpublished Ph.D thesis, UCD, Dublin.

Power, R. and Roche, M. (1996) *National Farm Survey 1995*, Teagasc, Dublin.

Rohan, P.K. (1986) *The Climate of Ireland*, Second Edition, Meteorological Service, Dublin.

Ross, M. (1969) A regional study of the relative prosperity of Irish farms of different sizes, *Economic and Social Review*, 1, 77-107.

Royal Irish Academy (1979) *Atlas of Ireland*, Royal Irish Academy, Dublin.

Rural Development Policy Advisory Group (1997) *Report of the Rural Development Advisory Group*, Stationery Office, Dublin.

Scully, J.J. and Swanson, E.R. (1964) Inter-area resource productivity comparison in Irish agriculture, *Farm Economist*, 10, 284-295.

Scully, J.J. (1969) The development of western Ireland, *Irish Geography*, 6 (1), 1-13.

Scully, J.J. (1971) *Agriculture in the West of Ireland*, Stationery Office, Dublin.

Stamp, L.D. (1931) *Agricultural Atlas of Ireland*, Gill, London.

Sweeney, J. (1987-88) Controls on the climate of Ireland, *Geographical Viewpoint*, 16, 60-72.

Sweeney, J. (1997) Ireland, in, Wheeler, D. and Mayes, J. (eds.) *Regional Climates of the British Isles,* Routledge, London.

Walsh, J.A. (1976) Spatial and temporal variations in crop production in the Republic of Ireland, *Irish Journal of Agricultural Economics and Rural Sociology*, 6, 55-74.

Walsh, J.A. (1984) Regional aspects of agricultural production in Ireland, *Irish Geography*, 17, 95-110.

Walsh, J.A. (1985) Uneven development of agriculture in Ireland, *Geographical Viewpoint,* 14, 36-65.

Walsh, J.A. (1989) Enterprise substitution in Irish Agriculture: sheep in the 1980s, *Irish Geography,* 22, 2, 106-109.

Walsh, J.A. (1992) Adoption and diffusion processes in the mechanisation of Irish agriculture, *Irish Geography*, 25, 1, 33-53.

Walsh, J.A. (1993) Modernisation and marginalisation under the Common Agricultural Policy: Irish agriculture in transition, in, Flognfeldt, T. and Nordgreen, R. (eds.), *Conditions for Development in Marginal Regions*, Oppland College, Norway.

Walsh, J.A. and Gillmor, D.A. (1993) Rural Ireland and the Common Agricultural Policy, in, King, R. (ed.) *Ireland, Europe and the Single Market*, Geographical Society of Ireland, Dublin.

Walsh, J.A. (1994) Agriculture as a land use in Ireland, in, Gillmor, D. and Fenton S. (eds.) *Rural Land Use on the Atlantic Periphery of Europe: Scotland and Ireland*, Royal Irish Academy, Dublin.

Walsh, J.A. (1995) *Regions in Ireland: A Statistical Profile*, Regional Studies Association (Irish Branch), Dublin.

APPENDIX

Map Compilation: Methods and Procedures

The compilation of the maps contained in this atlas involved the reconciliation of census data with digitised boundaries of DEDs and RDs for 1980 and 1991. This involved taking cognisance of changes in boundaries over the period as well as changes in the system of census enumeration between 1980 and 1991. This appendix outlines the pragmatic adjustments which had to be undertaken at various stages to deal with these changes. It also provides definitional information and discussion of the selection of class intervals.

Reconciling DED Numbers

The data enumerated at household level in the Census of Agriculture in 1991 have been aggregated by the Central Statistics Office into summary counts for 3,443 District Electoral Divisions (DEDs). These included six new districts and 330 that did not have any agricultural activity. DEDs without agricultural activity were primarily centred around the main urban areas and are illustrated as the purple districts in Figure 1 and in all subsequent maps. The new DEDs were located around Athy, Clonmel and Ennis. As the precise location of the boundaries for each of the new DEDs was not readily identifiable it was necessary to adopt a pragmatic approach to artificially subdivide the original DEDs and allocate a number of farms to the new districts.

Apart from the creation of new DEDs there is also a slight mismatch between the population and agricultural censuses in that agricultural data are not collected using exactly the same DEDs as the population census. In fact, the agricultural census has data for some DEDs that are no longer utilised in the Population census. This occurred around a few urban areas (Drogheda, Dundalk and Letterkenny) where for Census of Population purposes a few DEDs have been combined. The agricultural data were adjusted to take account of these changes.

Issues of Data Comparability

A census of agriculture had been conducted at five yearly intervals since 1960 and in fact on an annual basis for over 100 years from 1847 to 1953. However, changes in the method of data collection and in the way in which different variables are classified make comparability between census years difficult.

The 1991 Census of Agriculture was the first such census in Ireland to use the EU "Community Farm Typology" to classify farms. As such it affords a new and valuable insight into the structure of Irish agriculture. It was developed with the aim of classifying farms into homogeneous groups based on type of farming and also allows for the derivation of a measure of the "economic size" of farms. Economic size is measured by the application of "standard gross margins (SGMs)" to the agricultural activity of a farm. SGMs are essentially a monetary value assigned on a per hectare basis for crops and on a per head basis for livestock and include subsidies payable and "specific costs" directly involved in production. These specific or direct costs relate to such items as seeds and fertiliser in the case of crops and feedstuffs and veterinary expenses in the case of livestock. Indirect costs such as labour, machinery and buildings are excluded. The aggregation of the SGMs for each activity recorded on a farm gives a measure of the 'economic size' of the farm. It is usually expressed in terms of a "European Size Unit" which is again a European standardised coefficient equal to 1,200 ECU of SGM taking 1986 as the base year (CSO, 1994).

The "typology" is an expression of the relative importance of each activity's SGM to the total SGM of the farm. For example, a farm is regarded as 'specialist sheep' if sheep account for >2/3 of the total SGM of the farm. A complete explanation of the typology variables used in the Irish context and mapped in this atlas is contained in CSO (1994).

Table A.1: Comparison of number of holdings and number of farms enumerated in Census of Agriculture 1980 and 1991

Province	Total No. Holdings 1980	Total No. Farms 1991	% Change	Total Holdings <10acres 1980	Total Farms <10acres 1991	% Change	Actual Change
Leinster	66,645	42,856	-35.69	12,783	3,489	-72.7	-9,294
Munster	83,089	56,456	-32.05	12,309	3,613	-70.6	-8,696
Connacht	76,231	49,004	-35.71	9,928	2,793	-71.9	-7,135
Ulster (part)	37,593	22,262	-40.78	8,331	1,975	-76.3	-6,356
Ireland	263,558	170,578	-35.3	43,351	11,870	-72.6	-31,481

Source: Special tabulation by CSO.

Differences Between the 1991 Census and Previous Censuses

The task of preparing the maps of change had to take account of differences in methods of enumeration between censuses. The first major difference was that the 1991 Census of Agriculture used "farms" as opposed to "holdings". Under the holdings system all agricultural activity was recorded as being undertaken by the holders or registered owners of the land regardless of the fact that the land may have been rented out. Given the fact that farmers frequently rent in land and indeed can do so from different land owners it is reasonable to expect that there will be considerably fewer farmers than land owners in the State (CSO, 1994). This is reflected in a decline of 35 per cent between the number of holdings in 1980 compared to the number of farms in 1991 (Table A.1).

Another major difference was the size of holding/farm included in the census. In 1980 all holdings over one-quarter of an acre were included but in 1991 only farms over one hectare (2.47 acres) in size were included - unless they were involved in intensive agriculture. This had the effect of diminishing the total recorded agricultural area used (AAU) in the State from 5.704 million hectares in 1980 to 4.442 million hectares in 1991 (CSO, 1994). The final difference was the exclusion in 1991 of the total area of commonage from the AAU figure.

Reconciling the Differences in Agricultural Area (AAU)

While initial reaction to these figures might suggest that the two censuses are not comparable the CSO makes a reasonable argument for allowing comparison. The first point towards reconciling the differences is the removal of "insignificant farms" from the coverage. The number of holdings less than 10 acres (4 hectares) in 1980 was 43,351 as compared to 11,870 farms in 1991. The loss of these farms makes little difference, in real terms, to the overall recording of agricultural activity in the State.

Secondly, consideration of the figures for rough grazing land in the State helps to reconcile the figures further. In 1980 there was 1.008 million hectares of rough grazing land as compared to 0.641 million hectares in 1991 thus indicating that a considerable fraction (29 per cent) of the discrepancy in total AAU between the two censuses can be accounted for by this relatively less important land use. Thirdly, over the period since 1980 there has been a substantial increase in the area of woods and plantation. This increase, amounting to 120,000 hectares, was included in AAU in 1980.

Taking account of these considerations still leaves an obvious problem when directly comparing the two censuses. Using the above figures there is a discrepancy of 775,000 hectares in the total area farmed. The figures could be further reconciled if use is made of the 1980 EU Farm Structures Survey which attempted to estimate the number of 'farms' in 1980 and the corresponding area farmed. These estimates were 223,500 and 5.049 million hectares respectively. This brings the difference down to 120,000 hectares. Unfortunately, because these data are based on a sample survey they were not applicable to this work. Having highlighted the problems with the data, it is still fair to suggest that the change in methodology and the resultant discrepancy has had only a very small or indeed negligible effect on the recording of the overall agricultural activity of the State (CSO, 1994).

Change Maps

The change maps in this atlas were produced for 156 Rural Districts (RDs) with county Dublin treated as one. This was preferable to using DEDs as it minimised the effect of the changes in data collection. In analysing these maps one must bear in mind that there are some implications at a local level from the changed procedures in enumeration. In addition one must also consider the variation in land area across different RDs. For example, Rathdrum No. 2 in Wicklow has 3,852 hectares of AAU compared to 67,680 hectares in Cavan Rural District.

Interval Boundaries for Maps

The majority of maps in this volume are choropleth maps designed to simplify the complexity of the agricultural sector in Ireland and present it in a visually informative format. By its very nature choropleth mapping involves generalisation and some loss of detail. This loss of detail occurs on two levels. Firstly, since data are mapped within the boundaries of spatial units one is implicitly assuming homogeneity within these boundaries in the sense that no account is taken of internal variations. Secondly, all spatial units within a range of data values are grouped or 'classified' into a single category represented by a single colour. Thus an arbitrary selection of class intervals can introduce a risk that the map may exaggerate, distort or even conceal the true geographical pattern in the data.

There are a range of options for selecting appropriate 'break points' for the class intervals. The class intervals used in almost all maps in this volume, excluding those representing change from 1980-91, were devised using the 'Natural Break' option in MapInfo Professional. This utilises an algorithm advanced by Jenks and Caspall (1971) by which the average of each range is as close as possible to the values in that range. This ensures that the data in each range are 'clustered' as closely together as possible by minimising the internal variation in each range while maximising the variation between ranges (Cuff and Mattson, 1982; MapInfo, 1998).

SUBJECT INDEX

Séamus Lafferty is a former Teagasc Walsh Fellow based in the Department of Geography, National University of Ireland, Maynooth.

Patrick Commins is Head of Rural Development Research in the Rural Economy Research Centre, Teagasc, Dublin.

James A. Walsh is Professor and Head of the Department of Geography, National University of Ireland, Maynooth.

AGRICULTURE AND FOOD DEVELOPMENT AUTHORITY

NUI MAYNOOTH

Ollscoil na hÉireann Má Nuad

EUROPEAN UNION

European Agricultural
Guidance and Guarantee Fund

First published in 1999 by Teagasc, 19 Sandymount Avenue, Dublin 4, Ireland

in association with Department of Geography, National University of Ireland, Maynooth, County Kildare, Ireland